NetBeans IDE 8 Cookbook

Over 75 practical recipes to maximize your productivity
with NetBeans

David Salter

Rhawi Dantas

[PACKT] open source ✳
PUBLISHING   community experience distilled

BIRMINGHAM - MUMBAI

NetBeans IDE 8 Cookbook

First published: May 2011

Second edition: October 2014

Production reference: 1201014

Published by Packt Publishing Ltd.
Livery Place
35 Livery Street
Birmingham B3 2PB, UK.

ISBN 978-1-78216-776-1

www.packtpub.com

Cover image by Faiz Fattohi (faizfattohi@gmail.com)

Credits

Authors

David Salter

Rhawi Dantas

Reviewers

Ritwik Ghoshal

Petr Hejl

Tushar Joshi

Jonathan Lermitage

Hrushikesh Zadgaonkar

Commissioning Editor

Mary Jasmine Nadar

Acquisition Editor

Nikhil Karkal

Content Development Editor

Govindan K

Technical Editors

Tanvi Bhatt

Siddhi Rane

Copy Editors

Roshni Banerjee

Janbal Dharmaraj

Alfida Paiva

Laxmi Subramanian

Project Coordinator

Shipra Chawhan

Proofreaders

Paul Hindle

Chris Smith

Indexers

Monica Ajmera Mehta

Priya Sane

Production Coordinators

Manu Joseph

Komal Ramchandani

Shantanu N. Zagade

Cover Work

Shantanu N. Zagade

About the Authors

David Salter is an enterprise software developer and architect who has been developing software professionally since 1991. His relationship with Java goes right back to the beginning, using Java 1.0 for writing desktop applications and applets for interactive websites. He has been developing enterprise Java applications using both Java EE (and J2EE) and open source solutions since 2001. He wrote the book, *Seam 2.x Web Development, Packt Publishing*, and co-authored the book, *Building SOA-Based Composite Application Using NetBeans IDE 6, Packt Publishing*.

First and foremost, I would like to thank my wife and family for putting up with my many hours at the computer while writing this book. Special thanks and love to my wife for all her encouragement and support.

I'd also like to say thanks to all the people at Packt Publishing for helping me with this book. Thank you Nikhil for your encouragement from the beginning. Thanks also to Kinjal and Govindan for your hard work helping me to complete the book.

Finally, thanks to everyone who has worked on NetBeans to make it the product it is today. Without you, this book would not exist.

Rhawi Dantas is a software engineer from Recife, Brazil, with several years of Java development expertise, focused mainly on server-side development. He has a Bachelor's degree in Information Systems and is currently doing his Masters in Software Systems from Tampere University of Technology. He is also certified as SCJP, SCWCD, and SCSNI.

This is a small thank you to the three most important women in my life: Sônia Dantas, Paula Mäkinen-Dantas, and Maria Dantas. I would also like to thank the work of my editors, specially Jovita Pinto and Roger D'Souza, and all of the reviewers for their valuable contribution.

About the Reviewers

Ritwik Ghoshal is a senior security analyst at Oracle Corporation, responsible for Oracle Software and Hardware Security Assurance. His primary work areas are operating systems and desktop virtualization, along with developing vulnerability management and tracking tools. Before coming to Oracle in 2010, when the company acquired Sun Microsystems, he had worked at Sun as a part of Sun security engineering team and Solaris team since 2008. At Oracle, he continues to be responsible for all Sun Microsystems products and Oracle Linux and virtualization products. He earned a Bachelor's degree in Computer Science and Engineering in 2008 from Heritage Institute of Technology in Kolkata, India.

> I'm heavily indebted to my parents and Sara E Taverner for their continuous help and support.

Petr Hejl works as a software developer at Oracle Corporation. He is an experienced Java developer contributing to the NetBeans IDE in various areas, such as Java EE, JavaScript, and the core infrastructure.

His professional interests center on multithreading, API design, and code quality. In his free time, he created and still maintains the open source Checkstyle Beans plugin, integrating the Checkstyle tool into the NetBeans IDE.

He holds a Master's degree in Computer Science from the Czech Technical University in Prague.

> I'd like to thank my family, Tereza and Matěj, for all their love, help, and support.

Jonathan Lermitage is a 30-year-old programmer from France. He has worked for 5 years with the Java SOA and BPM ecosystem for a medium-sized company. Now, he is working for one of the European e-business leaders in order to modernize their Java EE products. Also, he is continuing his education in order to become an engineer in scientific computing, his first passion.

He wrote the book, *Instant JRebel, Packt Publishing*. He also worked as a technical reviewer on *Instant NetBeans IDE How-to, Packt Publishing*, a book written by Atul Palandurkar.

Living with a computing fanatic is not easy every day, so I thank my marvelous girlfriend for all her patience and encouragement.

Hrushikesh Zadgaonkar is a senior software engineer at Persistent Systems. He has completed BE from RCOEM, Nagpur, and MS from Birla Institute of Technology and Science, Pilani, in Computer Science. He is a NetBeans Certified Associate and has worked on the NetBeans platform. He was a Microsoft Student Partner and has been constantly working on distinct domains such as .NET, Android, iOS, and automation in Robotium extensively.

He is an author of the book, *Robotium Automated Testing by Android, Packt Publishing*. He is also a semifinalist of the Touch and Tablet Accessibility Award organized as part of Imagine Cup 2010.

He has several papers published in various international journals. His leisure activities include blogging, reading articles, playing tabla, guitar, and sports such as Cricket, Football, and Snooker.

You can contact him at hzadgaonkar@gmail.com and you can follow him on Twitter at @MsWizKid.

I would like to thank my mother, Bharati Zadgaonkar, and wife, Arti Zadgaonkar, for their continuous help and encouragement.

www.PacktPub.com

Support files, eBooks, discount offers, and more

You might want to visit www.PacktPub.com for support files and downloads related to your book.

Did you know that Packt offers eBook versions of every book published, with PDF and ePub files available? You can upgrade to the eBook version at www.PacktPub.com and as a print book customer, you are entitled to a discount on the eBook copy. Get in touch with us at service@packtpub.com for more details.

At www.PacktPub.com, you can also read a collection of free technical articles, sign up for a range of free newsletters, and receive exclusive discounts and offers on Packt books and eBooks.

http://PacktLib.PacktPub.com

Do you need instant solutions to your IT questions? PacktLib is Packt's online digital book library. Here, you can access, read, and search across Packt's entire library of books.

Why Subscribe?

► Fully searchable across every book published by Packt

► Copy and paste, print, and bookmark content

► On demand and accessible via web browser

Free Access for Packt account holders

If you have an account with Packt at www.PacktPub.com, you can use this to access PacktLib today and view nine entirely free books. Simply use your login credentials for immediate access.

Table of Contents

Preface

NetBeans IDE is the only IDE that can be downloaded alongside Java itself. It supports all of the latest standards such as Java SE 8, Java EE 7, and Java ME 8, providing a comprehensive set of development tools for the modern-day Java developer.

This book provides a wide-ranging set of recipes that can help you to develop better applications and become more productive in your work. From the start to the end of a Java project's development lifecycle, this book shows how to perform many different tasks with the NetBeans IDE, discovering mobile, desktop, and enterprise Java along the way.

The book is packed with over 75 practical recipes specifically designed to maximize developer productivity with NetBeans. Each recipe is fully explained, providing clear steps and examples throughout. In addition to the recipes, there are many different techniques and tips included, all of which will allow you to progress to becoming an effective NetBeans IDE user.

What this book covers

Chapter 1, Using NetBeans Projects, takes you through the process of creating Java projects. In this chapter, you will learn how to use Apache ANT, Maven, and NetBeans itself for creating projects, along with details on how to import projects from Eclipse.

Chapter 2, Java Development with NetBeans, teaches you how to use NetBeans effectively. Having created Java projects in the previous chapter, you will learn how to create classes, packages, and interfaces. You will learn how to run and debug the code and how to efficiently manage the Java code.

Chapter 3, NetBeans Productivity, explains the different techniques that NetBeans offers for code editing and refactoring. You will see how to use the many different refactoring tools in NetBeans along with shortcuts to quickly implement standard code.

Chapter 4, Developing Desktop Applications with NetBeans, shows you how to develop desktop Swing applications and deploy them outside of NetBeans.

Chapter 5, NetBeans Enterprise Application Development, teaches you how to integrate different Java EE applications servers into NetBeans and how to create Java EE web and EJB applications.

Chapter 6, Managing Databases with NetBeans, describes how to connect to different databases such as Oracle and MySQL. You will also see how to manage databases from within NetBeans and how to run ad hoc SQL queries against them.

Chapter 7, NetBeans JavaFX, teaches you how to create and deploy JavaFX applications. You'll also learn how to integrate Oracle's Scene Builder into NetBeans allowing you to style JavaFX applications.

Chapter 8, NetBeans Mobile Development, explains how to add Java ME support into NetBeans and how to develop MIDP and Android applications.

Chapter 9, Version Control, explains the procedures necessary for working with revision control systems such as Git and Subversion. You will learn many different techniques required such as cloning repositories, checking in files, and reviewing project changes—all from within NetBeans.

Chapter 10, NetBeans Testing and Profiling, describes how to test Java applications within NetBeans using JUnit and TestNG. After learning how to write tests for applications, you will learn how to profile their CPU and memory usage.

Chapter 11, Using External Web Services, shows how to invoke external third-party web services such as Flickr and the Google Geocoding API directly from within NetBeans. You'll learn how consuming a web service is as simple as dragging-and-dropping it into an application.

Chapter 12, Extending NetBeans, describes what to do in the rare situation when NetBeans doesn't provide all of the functionality you need. You will learn how to write a NetBeans plugin and how to distribute it to other NetBeans users.

What you need for this book

To complete the recipes within this book, you will need to download and install NetBeans IDE 8. NetBeans is provided in three different download bundles: Java SE, Java EE, and the All bundle. Some of the recipes in this book require specific versions of NetBeans due to the technologies used. For example, the Java EE or All version of NetBeans is required for the recipes explaining Java EE concepts and techniques. For each recipe, the version of NetBeans that is required is specified.

Each of the different download bundles of NetBeans can be downloaded from `https://netbeans.org/downloads`.

Who this book is for

This book is intended for Java developers of any level who are using NetBeans and want to learn how to get the most out of the IDE. Learning NetBeans effectively will help to provide a firm foundation for your application development activities.

This book assumes some knowledge of Java development and does not try to teach Java programming.

Conventions

In this book, you will find a number of styles of text that distinguish between different kinds of information. Here are some examples of these styles, and an explanation of their meaning.

Code words in text, database table names, folder names, filenames, file extensions, pathnames, dummy URLs, user input, and Twitter handles are shown as follows: "Ensure that the `BookMarks.java` file is open for editing."

A block of code is set as follows:

```
public static void main(String[] args) {
  List<String> l = new ArrayList<String>();
  l.add("Hello");
  l.add("World");
}
```

When we wish to draw your attention to a particular part of a code block, the relevant lines or items are set in bold:

```
<html xmlns="http://www.w3.org/1999/xhtml"
      xmlns:h="http://xmlns.jcp.org/jsf/html"
      xmlns:f="http://xmlns.jcp.org/jsf/core">
```

Any command-line input or output is written as follows:

```
netbeans --laf com.sun.java.swing.plaf.motif.MotifLookAndFeel
```

New terms and **important words** are shown in bold. Words that you see on the screen, in menus or dialog boxes for example, appear in the text like this: "Expanding the project within the **Projects** explorer displays a list of **Source Packages** within the project and **Libraries** used by the project."

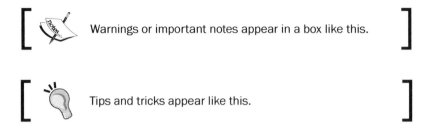

Warnings or important notes appear in a box like this.

Tips and tricks appear like this.

Reader feedback

Feedback from our readers is always welcome. Let us know what you think about this book—what you liked or may have disliked. Reader feedback is important for us to develop titles that you really get the most out of.

To send us general feedback, simply send an e-mail to feedback@packtpub.com, and mention the book title via the subject of your message.

If there is a topic that you have expertise in and you are interested in either writing or contributing to a book, see our author guide on www.packtpub.com/authors.

Customer support

Now that you are the proud owner of a Packt book, we have a number of things to help you to get the most from your purchase.

Downloading the example code

You can download the example code files for all Packt books you have purchased from your account at http://www.packtpub.com. If you purchased this book elsewhere, you can visit http://www.packtpub.com/support and register to have the files e-mailed directly to you.

Downloading the color images of this book

We also provide you a PDF file that has color images of the screenshots/diagrams used in this book. The color images will help you better understand the changes in the output. You can download this file from https://www.packtpub.com/sites/default/files/downloads/7761OS_ColoredImages.pdf.

Errata

Although we have taken every care to ensure the accuracy of our content, mistakes do happen. If you find a mistake in one of our books—maybe a mistake in the text or the code—we would be grateful if you would report this to us. By doing so, you can save other readers from frustration and help us improve subsequent versions of this book. If you find any errata, please report them by visiting http://www.packtpub.com/submit-errata, selecting your book, clicking on the **errata submission form** link, and entering the details of your errata. Once your errata are verified, your submission will be accepted and the errata will be uploaded on our website, or added to any list of existing errata, under the Errata section of that title. Any existing errata can be viewed by selecting your title from http://www.packtpub.com/support.

Piracy

Piracy of copyright material on the Internet is an ongoing problem across all media. At Packt, we take the protection of our copyright and licenses very seriously. If you come across any illegal copies of our works, in any form, on the Internet, please provide us with the location address or website name immediately so that we can pursue a remedy.

Please contact us at copyright@packtpub.com with a link to the suspected pirated material.

We appreciate your help in protecting our authors, and our ability to bring you valuable content.

Questions

You can contact us at questions@packtpub.com if you are having a problem with any aspect of the book, and we will do our best to address it.

1
Using NetBeans Projects

In this chapter, we will cover the following recipes:

- ▶ Creating a Java application
- ▶ Creating a Maven application
- ▶ Using Maven projects
- ▶ Creating a Free-Form application
- ▶ Creating a library
- ▶ Importing an Eclipse project

Introduction

The NetBeans IDE is a free, open source, Java-based **Integrated Development Environment** (**IDE**) that is used the world over to develop Java, PHP, C/C++, HTML, and other applications.

One of the first tasks when using NetBeans is to create projects or libraries or import projects from Eclipse. In this chapter, we will discuss how to create different types of projects based on different build tools (NetBeans, Maven, and Ant), how to create class libraries, and how to import both existing Eclipse and Maven projects.

To follow the recipes in this chapter, you can use any of the Java NetBeans download bundles (Java SE, Java EE, and All). All of these NetBeans versions can be downloaded from `https://netbeans.org/downloads/`.

Creating a Java application

Creating a Java application using the NetBeans standard project format is the simplest way to start developing Java applications with NetBeans.

This recipe shows how to create a Java application using the NetBeans project format. The NetBeans 8, Java SE version was used for this recipe. If you are using a different version of NetBeans, you may have more project types available for selection while creating a project.

Getting ready

To get started, ensure that one of the Java bundles of NetBeans (Java SE, Java EE, or the All bundle) is running. You need not have any projects created to start this recipe.

How to do it...

1. Click on **File** and then click on **New Project...**.
2. On the resultant dialog, select the **Java** category and the **Java Application** project, as shown in the following screenshot:

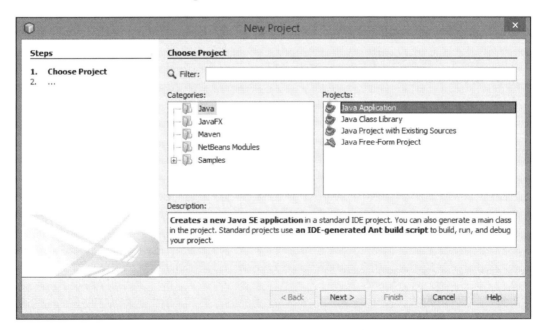

3. Click on **Next**.

4. On the resultant dialog, enter `MyFirstApp` in the **Project Name** field and ensure that a sensible project location is specified in the **Project Location** field.

5. Ensure that **Create Main Class** is selected and enter `com.davidsalter.cookbook.myfirstapp.Main` as the **Create Main Class** name.

> NetBeans will automatically suggest a **Create Main Class** name `myfirstapp.MyFirstApp` using the project name for both the package and class names. The best practice for Java package naming is to use your companies' reversed Internet domain name followed by some identification for your application. Hence, the `com.davidsalter.cookbook.myfirstapp` package name is a good choice of a package name. Without using reverse domain names for packages, it's easy to see how different people could create packages all with the same name, leading to name collisions.

The **New Java Application** wizard is shown in the following screenshot:

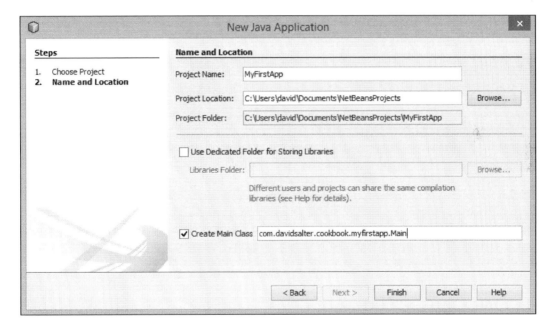

How it works...

Creating a Java application using the **New Java Application** wizard creates a new NetBeans project that is visible within the **Projects** explorer within the main NetBeans window, as shown in the following screenshot:

Expanding the project within the **Projects** explorer displays a list of **Source Packages** within the project and **Libraries** used by the project. For a freshly created project, the **Source Packages** node will display only **<default package>** if the user did not select the **Create Main Class** option at the time of project creation. If the **Create Main Class** option was selected, as we did in this recipe, then the package structure used for the main class will be displayed within the hierarchy.

There's more...

While creating a new project, NetBeans provides the **Create Main Class** option. If this option is selected, then the name of a class can be specified into which NetBeans will create a `main` method.

Within the **New Java Application** wizard, the user has the **Use Dedicated Folder for Storing Libraries** option. When this option is selected, NetBeans will create a `lib` folder (usually within the project's structure) in which all libraries used by the project are placed. This option is useful when the developer wishes to share the project with other parties or wants to build the project outside of NetBeans, for example, within a Continuous Integration environment. As all of the libraries used by the project are stored within the same location, additional (often complex) configuration is not required to access any project dependencies.

When projects are created using the **New Java Application** wizard, Ant is used as the build tool for the project and a standard build file (`build.xml`) is created at the root of the project, with a build implementation Ant file (`build-impl.xml`) created within the `nbproject` folder of the project. It's not recommended that you edit the contents of the `build-impl.xml` file directly; it is not usually required for a developer to modify any of these build scripts. If you wish to override any of the targets within the `build-impl.xml` file, they should be defined within the `build.xml` file. Any properties that you want to change from within the `build-impl.xml` file should be defined within the `project.properties` file.

Opening the **Files** explorer shows all of the files within the project. The project build files can be seen and selected for editing (if required) from within this window, as shown in the following screenshot:

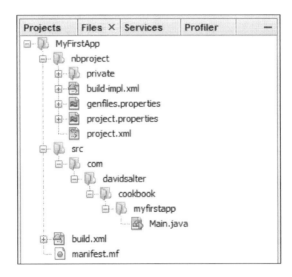

Many of the properties defined within the `project.properties` file can also be edited within the IDE by right-clicking on the project in either the **Projects** or **Files** explorer and selecting the **Properties** option.

Creating a Maven application

Many Java developers find that Maven provides superior build and project management tools that IDEs do not offer. The NetBeans IDE therefore offers the ability to create and manage Maven projects directly from within the IDE, thus offering the best combination of tools. This recipe shows how to create a Maven project from within the NetBeans IDE.

Getting ready

To get started, ensure that one of the Java bundles of NetBeans (Java SE, Java EE, or the All bundle) is running. You do not have to have any projects created to start this recipe.

How to do it...

1. Click on **File** and then click on **New Project...**.

2. On the resultant dialog, select the **Maven** category and the **Project from Archetype** project, as shown in the following screenshot:

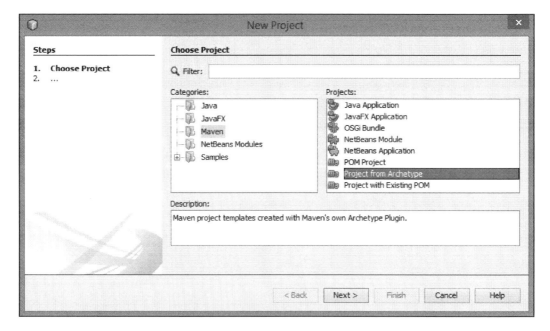

3. Click on **Next**.

4. In the **Search** field, enter `maven-archetype-quickstart` and then select it in the **Known Archetypes** field, as shown in the following screenshot:

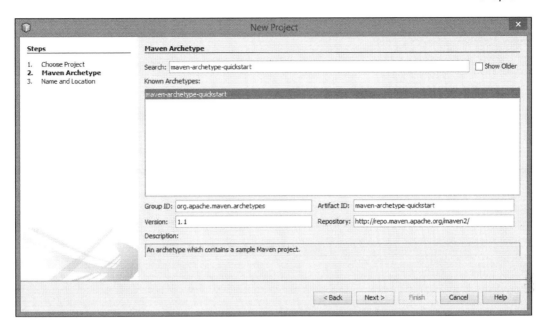

5. Click on **Next**.

6. On the resultant dialog, enter a project name, group ID, version, and package, as shown in the following screenshot:

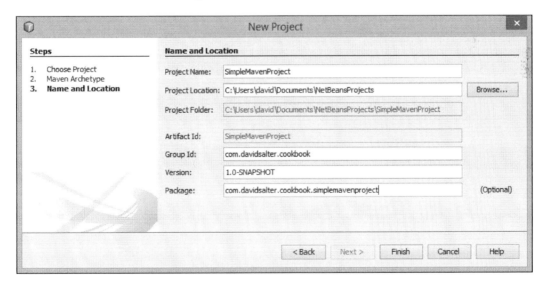

7. Click on the **Finish** button to create the project.

How it works...

NetBeans comes bundled with a copy of Maven that is used to create and manage projects. The current version of Maven bundled with NetBeans 8 is version 3.0.5. This version number can be checked by navigating to **Tools** | **Options** from the NetBeans main menu. (On the Mac, this screen is accessed by navigating to **NetBeans** | **Preferences**.) On the resulting dialog (shown in the following screenshot), click on **Java** and then select the **Maven** tab to see the version of Maven bundled with NetBeans:

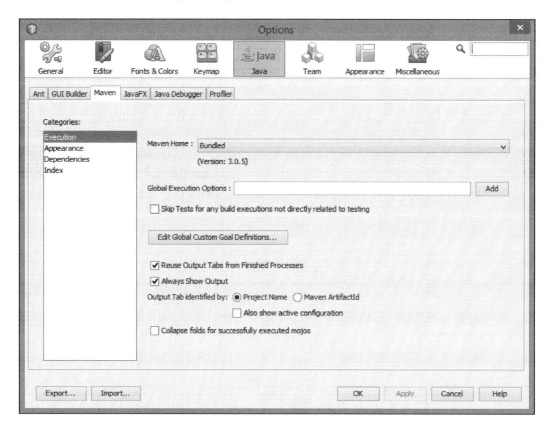

As when creating a Java project using the **New Project** wizard, when a Maven project has been created, it is automatically opened within the **Projects** explorer. The list of nodes available within the project, however, depends upon the type of Maven project created. For most Maven project types (in Maven terms, these are called **archetypes**), the **Source Packages**, **Test Packages**, **Dependencies**, **Test Dependencies**, **Java Dependencies**, and **Project Files** nodes will be created as shown in the following screenshot:

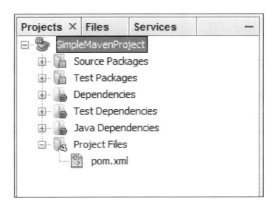

Within the **Project Files** node, we have the pom.xml file that was created by the **New Project** wizard. The pom.xml file can be opened by double-clicking on it within the project hierarchy, or by right-clicking on the project and selecting the **Open POM** menu option. In addition to editing, the NetBeans pom.xml editor windows allow us to display a graph of all the artefacts used by the Maven project. This can be very useful when trying to identify what dependencies exist within a project. NetBeans also provides an **Effective** tab on the pom.xml editor. This window shows the inherited information and provides a complete view of what the pom.xml file looks like, including listing any plugins used by Maven.

If we look in the **Output** window after the project has been created, we can see that the bundled copy of Maven has been used to create a Maven project.

There's more...

Maven uses a set of executable **goals** to manage the lifecycle of a project. These goals can be chained to each other to perform a set of project management tasks.

For example, the install goal is typically used to build a project, whereas the clean goal is typically used to clean a project. If a developer wanted to clean and then build a project, he/she would typically execute these goals sequentially on the command line by running the Maven clean install goals together.

The command line is not so user friendly, so fortunately NetBeans allows us to manage these goals in a much nicer fashion. Right-click on a Maven project within the **Projects** explorer and select **Properties**. On the resultant dialog, select the **Actions** node to see and edit the Maven goals that are executed for different NetBeans actions (**Build project**, **Clean project**, **Test project**, and so on), as shown in the following screenshot:

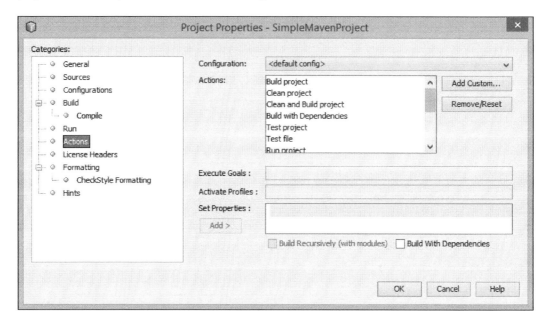

These goals are mapped to the standard NetBeans IDE project build options. So, for example, right-clicking on a project and selecting **Build** will execute the Maven `install` goal.

For the most common project-related tasks (build, clean, test, and so on), developers can therefore use the standard NetBeans button and keyboard shortcuts.

Invoking Maven goals

Within the **Navigator** explorer, a list of commonly used goals is displayed. Double-clicking on any of these goals will execute it against the current project. Toggling **Show help goals** and **Show lifecycle bound goals** determines the set of goals that are shown in the **Navigator** explorer:

Invoking custom Maven goals

Sometimes, when using Maven, a developer will want to run additional goals outside the normal build/test/deploy goals. These would include, for example, running code analysis against a project. NetBeans allows both global and custom goals to be defined, which can easily be executed against a project.

To define a global goal, select **Tools** and then select the **Options** menu item. On the **Options** dialog box, select **Java** and then select the **Maven** tab. On the resultant dialog, click on the **Edit Global Custom Goal Definitions...** button.

On the **Global Maven Goal definitions** dialog, actions can be added and removed. For each action, a specific Maven goal (or goals) can be defined.

To execute any of these global goals against a project, right-click on the project in the **Projects** explorer and select the **Custom** menu option. All of the global goals that have been defined will be available here for execution against the project.

Custom goals can be defined on a per project basis. To define custom goals, right-click on the project and select **Custom** and then select the **Goals...** menu option. Custom goals can be stored within a project by selecting the **Remember as** checkbox. Unlike global goals, custom goals are stored within a project and are therefore distributed with the project when it is supplied to other people.

Using a different installation of Maven

If you wish to use a different version of Maven than the one bundled with NetBeans, you can select the version to use from the Maven properties. You may wish to use a different version of Maven if you already have a different version of Maven installed outside of NetBeans, or you have a local copy of Maven that is differently configured especially for your environment.

Select **Tools** and then select the **Options** menu item from the main NetBeans menu. On the **Options** dialog, select **Java** and then click on the **Maven** tab. Under the **Maven Home** drop-down list, select the **Browse...** option and choose the installation of Maven that you wish to use.

Using Maven projects

Given the open nature of the Java platform, it is quite common for Java developers to work on projects that were not created within NetBeans, or that do not employ the NetBeans project structure.

One of the most common Java build and management tool is Maven (see the *Creating a Maven application* recipe for more information on Maven), and as such a growing number of projects are created using it. These include both single module projects (where a single .jar file is generated) and complex multimodule projects (which may include .war, .ear, .jar, and more!).

This recipe shows how a Maven project can be loaded within NetBeans and subsequently managed via the NetBeans user interface.

Getting ready

To complete this recipe, you need a Maven project on your local machine. It does not matter whether the project is a single or multimodule Maven project.

How to do it...

1. Click on **File** and then on **New Project...**.
2. On the resultant dialog, select the **Maven** category and select the **Project with Existing POM** project.
3. Click on **Next**.
4. Click on the **Finish** button.
5. Using the **Open Project** window, browse to the top-level pom.xml file for the project and click on **Open Project**.
6. The Maven project will now be loaded and will be shown in the **Projects** explorer.

How it works...

Loading and using a Maven project in NetBeans is an easy way to utilize the power of Maven with the convenience of NetBeans.

After loading a Maven project into NetBeans in this way, the project still remains intact as a Maven project. You can still use the project outside of NetBeans as a standard Maven project.

When a Maven project is loaded into NetBeans, the project's icon in the **Projects** explorer indicates that this is a Maven project. Opening up the project node for a multimodule Maven project will show all the child Maven modules. Right-clicking on a child module and selecting the **Open POM** option opens the child module as a top-level project that can then be managed (build, test, debug, and so on) as a standard Maven project.

There's more...

In addition to using the **New Project** wizard, Maven projects can also be opened simply by going to **File** | **Open Project** from the NetBeans main menu.

Creating a Free-Form application

For many projects, Apache Ant is used as the build tool (Ant is used as the internal build tool for NetBeans projects). It is not uncommon for these projects to have custom Ant build scripts that are used to build, test, and deploy the projects.

Rather than having to amend the structure of existing projects, NetBeans provides the facility to create a Free-Form project. In a Free-Form project, NetBeans invokes Ant targets to perform build options.

The Ant script used in these types of projects must be managed independently of NetBeans, and any changes required to the build procedure must be directly defined within the projects' build script.

 Free-Form projects are only recommended when an existing Ant project has a fixed structure, but the developer wants to use NetBeans for further development of the project. For smaller projects, creating a new NetBeans project or a Maven project may be a better option.

This recipe shows how to create a Free-Form project from within the NetBeans IDE by importing an existing Ant project.

Getting ready

This recipe assumes that you have an existing Java project that uses Ant as the build tool and shows you how to import the project into a NetBeans Free-Form project.

How to do it...

1. Click on **File** and then click on **New Project...**.

2. On the resultant dialog, select the **Java** category and select the **Java Free-Form Project** project, as shown in the following screenshot:

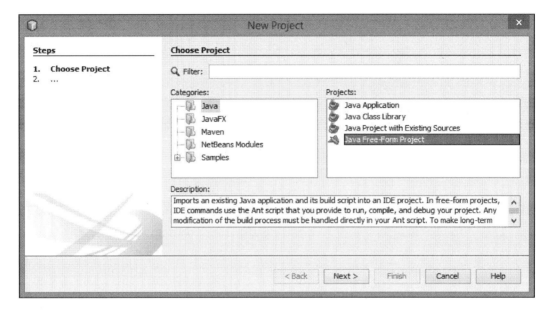

3. Click on **Next**.

4. Browse for the Ant project's location. NetBeans should then parse the `build.xml` file for the project and populate the **Build Script**, **Project Name**, and **Project Folder** options.

5. Click on **Next**.

6. Five NetBeans actions are now shown (**Build Project**, **Clean Project**, **Generate Javadoc**, **Run Project**, and **Test Project**). Select the Ant targets for these project actions. If there is no Ant build target for a specific action (for example, the Ant build script has no ability to generate Javadoc), then leave the action blank.

7. Click on **Next**.

8. Enter **Source Package Folders** and **Test Package Folders** for the project. As with the previous stage, NetBeans will attempt to work out these values from the `build.xml` file.

9. Click on **Next**.

10. If there are any additional classpath entries required, specify them as **Java Sources Classpath**.

11. Click on **Next**.

12. From the **Output JARs of Folders Containing Compiled Classes** field, select the folders that contain the compiled classes or `.jar` files.

13. If any Javadoc is generated during the build process, enter the location in the **Javadoc Output** field.

14. Click on **Finish** for NetBeans to create the Free-Form project.

How it works...

When a Free-Form project is created, NetBeans creates a special type of project that uses a custom Ant script to build the project. This project can have the source code stored wherever it is defined by the Ant script and does not have to follow the code layout guidelines of NetBeans.

As with other types of projects created within NetBeans, once the project is created, it is opened and shown in the **Projects** explorer, as shown in the following screenshot:

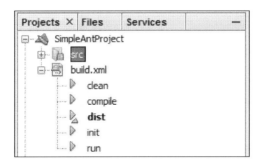

As long as the relevant mappings were defined correctly between NetBeans actions and the Ant targets, the developer can build, clean, run, test, and generate Javadoc from within the IDE using the standard menu items and keyboard shortcuts.

Selecting the `build.xml` file within the **Projects** explorer shows all of the Ant targets that have been defined within the file. Double-clicking on any of these will run the target.

It is important to note that any changes made to the project settings via NetBeans, for example, adding extra dependencies to the project or additional source roots, will not affect the way the project is build. The project is built exactly as defined within the `build.xml` file. This can sometimes lead to confusion; for example, NetBeans may show that there are no missing dependencies for a project, but the project itself will not build due to missing dependencies. It is important to remember that it is the Ant file itself (not NetBeans) that defines how the project is built.

There's more...

As stated in the previous section, it's important to remember that, with Free-Form projects, the project is built by Ant as defined within the `build.xml` file. Any changes to the project's metadata within NetBeans will not affect how the project is built.

To add extra source nodes to a project or to add additional dependencies, it is important that these are first defined within the `build.xml` file and then added at the NetBeans project level. This is achieved within NetBeans by right-clicking on a Free-Form project and selecting **Properties**. The resulting dialog box allows all of the configuration options defined at the project creation to be modified.

Using a different version of Ant

NetBeans is bundled with a version of Ant. This enables developers to use Ant from within NetBeans without having to install a separate copy.

If you wish to use a different version of Ant within Free-Form projects, this can be configured by selecting **Tools** and then clicking on **Options** from the main NetBeans menu. On the **Options** dialog box, select **Java** and then select the **Ant** tab.

Within this **Options** dialog box, a different version of Ant can be specified together with any classpath or properties required to build your projects.

To quickly change back to the default version of Ant supplied with NetBeans, click on the **Ant Home Default** button within the **Java** section of the **Options** dialog box.

Creating a library

When developing large applications, it's often necessary to utilize third-party libraries. Sometimes, third-party libraries can be distributed as source code that can be dropped into an application, but more often, they are distributed as a set of .jar files.

NetBeans comes bundled with several class libraries (such as Hibernate, Spring, and TestNG), but it also allows developers to create their own sets of class libraries that can be easily added to projects.

This recipe shows how to create a new library within NetBeans that can then be subsequently used by NetBeans projects. This recipe does not involve writing any Java code, but describes the procedure of creating a library from existing code that other NetBeans projects can then reference.

Getting ready

This recipe assumes that you have a third-party library which is provided as a set of one or more .jar files that you wish to use within a NetBeans project.

If you do not have a suitable third-party library, a sample library is provided as a part of the download bundle for this book.

Downloading the example code

You can download the example code files for all Packt books you have purchased from your account at http://www.packtpub.com. If you purchased this book elsewhere, you can visit http://www.packtpub.com/support and register to have the files e-mailed directly to you.

How to do it...

1. Click on **Tools** and then click on **Libraries** on the NetBeans main menu. The **Ant Library Manager** dialog is displayed as shown in the following screenshot:

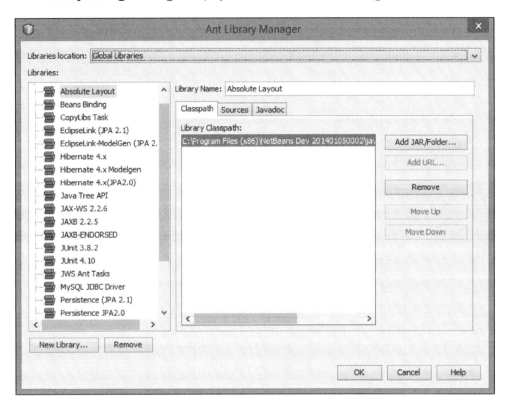

2. Click on the **New Library...** button.

3. Enter the name of the library to be created into the **Library Name** field as shown in the following screenshot:

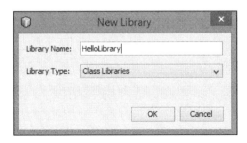

4. Click on the **OK** button to create the library.

5. The library has now been created and given a name as specified in step 3. This name is displayed in the **Library Name** field. Now, we need to add some content to the library.

6. Click on the **Add JAR/Folder** button.

7. Using the **Browse JAR/Folder** dialog box, select a .jar file or folder containing the third-party library content that you wish to add to the NetBeans library.

8. Repeat step 7 for any additional .jar files or folders that you wish to add to the library.

9. Click on the **OK** button to complete creation of the library.

How it works...

A class library in NetBeans is an easy way to add a set of .jar files or folders to the classpath. When a class library has been defined as detailed in this recipe, it can be added to a project by right-clicking on the project's **Libraries** node within the **Projects** explorer and selecting **Add Library...**. NetBeans will then append the .jar files and folders from the library into the project's classpath at both compile time and runtime (if the project is runnable).

There's more...

In addition to adding class libraries to a project to extend the classpath, it is also possible to reference projects from a NetBeans project. If for example, you have a NetBeans project that creates a .jar file, this can be added into the classpath of a different NetBeans project by right-clicking on the **Libraries** node in the **Projects** explorer and selecting **Add Project...**. The build artifacts from this selected project will then be added to the classpath of the original project.

Importing an Eclipse project

If you wish to work alongside Eclipse, NetBeans lets you use the **Project Import** functionality.

This functionality will import one or more projects created by the Eclipse IDE simply by specifying the workspace in which they are housed.

Getting ready

A valid Eclipse project with sources and dependencies must be used in order to continue with this recipe.

How to do it...

1. Click on **File** and then click on **Import Project** and **Eclipse Project...**.

2. In the **Import Eclipse Project** window, select **Import Projects from Workspace**.

3. Click on the **Browse...** button. An **Open** dialog box will pop up from where you can select the workspace.

4. After selecting a valid workspace project, click on the **Next** button.

5. In the **Projects to Import** section, select the projects you want to import.

6. Select **Store NetBeans project data inside Eclipse project folders**.

7. Click on the **Finish** button.

How it works...

By selecting the workspace location, NetBeans will then analyze and convert the metadata created by Eclipse. The following screenshot shows the **Import Eclipse Project** window:

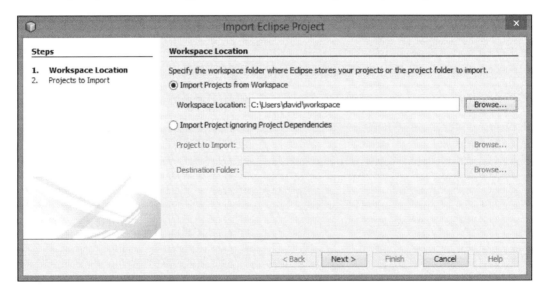

The project structure, along with the dependencies, will be available for NetBeans usage. It is important to notice that NetBeans will not change the way the Eclipse project behaves.

On selecting the **Store NetBeans project data inside Eclipse project folders** option, NetBeans will create its own structure inside the Eclipse folder structure. Select this option if you want to distribute the NetBeans project directory in a version control system. This ensures that the libraries and configuration files used by Eclipse and NetBeans are the same.

The following screenshot shows the **Projects to Import** section:

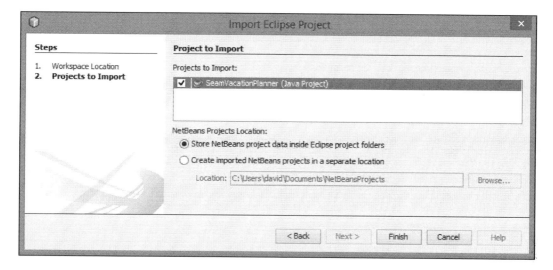

It is also possible to use NetBeans without placing its configuration files inside Eclipse's workspace. If this is the desired outcome, then select **Create imported NetBeans projects in a separate location** and then click on **Browse** to select the folder where NetBeans configurations will exist.

The imported Eclipse projects will then be placed on the **Projects** tab on the left-hand side.

In the *There's more...* section, there is a list of some errors that might occur while importing an Eclipse project.

There's more...

Now, let's talk about some other options as well as some pieces of general information that are relevant to this task.

Synchronizing Eclipse

With multiple developers working on a project, it is common that changes to a project happen from time to time. When this happens, NetBeans can resynchronize the projects by selecting **Import Project** and then **Resynchronize Eclipse Projects** from the main **File** menu.

After following these steps, the classpaths of all the projects imported into Eclipse will be in sync. However, changes to your local project will not be synchronized back. This way, NetBeans ensures that the local configurations will not damage the parent project.

Errors when importing Eclipse projects

When importing Eclipse projects, some importing errors might come up. Many of these errors are not specific to our recipe, but the following notes might come in handy while developing future projects. Some of the errors are as follows:

▶ **Resolve Missing Server Problem**

This error is solved by just right-clicking on the project node and browsing to the folder where the server is installed.

▶ **Resolve Reference Problems**

This error occurs when libraries are missing from the project classpath. Solving this is very similar to solving the missing server problem. Right-click on the project node and select **Resolve Reference Problem**, and then select the folder where the library is. Sometimes, you may have to create libraries to add to the project. If you are unsure on how to create libraries, check out the *Creating a library* recipe discussed earlier in this chapter.

▶ **Eclipse platform for Project Name cannot be used. It is a JRE and the NetBeans project requires a JDK. NetBeans will use the default platform.**

This error occurs when the Eclipse project is configured with a JRE instead of JDK. To solve this, click on **Tools** and select **Java Platforms**. The **Java Platform Manager** dialog will be shown. Click on **Add Platform...** and from the options, select the correct Java platform on which the application is being developed.

2
Java Development with NetBeans

In this chapter, we will cover the following recipes:

- ▶ Creating a package
- ▶ Creating a class
- ▶ Creating an interface
- ▶ Running a file
- ▶ Debugging a class
- ▶ Formatting the code
- ▶ Collapsing and expanding code folds
- ▶ Toggling comments
- ▶ Fixing and organizing imports
- ▶ Creating file headers
- ▶ Changing the look and feel of NetBeans

Introduction

In this chapter, we will look at using the NetBeans IDE for Java development and see what options are available to assist in a Java developer's daily routine.

We will start by looking at how to create classes, packages, and interfaces. We will look at how to run individual files and projects and also how to debug them.

We will then look at code management and see how we can organize the code more effectively using code folds and how we can toggle comments, fix imports, and define file headers.

Finally, we'll take a look at how we can customize the look and feel of NetBeans in order to help us be more comfortable with the IDE. The more comfortable we are with the IDE, the more productive we'll be.

Creating a package

Everything is better when organized. With this in mind, we will check how to create packages using the IDE.

Besides being more organized, it is a bad coding practice to leave all classes in the same package or in the root package.

How to do it...

First, we will need to create a new project, so please refer to the recipes in *Chapter 1, Using NetBeans Projects*, for creating Java projects. When naming the project, enter `CreatingPackages`. When the **Projects** explorer shows the `CreatingPackages` project, expand the `CreatingPackages` node if not yet expanded. When creating the project, it is not necessary to create a main class.

Now, we will create a package for our source code with the following steps:

1. Within the **Projects** explorer, expand the `CreatingPackages` node (if not yet expanded) and the **Source Packages** node within it.
2. Right-click on the **<default package>** node.
3. Select **New** and then click on **Java Package...**.
4. In the **Package Name** text field, enter `com.davidsalter.cookbook.creatingpackages.gui`.
5. Leave the **Location** set as **Source Packages**.
6. Click on **Finish**.

   A new empty package will be shown right under the **Source Packages** node.

   Finally, add a package for our unit test source code with the following steps:

7. Expand the **Test Packages** node (if not yet expanded).

 If the **Test Packages** node is not shown, right-click on the `CreatingPackages` node within the **Projects** explorer and create a new folder called `Test`. The **Test Packages** node within the project will then be displayed correctly.

8. Right-click on **Test Packages**.

9. Select **New** and then click on **Java Package...**.

10. In the **Package Name** text field, type `com.davidsalter.cookbook.creatingpackages.gui`.

11. Leave the **Location** set as **Test Packages**.

12. Click on **Finish**.

A new empty test package named `com.davidsalter.cookbook.creatingpackages.gui` is shown beneath the **Test Packages** node.

The final setup should look like the following screenshot:

How it works...

This recipe shows two ways of creating a package: one, by clicking on the desired folder destination where the package will reside, and the other, by clicking where the root node of the package will be.

By right-clicking on **<default package>**, NetBeans will understand that we wish to create a package under the current one and will automatically append the full path of the packages in the **Package Name** field. The developer then needs to only type the rest of the path. This saves a lot of time when the project grows and nested packages start to spread.

The second option is to right-click directly on the desired node in the **Packages** explorer. In our example, we are creating a package under the **Test Packages** node. Right-clicking on the **Test Packages** node will trigger a clean package name and it is up to the developer to decide what the full path is going to be.

There's more...

It is also possible to create packages in the **Files** explorer with a new class creation wizard.

The Files explorer

By navigating to the **Files** explorer, it is possible to see how the project structure is organized, similar to the **Projects** explorer. It is also possible to create a package using this view by following the same steps described previously.

The **Files** explorer differs from the **Projects** explorer in the sense that the files are presented as they exist in the filesystem. The **Projects** view, on the other hand, presents the files as they are organized from the project perspective.

Automatic creation of packages

It is also possible to create packages when a new Java source file is created by the IDE.

When creating new source files and new test classes, NetBeans will automatically create the relevant package for the file in the project if it does not already exist. If the file being created is a test class, NetBeans will create the package underneath the **Test Packages** node. Otherwise, the package will be created underneath the **Source Packages** node.

Creating a class

One of the most repetitive tasks in software development is creating classes. Once again, with NetBeans wizards, creation of classes is very easy and straightforward.

Getting ready

It is necessary to have a project in order to create a class; so, if you are unsure on how to do this, please check the recipes in *Chapter 1, Using NetBeans Projects*. To help follow this recipe, when creating a project, enter `CreatingClasses` as the project name. When creating the project, ensure the **Create Main Class** option is not selected.

How to do it...

When the **Projects** explorer shows the `CreatingClasses` project, expand the `CreatingClasses` node if not yet expanded and perform the following steps:

1. Right-click on the `CreatingClasses` project, and select **New** and **Java Class...**.
2. On the **New Java Class** window, type `Recipe` under the **Class Name** field.
3. On the **Package** selection, enter `com.davidsalter.cookbook.creatingclasses`.
4. Click on **Finish**.

We can see the **New Java Class** window in the following screenshot:

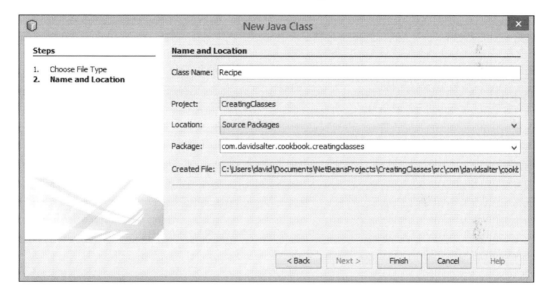

How it works...

The class is created relative to the path of the item we right-click on. Having said that, this example shows that it is also possible to create packages during class creation.

The class created by NetBeans is a very basic one. NetBeans has added comments and package name, along with the class declaration.

Creating an interface

A good development practice is to use interfaces to group together related functions. Coding to an interface allows a developer to easily switch the implementation to another defined by an interface and helps to keep the contract between code modules.

An **interface** defines a set of related methods that have no bodies that a Java class can then implement. NetBeans allows us to create an empty interface in a similar fashion to creating an empty class as described in the *Creating a class* recipe earlier in this chapter.

Getting ready

It is necessary to have a project in order to create an interface; so, if you are unsure on how to do this, please check the recipes in *Chapter 1, Using NetBeans Projects*. To help follow this recipe, when creating a project, enter `CreatingInterfaces` as the project name.

How to do it...

When the **Projects** explorer shows the `CreatingInterfaces` project, expand the `CreatingInterfaces` node if not yet expanded.

Let's now create an interface:

1. Right-click on the `CreatingInterfaces` project, and select **New** and **Java Interface...**.

2. On the **New Java Interface** window, type `Book` under the **Class Name** field (NetBeans displays the title of the field as **Class Name** even though we are actually creating an interface).

> In some programming languages, the best practice is to prefix interfaces with a capital `I` to indicate that a file is indeed an interface. In Java, this practice is not as common as in other languages and generally interfaces are named after nouns such as `Car` or `User`. Implementing classes usually use specific instances of the interface name such as `SportsCar` or `Manager`. It's a personal preference on whether you prefix classes with an `I`; however, in this book, I do not preface interfaces with an `I`.

3. In the **Package** section, enter `com.davidsalter.cookbook.creatinginterfaces`, as shown in the following screenshot:

4. Click on **Finish**.

We have now created a blank interface called `Book`. Edit the `Book.java` file by double-clicking on it in the **Projects** explorer and add the following two method signatures to the interface:

```
int getNumberPages();
void read();
```

The interface now has two methods defined within it. An interface, however, is not much use without a class that implements it, so let's implement the `Book` interface with the following steps:

1. Click on the line defining the interface so that a light bulb is displayed in the left-hand side margin.

2. Click on the light bulb so that the **Implement Interface** hint is displayed, as shown in the following screenshot:

```
     public interface Book {
14        Implement Interface    ►   ();
15        void read();
16   }
17
```

3. Click on the **Implement Interface** hint to display the **Implement Interface** dialog.

4. Enter the **Class Name** field as Paperback and leave the **Package Name** field as it is.

5. Click on **OK**.

How it works...

A new Java class called Paperback will now be created that implements the Book interface.

A method is created within the class for each of the methods defined within the interface. Each of the methods in the class throws an UnsupportedOperationException to indicate that no code has been written for the method yet—it is up to the developer to fully implement the method bodies.

There's more...

After implementing an interface, a gray **I** in a circle is displayed next to all of the methods in the interface that have an implementation. Clicking on this will open up the implementation of the interface in the Java editor. Similarly, when looking at an implementation of an interface, a green **I** in a circle is displayed next to the method name. Clicking on this will open up the interface file within the Java editor, as shown in the following screenshot:

```
10      public class Paperback implements Book {
11
12          @Override
            public int getNumberPages() {
14              throw new UnsupportedOperationException("
15          }
```

Running a file

Once we have created some code as a part of our application, the next stage is to run the code. NetBeans allows developers to run either a file (with a main method) or a project. In this recipe, we'll see how this can be achieved.

Getting ready

It is necessary to have a project in order to run a file. If you are unsure on how to create a project, please check the recipes in *Chapter 1, Using NetBeans Projects*. To help follow this recipe, when creating a project, enter RunningFiles as the project name and ensure that the **Create Main Class** option called com.davidsalter.cookbook.runningfiles. RunningFiles is selected.

How to do it...

1. Right-click on the `RunningFiles` project, and select **New** and **Java Class...**.

2. On the **New Java Class** window, type `Application` under the **Class Name** field.

3. On the package selection, enter `com.davidsalter.cookbook.runningfiles`.

4. Edit the `Application.java` file and add a `main` method:

```
public static void main(String[] args) {
   System.out.println("This is called from Application");
}
```

There should now be two files within the project that have a `main` method within them, `Application.java` and `RunningFiles.java`.

5. Right-click on the `Application.java` file in the **Projects** explorer and select **Run File**.

Notice that the `Application.java` file is executed with the `println` statement we added in step 4 being displayed in the **Output** window.

6. Edit the `RunningFiles.java` file and change the `main` method to:

```
public static void main(String[] args) {
   System.out.println("This is called from RunningFiles");
}
```

7. Run the project by clicking on the **Run** menu option and then the **Run Project** menu option or by pressing *F6*.

Notice that the `RunningFiles.java` file is executed with the `println` statement we added in step 6 being displayed in the **Output** window.

How it works...

In this recipe, we've shown how you can either run a file or a run a project. When running a file, the Java class that is selected to be run is executed as long as it has a `main` method in it.

When we choose to run a project, NetBeans executes the file that is specified as **Main Class** on the **Project Properties** dialog under the **Run** node. Right-click on the project in the **Projects** explorer and select **Properties** to see the following dialog:

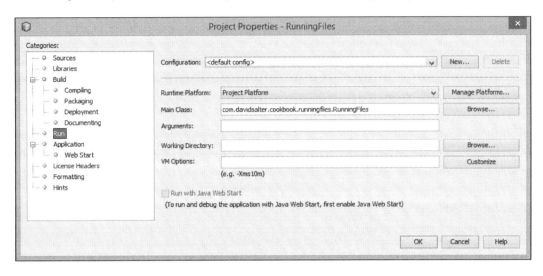

In this **Properties** dialog, we can also specify any arguments that need to be passed to the main method of our application. These arguments are specified within the **Arguments** field.

When the project was created, the **Main Class** field was set to com.davidsalter. cookbook.runningfiles.RunningFiles and not to any subsequent main classes that we may have added. This explains why running a class and running the project do not necessarily perform the same operation.

There's more...

If we have a project with more than one **Main Class** within it, we can use the **Project Properties** dialog to select the class that will be executed when *F6* or the **Run Project** option is selected. Click the **Browse...** button next to the **Main Class** input on the **Project Properties** dialog. On the resultant dialog, a list of all the main classes within a project is shown. Select the one that you wish to use as **Main Class** for the project. We can see the **Browse Main Classes** window in the following screenshot:

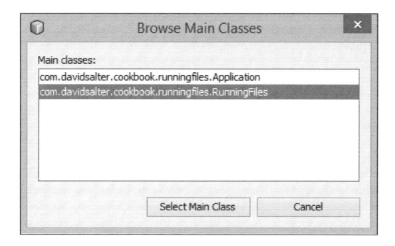

In addition to creating a blank Java class and then adding a `main` method into it manually, NetBeans provides a wizard to automatically create a new class with a `main` method in it. This is achieved by right-clicking on a project and selecting **New** and then **Other** and then selecting **Java** from the list of categories and **New Main Class** as the file type.

In this recipe, we've seen how a main class can be executed from within NetBeans. Later on in this book, we'll see how a web project and a mobile project can be executed.

Debugging a class

It is possible to set breakpoints and watches in NetBeans and, on execution, check what the value of a given variable or object is.

The NetBeans debugger also lets the developer follow method calls and execute code one line at a time giving a fine-grained visualization on how the code is running.

This is one of the features where NetBeans shines in comparison to other IDEs; so, without further ado, let's dive in. NetBeans has already included many of the plugins, performance tools, and servers that are used for easing the process of setup and debugging.

Getting ready

We will be using a **Java Application** project for this example. Since we are just showcasing the capabilities of the debugger, we won't be using anything complicated; so, a normal **Java Application** project will suffice. If you're unsure on how to create one, please check the *Creating a Java application* recipe of *Chapter 1, Using NetBeans Projects*.

We are also going to need a Java class. If the *Creating a Java application* recipe was used, then a main class is already generated and that one can be used for our example. If a project already exists, then it is possible to follow the *Creating a class* recipe in order to get a clean class for the work to proceed. The automatically generated class will be our main class, so the class name to use for the clean class is `HowToDebug.java`.

If the *Creating a Java application* recipe is followed, the project name should be `HowToDebug` with the main class being called `com.davidsalter.cookbook.howtodebug.HowToDebug.java`. All of the other default setting present on the wizards should be left untouched.

How to do it...

We will need another class to demonstrate how to set up breakpoints in other objects. For this, perform the following steps:

1. Right-click on **Source Packages**, under the `HowToDebug` project, select **New** and **Java Class...**.
2. On the **New Java Class** window, type `Person` under the **Class Name** field.
3. On package selection, click on the dropdown and select `com.davidsalter.cookbook.howtodebug`.
4. Click on **Finish**.

The `Person.java` file will show up on the Java editor.

Inside the `Person` class declaration, write:

```
int age;
String name;
```

Now, let's refactor our class by encapsulating the fields:

1. Right-click on the `Person` class inside the Java editor.
2. Select **Refactor** and then click on **Encapsulate Fields...**.
3. Then click on **Select All** and **Refactor**. Getters and setters for the `age` and `name` instance variables will be added to `Person.java` and the variables will have the visibility modifiers set to `private`.
4. Open `HowToDebug.java`. Inside the `main` method, enter the following lines of code:
   ```
   Person person1 = new Person();
   Person person2 = new Person();

   person1.setName("David");
   person1.setAge(21);
   person2.setName(null);
   person2.setAge(32);
   ```

It is not a good practice to set variables with null values, but for the purpose of this example, we will do it this one time.

We will now use a **watch** to observe a specific variable's value. A watch is exactly what the name says, it "watches" a specific variable for the entire lifetime of the application and displays its value in the **Variables** view.

To add a watch, simply:

1. Select the `person1` variable.

2. There are two ways to add a watch: On the top bar, click on **Debug** and then select **New Watch...** or press *Ctrl + Shift + F7* (*Command + Shift + F7* on a Mac) and click on **OK**, as shown in the following screenshot. The `person1` variable will be added to the **Variables** view.

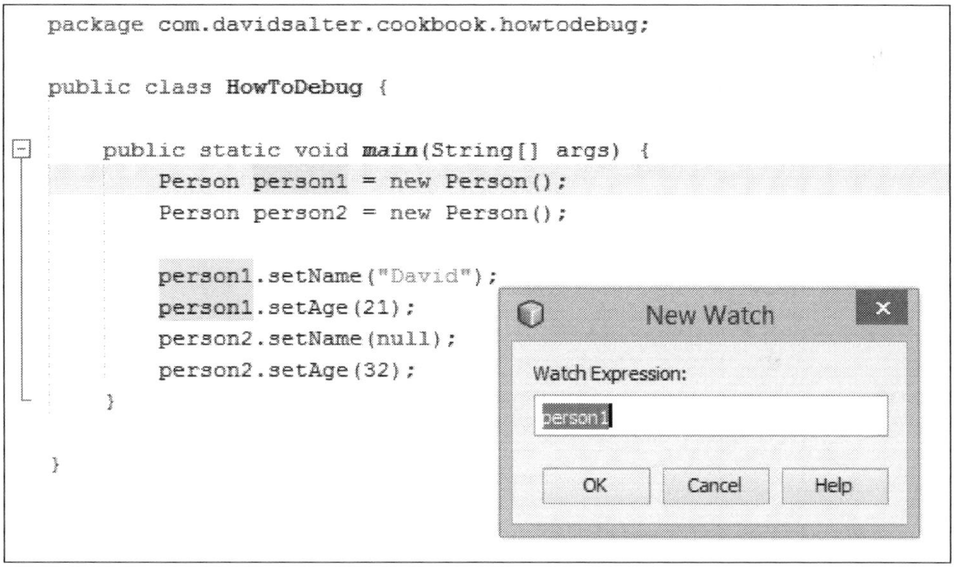

```
package com.davidsalter.cookbook.howtodebug;

public class HowToDebug {

    public static void main(String[] args) {
        Person person1 = new Person();
        Person person2 = new Person();

        person1.setName("David");
        person1.setAge(21);
        person2.setName(null);
        person2.setAge(32);
    }

}
```

New Watch

Watch Expression:

person1

OK   Cancel   Help

For our first breakpoint, click on the left-hand side bar, where the line numbers are placed, specifically on the following line:

```
person2.setName(null);
```

A breakpoint will be added to the side bar and a long pink line will specify the breakpoint location, as shown in the following screenshot:

```
7       package com.davidsalter.cookbook.howtodebug;
8
9       public class HowToDebug {
10
11          public static void main(String[] args) {
12              Person person1 = new Person();
13              Person person2 = new Person();
14
15              person1.setName("David");
16              person1.setAge(21);
                person2.setName(null);
18              person2.setAge(32);
19          }
20
21      }
```

Then, add another breakpoint, but this time to `Person.java`. Add the breakpoint to the line:

```
this.age = age;
```

This line is highlighted in the following screenshot:

```
24      /**
25       * @param age the age to set
26       */
27      public void setAge(int age) {
            this.age = age;
29      }
30
```

Finally, let's debug our example. Open `HowToDebug.java` and press *Ctrl + Shift + F5* (*Command + Shift + F5* on a Mac).

 Instead of using keyboard shortcuts, a file can be debugged by selecting the **Debug** option and then **Debug File** menu option, or by clicking on the **Debug Project** button (📦)in the toolbar.

How it works...

Upon the debug mode execution, NetBeans stops the execution at the first breakpoint.

The breakpoint tells NetBeans to temporarily halt the program and let the developer examine the contents of variables and watches at that point.

In our example, NetBeans will look like the following screenshot:

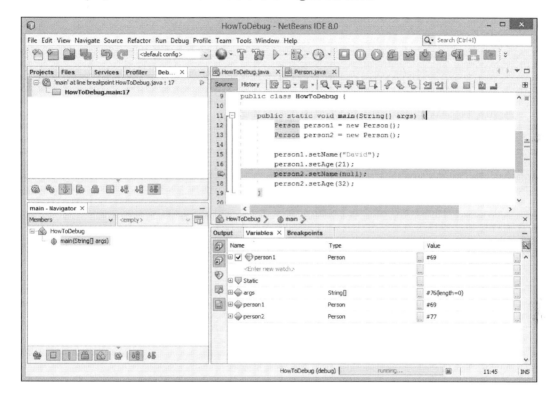

It is possible to see our watch, shown with a blue diamond icon, and also the normal variables, shown with a green lozenge. It is possible to expand the watch or variables to check the contents of an object at runtime.

The execution point is highlighted in green. To jump one line of code in the execution, press *F8*. To continue, press *F5*; NetBeans will resume the debugging process until another breakpoint is found, at which point the execution will once again stop so that the developer can have another chance to examine the execution. In our example, the execution will continue until the `Person` class's set method for age is reached. To continue with the execution, just press *F5* one more time and the program execution will continue until the end, since we do not have any other breakpoints.

To remove a breakpoint, simply click on it and it will disappear.

There's more...

What if I want a breakpoint when my variable reaches a certain value? Watches are too complicated, is there something easier? Does NetBeans debug other types of applications? Can I debug applications rather than main classes?

Conditional breakpoints

It is possible to create breakpoints with conditions.

Just right-click on the breakpoint, select **Breakpoint**, and then **Properties**. A **Breakpoint Properties** window will show up, with a section where the conditions can be specified. We can see the **Breakpoint Properties** window in the following screenshot:

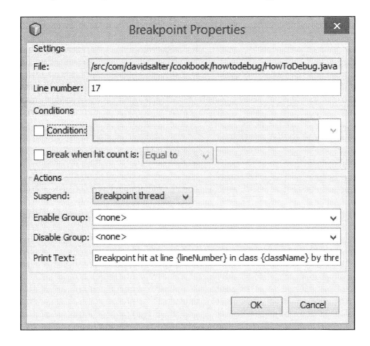

Other ways to check variable content

It is also possible to check the contents of a variable without needing to watch the **Variables** view. When the execution stops, just place the mouse cursor over the variable. A tooltip will be shown with the variable result.

This is very fast and useful especially when you first start debugging, and don't know what watches are needed yet.

Different kinds of debuggable applications

In this recipe, we used a Java Desktop application as a base for our example. However, debugging can also be used with different applications, such as web and mobile applications.

Debugging the application rather than a class

In the earlier discussion, we showed how to debug a file by pressing *Ctrl + Shift + F5*. This is an excellent way for debugging classes with a `main` method in them. For other application types, such as web applications, there is no `main` method and so a class cannot be debugged on its own. In this case, the application can be debugged rather than a class.

To start debugging an application rather than a class, press *Ctrl + F5* instead of *Ctrl + Shift + F5*.

When debugging an application with a single `main` method, the option to debug a class and the option to debug the application will both operate identically.

Formatting the code

Once we've written and run/debugged some of our code, it's generally a good idea to check that the code follows some layout guidelines.

In this recipe, we'll see how we can quickly and easily format the code so that all of our code has a standard layout making it easier for us and others to read.

Getting ready

It is necessary to have a project in order to format the code within it. If you are unsure on how to create a project, please check the recipes in *Chapter 1, Using NetBeans Projects*. To help follow this recipe, when creating a project, enter `FormattingCode` as the project name and ensure that the option to create a main class called `com.davidsalter.cookbook.formattingcode.FormattingCode` is selected.

How to do it...

1. Expand the **Source Packages** node within the `FormattingCode` project and select the `FormattingCode.java` class to be edited in the Java code editor.

2. Edit the empty `main` method in the class to have the following contents (note that the layout of the code here is deliberately bad with each line starting in the first column of the editor):

```
public static void main(String[] args)
{
for (int i = 0; i < 10; i++)
{
System.out.println("i="+i);
}
}
```

3. Right-click in the code editor and select **Format**.

4. The code in the editor window will now be formatted according to the Java code guidelines. For example, you can see that each line is now indented correctly and the opening brace symbols, {, have been placed at the end of the first line of the block they belong to rather than being on lines on their own.

How it works...

NetBeans maintains a list of code formatting rules that can be applied to different file types. When the **Format** action is invoked, these formatting rules are applied to the currently open file.

The formatting rules include options such as where to place braces, how to align code and the order of members in a class. All of these formatting rules can be customized if the default is not to your liking. To customize the formatting rules, select **Tools** and then **Options** from the main menu. On the **Options** dialog, select the **Editor** option and the **Formatting** tab.

Project-specific formatting rules can be defined by right-clicking on a project and selecting **Properties**. On the **Formatting** section of the **Properties** dialog, the user can select to use **Global options**, or to **Use project specific options**.

A shortcut for formatting a file is pressing *Alt + Shift + F* rather than right-clicking on the file and selecting **Format**.

Collapsing and expanding code folds

When you've written a lot of code, it's useful to be able to group sections of code together that can be collapsed and expanded at will. Code folds allow you to hide sections of code to make the code that you are looking at easier to understand. NetBeans allows any amount of code to be defined within a code fold, and indeed automatically generates code folds for comments, classes, and methods as will be seen in this recipe.

Getting ready

It is necessary to have a project with some Java code within it in order to see code folds in action. If you are unsure on how to create a project, please check the recipes in *Chapter 1, Using NetBeans Projects*. To help follow this recipe, when creating a project, enter `CodeFolds` as the project name and ensure that the option to create a main class called `com.davidsalter.cookbook.codefolds.CodeFolds` is selected.

How to do it...

1. Expand the **Source Packages** node within the `CodeFolds` project and select the `CodeFolds.java` class to be edited in the Java code editor.

2. Edit the empty `main` method in the class to have the following content:

```java
public static void main(String[] args) {

    int total = 0;
    int maximumCount = 10;

    for ( int i = 0; i < maximumCount; i++) {
        total += i;
    }

    System.out.println("Total: "+total);
}
```

3. Examine the code in the Java editor and you will see that there is a minus sign, `-`, in the left-hand side margin at the start of the `main` method indicating the start of a code fold. The code fold continues to the end of the method.

4. Edit the code, and enclose the `for` statement block within a code fold as shown in the following code:

```java
// <editor-fold desc="Basic summing algorithm.">
for ( int i = 0; i < maximumCount; i++) {
    total += i;
}
// </editor-fold>
```

5. The `main` method should now look like the following screenshot:

```
public static void main(String[] args) {

    int total = 0;
    int maximumCount = 10;

    // <editor-fold desc="Basic summing algorithm.">
    for ( int i = 0; i < maximumCount; i++) {
        total += i;
    }
    // </editor-fold>

    System.out.println("Total: "+total);
}
```

6. Click on – in the border to collapse the code fold as shown in the following screenshot:

```
public static void main(String[] args) {

    int total = 0;
    int maximumCount = 10;

    Basic summing algorithm.

    System.out.println("Total: "+total);
}
```

How it works...

Adding an `<editor-fold>` element around a section of code within the NetBeans editor allows the code to be collapsed and expanded using the **+** and **–** buttons in the left-hand side margin.

If a description for a code fold is required, then the `desc` attribute of the `<editor-fold>` element can be used to hold that description. When the code is collapsed, the description is displayed within the editor. If no description is specified, then the first line of the code fold together with the number of lines collapsed is displayed instead of a description.

By default, when a file is opened up within the Java editor, all of the code folds are displayed in an expanded fashion. If you have some code that you wish to be collapsed when the file is opened up (perhaps this could be some variable declarations or initialization code), then this can be achieved by adding the `defaultstate="collapsed"` attribute onto a `<editor-fold>` element. NetBeans allows you to define both a description and a default collapsed state on a piece of code.

There's more...

Clicking on **View** and the **Code Folds** menu item displays a menu showing all of the operations that can be performed against code folds within the currently open file. This menu shows options for collapsing the current fold, collapsing all folds, collapsing only Javadoc folds, and so on.

Toggling comments

When writing code, it is sometimes useful to comment out code to see what effect it will have on a running application while still keeping the original code. NetBeans provides an easy way to comment out and remove comments from multiple lines of code as seen in this recipe.

Getting ready

To complete this recipe, you need to have a NetBeans project with some Java code in it that can be commented out. If you do not have a suitable project, you can create one using any of the recipes in *Chapter 1, Using NetBeans Projects*, of this book.

How to do it...

1. Using the mouse, click on a single line of code within a Java source file.
2. Press *Ctrl + Shift + C*.
3. Note that the commenting state of the line you have selected is toggled. That is, if you selected an uncommented line of code it will now be commented out. If you selected a commented out line of code, it will now not be commented.
4. Using the mouse, highlight several lines of code within a Java source file.
5. Press *Ctrl + Shift + C*.
6. Note that the commenting state of the lines that you have selected is again toggled just like in step 3.

How it works...

Pressing *Ctrl* + *Shift* + *C* on a line, or a set of lines will comment out/remove comments from the selected line(s).

Be careful when commenting out sections of lines that include both commented and uncommented lines within them. In these instances, toggling of comments may not necessarily occur on a line-by-line basis as the first press of *Ctrl* + *Shift* + *C* will comment out all of the lines that are selected even if they are already commented out. You will see that some lines are therefore commented out twice. Subsequently, pressing *Ctrl* + *Shift* + *C* will undo the commenting that has just been performed.

An alternative key combination to *Ctrl* + *Shift* + *C* is *Ctrl* + */*. Both of these key combinations perform the same action.

Fixing and organizing imports

With anything more than a very basic application, a developer needs to import other packages into their classes for them to function correctly. This quickly leads to a number of `import` statements at the top of a class file. NetBeans offers facilities to automatically add `import` statements (fix imports), in order to save developer time, and the ability to tidy up the `import` statements (organize imports).

Getting ready

It is necessary to have a project with valid Java source code in order to fix and organize imports. If you are unsure on how to create a project, please check the recipes in *Chapter 1*, *Using NetBeans Projects*. To help follow this recipe, when creating a project, enter `UsingImports` as the project name and ensure that the option to create a main class called `com.davidsalter.cookbook.usingimports.UsingImports` is selected.

How to do it...

1. Expand the `UsingImports` project, and open the `UsingImports.java` class for editing.

2. Edit the `main` method in `UsingImports.java` to be as follows:

```
public static void main(String[] args) {
  List<String> l = new ArrayList<String>();
  l.add("Hello");
  l.add("World");
}
```

3. Note that the Java types `List` and `ArrayList` are underlined in red to indicate that an error has occurred here in the source code. The reason for the error here is that the classes have not been defined by their respective packages being imported.

4. Press *Ctrl + Shift + I* (or click on **Source** from the main menu and then click on **Fix Imports**) to open up the **Fix All Imports** dialog:

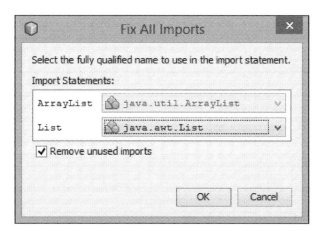

5. Ensure that the import for `ArrayList` is `java.util.ArrayList` and the import for `List` is `java.util.List` (these are the default options, but notice that there is also a `java.awt.List` class—this is not what we intend in this instance).

6. Click on the **OK** button.

At this point, the **Fix All Imports** dialog will close and you will see that the import statements for `ArrayList` and `List` have been added to the top of the `UsingImports` class.

In addition to fixing the `import` statements in a class file, NetBeans can also organize the imports with the following steps:

1. Edit the `UsingImports.java` file and swap the order of the imports so that the import for `java.util.List` is the first `import` statement.

2. Click on the **Source** menu and then the **Organize Imports** option.

You will now see in the source code window that NetBeans has organized the `import` statements into alphabetical order again with the `import` statement for `java.util.ArrayList` being first.

How it works...

When selecting to **Organize Imports**, NetBeans will order the imports into alphabetical order and perform any other organization as defined by the code formatting rules. For example, if more than three imports are made from the same package, NetBeans can be configured to replace all imports from that package with a star import (`import package.*`). The import organization rules can be defined within the NetBeans options. To access these options, select **Tools** and then **Options** menu item. Select the **Editor** option and then the **Formatting** tab choosing **Imports** as the category on this tab.

Performing a **Fix Imports** option will not only add any missing imports, it will also organize the imports as if the **Organize Imports** action had been performed,

There's more...

Imports can automatically be organized when a file is saved. To enable this option, click **Tools** and then **Options** from the main NetBeans menu. Select the **Editor** option and then the **On Save** tab. Ensure that the **Organize Imports** checkbox is checked to organize the imports in a file and that the **Remove Unused Imports** checkbox is checked to remove any unnecessary `import` statements, as shown in the following screenshot:

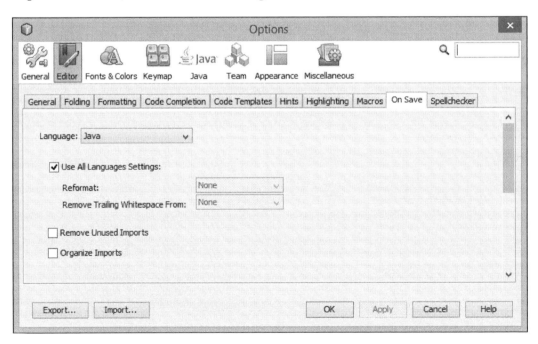

When a line of code is typed into a Java class file, NetBeans parses the line to determine if any additional classes need to be imported into the current class. These additional classes determine which imports are added to a class using the **Fix Imports** action. In addition to fixing all of the imports in one operation, each source line that requires an import has a light bulb displayed in the left-hand side margin. Clicking on the light bulb with the left mouse button will display a list of hints on how to fix any errors on the current line. Included in this list of fixes is the ability to individually add missing `import` statements.

Creating file headers

When writing open source software, or closed source software that belongs to a specific company or person, it is very useful to add a header to a file that consists, at a minimum, of the license terms for the file. NetBeans comes preconfigured with the major license terms that can be automatically applied to the beginning of files, but also allows custom headers to be defined.

Getting ready

It is necessary to have a project with valid Java source code in order to define file headers as they are defined on a per-project basis. If you are unsure on how to create a project, please check the recipes in *Chapter 1, Using NetBeans Projects*. To help follow this recipe, when creating a project, enter `UsingHeaders` as the project name and ensure that a main class is not created.

How to do it...

1. Right-click on the `UsingHeaders` project in the **Projects** explorer and select **Properties**. The **Project Properties** dialog will be displayed.

2. Select the **License Headers** category.

3. To apply one of the in-build open source headers to all new files created within NetBeans, select a license from the **Use global license** dropdown and then click on the **OK** button.

NetBeans comes preconfigured with the following license headers for open source software:

- ❑ **Apache License 2.0**
- ❑ **BSD 2-Clause License**
- ❑ **NetBeans CDDL/GPL**
- ❑ **Eclipse Public License 1.0**
- ❑ **General Public License 2.0**
- ❑ **General Public License 3.0**
- ❑ **Lesser GPL 2.1**
- ❑ **MIT License**

4. Right-click on the `UsingHeaders` project, and select **New** and then **Java Class**.

5. Enter the **Class Name** field as `WithHeaders` and the **Package** field as `com.davidsalter.cookbook.withheaders`.

6. The class will now be created and opened within the Java editor. You will see that the license header selected in step 3 is automatically applied to the file.

There's more...

In addition to using the standard open source license headers, custom file headers can be used. On the **Project Properties** dialog, selecting the **Edit global licenses** button allows the developer to edit and add to the collection of predefined license headers.

If a license file is stored alongside the project as a file, then this can be used as the default file header by selecting the **Use project location** option within the **Project Properties** dialog.

Changing the look and feel of NetBeans

Java provides a set of different **Look and Feel** styles that can be applied to applications. These **Look and Feel** styles change the way that user interface components are displayed within the application (the look) and how they behave (the feel). Java provides native **Look and Feel** components (for example, on Windows or on Mac OS X) as well as custom-styled components. Additional **Look and Feel** styles can be designed in addition to the ones provided by default with Java.

Getting ready

To change the look and feel of NetBeans, no specific projects are required to be loaded. All that is required is a running copy of NetBeans.

How to do it...

1. Click on **Tools** and then **Options** within the main NetBeans menu.

2. On the **Options** dialog, select the **Appearance** option.

3. Select the **Look and Feel** tab, which is displayed in the following screenshot:

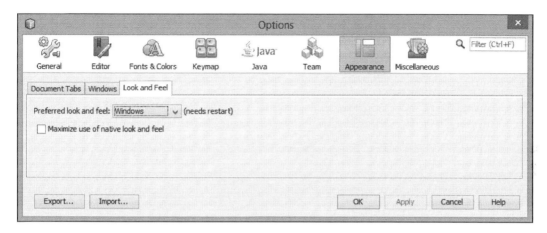

4. Select the required option from the **Preferred look and feel** drop-down box.

5. Restart NetBeans for the changes to take effect.

How it works...

Specifying the look and feel within the NetBeans options changes the default look and feel that is used when NetBeans starts up. This is the reason that a restart of NetBeans is required after changing the look and feel. At startup time, NetBeans invokes the standard Java `UIManager` class to set the application look and feel.

There's more...

When selecting the **Look and Feel** tab via the **Options** dialog, selecting **Maximize use of native look and feel** ensures that NetBeans uses the maximum number of native controls available to the Java runtime.

In addition to changing the look and feel of NetBeans via the application's user interface as described by this recipe, it is also possible to change the look and feel via the command line or via the NetBeans startup options. When the look and feel is changed via the command line, it is not possible to override this within the application as described by this recipe.

To change look and feel via the command line, start NetBeans with the `-laf` parameter specifying the full class name to the look and feel required. For example, to start NetBeans using the `Motif` look and feel, start NetBeans as:

```
netbeans --laf com.sun.java.swing.plaf.motif.MotifLookAndFeel
```

Notice the double - sign required here to specify the **Look and Feel** parameter is being passed to NetBeans. If a single – sign is used, the look and feel will not be changed.

To change the look and feel via the NetBeans configuration options, edit the `netbeans.conf` file located within the NetBeans installation and add the `-laf` option into the `netbeans_default_options` parameter as:

```
netbeans_default_options="--laf
javax.swing.plaf.metal.MetalLookAndFeel
 -J-client -J-Xss2m -J-Xms32m -J-XX:PermSize=32m -J-
Dnetbeans.logger.console=true -J-ea -J-
Dapple.laf.useScreenMenuBar=true -J-
Dapple.awt.graphics.UseQuartz=true -J-Dsun.java2d.noddraw=true -J-
Dsun.java2d.dpiaware=true -J-Dsun.zip.disableMemoryMapping=true -
J-Dnetbeans.extbrowser.manual_chrome_plugin_install=yes"
```

For details on the different **Look and Feel** classes that are available, check out `http://docs.oracle.com/javase/tutorial/uiswing/lookandfeel/plaf.html`.

3
NetBeans Productivity

In this chapter, we will cover the following recipes:

- ▶ Creating a constructor
- ▶ Creating a logger
- ▶ Creating a `toString()` method
- ▶ Creating a property
- ▶ Overriding a method
- ▶ Rename refactoring
- ▶ Move refactoring
- ▶ Copy refactoring
- ▶ Delete refactoring
- ▶ Change parameters refactoring
- ▶ Pull up / push down refactoring
- ▶ Extract interface refactoring
- ▶ Encapsulate fields refactoring
- ▶ Replacing a constructor with the Factory pattern

Introduction

In the first two chapters, we looked at how to create projects and how to create Java artifacts (classes, packages, and so on).

In this chapter, we'll move on and show how NetBeans can improve developer productivity by describing some different shortcuts for generating code. We'll generate constructors, loggers, `toString()` methods, and properties.

After looking at these shortcuts, we'll see some of the different types of code refactoring that can be achieved with NetBeans.

Creating a constructor

When creating a class that maintains any state (that is almost any class that has class members), it can be very useful to create a constructor that can perform any required initialization.

Creating constructors is not tricky; however, NetBeans provides a handy shortcut to save time and increase developer productivity.

Getting ready

First we will need to create a new project, so please refer to the recipes in *Chapter 1, Using NetBeans Projects*, for creating Java projects. To help follow this recipe, when creating a project, enter CreatingConstructors as the project name.

How to do it...

When the **Projects** explorer shows the CreatingConstructors project, expand the CreatingConstructors node if it is not already expanded.

We will now create an empty class and show how constructors can be added to it with the following steps:

1. Right-click on the CreatingConstructors project, and select **New** and **Java Class...**.

2. On the **New Java Class** dialog, type Shape under the **Class Name** field.

3. On the **Package** selection, enter com.davidsalter.cookbook.refactor. creatingconstructors.

4. Click on **Finish** and the new class will be created and opened in the editor.

5. Right-click within the body of the class and select **Insert Code...**.

6. On the pop-up **Generate** window, click on **Constructor...**.

   At this stage, the pop-up **Generate** window will close and you will see that a blank constructor has been added to the Shape class. Since NetBeans has no knowledge of what we want to do with the constructor, it has left its implementation empty.

   Let's now add some member variables to the class and show how NetBeans can make a constructor that will allow us to set these variables.

7. Within the `Shape` class, add the following code immediately before the `Shape()` constructor:

```
int numberOfSides;
float area;
```

8. Right-click within the body of the class and select **Insert Code...**.

9. On the pop-up **Generate** window, click on **Constructor...**.

Unlike the first time we chose to insert a constructor, this time NetBeans has displayed the **Generate Constructor** dialog:

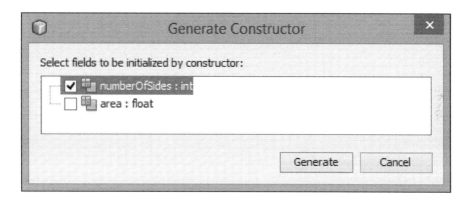

10. On the **Generate Constructor** dialog, check the **numberOfSides : int** field, leaving the **area : float** field unchecked.

11. Click on **Generate**.

12. The **Generate Constructor** dialog will now close and a new constructor will be added to the `Shape.java` class. The new constructor will look like the following code:

```
public Shape(int numberOfSides) {
    this.numberOfSides = numberOfSides;
}
```

How it works...

When creating a constructor, NetBeans first checks to see if there are any member variables within the class. If there are none, then a blank default constructor will be created for the class. If, however, there are member variables within the class, NetBeans provides the developer with the option of choosing which member variables can be initialized as part of the constructor.

Creating a constructor in this way can be performed multiple times if you wish to initialize different variables with different constructors. If you find yourself creating multiple different constructors, it may, however, be an indication that you need to rethink your design of the class.

There's more...

Instead of right-clicking within the body of a class and selecting **Insert Code...**, the shortcut key *Alt + Insert* can be used.

Creating a logger

When developing code, it can be useful to output log information either to the terminal, or more usefully in the case of web applications, to a logfile. NetBeans allows developers to easily make use of loggers within classes by creating a logger member within a class.

Getting ready

First we will need to create a new project, so please refer to the recipes in *Chapter 1, Using NetBeans Projects*, for creating Java projects. To help follow this recipe, when creating a project, enter `CreatingLoggers` as the project name and ensure that a main class called `com.davidsalter.cookbook.creatingloggers.CreatingLoggers` is created.

How to do it...

When the **Projects** explorer shows the `CreatingLoggers` project, expand the `CreatingLoggers` node if not yet expanded and perform the following steps:

1. Double-click on the `CreatingLoggers.java` class file within the **Projects** explorer to open it for editing.

2. Right-click within the body of the class and select **Insert Code...**.

3. On the pop-up **Generate** window, click on **Logger...**.

   At this stage, the pop-up **Generate** window will close and a logger will be added to the end of the class together with the relevant `import` statement at the beginning of the class. The following statement will be added:

   ```
   private static final Logger LOG =
       Logger.getLogger(CreatingLoggers.class.getName());
   ```

 For more information of Java logging, check out Oracle's *Java Logging Technology* page at `http://docs.oracle.com/javase/7/docs/technotes/guides/logging/`.

Now that we have created a logger within a class, information can be sent to the logger.

4. Change the body of the `main` method within the `CreatingLoggers.java` file to be:

    ```
    LOG.warning("This is a warning");
    LOG.info("This is information");
    ```

5. Run the main class by pressing *Shift + F6* and notice that the log information is output to the **Output** window.

Creating a toString() method

A useful technique to aid debugging Java applications is to add a `toString()` method onto a class so that useful information can be output to help describe the class. Typically, a `toString()` implementation would output any ID that an object has together with the description of the object. NetBeans provides facilities to allow developers to easily add and customize `toString()` methods within classes.

Getting ready

First we will need to create a new project, so please refer to the recipes in *Chapter 1, Using NetBeans Projects*, for creating Java projects. To help follow this recipe, when creating a project, enter `CreatingToString` as the project name and ensure that a main class called `com.davidsalter.cookbook.creatingtostring.CreatingToString` is created.

How to do it...

To show how to create a `toString()` method within NetBeans and how to define the implementation of the method, let's first add a `Person` class that could represent a person in a database table with the following steps:

1. Right-click on the `CreatingToString` project, and select **New** and **Java Class...**.

2. On the **New Java Class** dialog, type `Person` as the **Class Name** field.

3. In the **Package** section, select `com.davidsalter.cookbook.creatingtostring`.

4. Click on **Finish**.

5. Add the following as the body of the `Person` class:

```
private int id;
private String firstName;
private String lastName;

public Person(int id, String firstName, String lastName) {
   this.id = id;
   this.firstName = firstName;
   this.lastName = lastName;
}
```

6. Right-click within the body of the class and select **Insert Code...**.

7. On the pop-up **Generate** window, select **toString...**. NetBeans will now display the **Generate toString()** dialog:

8. Check the `id`, `firstName`, and `lastName` fields to be included in the `toString()` implementation.

9. Click on **Generate**.

    Upon clicking the **Generate** button, the **Generate toString()** dialog will close and the `Person.java` class will be updated with a new `toString()` method that outputs the selected fields—in this case, `id`, `firstName`, and `lastName`.

    Let's now write some code that shows this method in operation.

10. Double-click on the `CreatingToString.java` file within the **Projects** explorer to open it up for editing.

11. Add the following as the body of the `main` method:

```
Person person = new Person(1, "David", "Salter");
System.out.println(person.toString());
```

12. Press *Shift + F6* to run the main class and notice the `toString()` method's output in the **Output** window, which will display the following output:

```
run:
Person{id=1, firstName=David, lastName=Salter}
BUILD SUCCESSFUL (total time: 1 second)
```

There's more...

This recipe shows how a `toString()` method can easily be added to a class. It should be noted, however, that only one `toString()` method can be added to a class using this technique. If you attempt to add a `toString()` method to a class that already implements the method, then the pop-up **Generate** window will not show the **toString()** option.

Creating a property

In this recipe, we'll see how we can create properties directly within a class without having to first add fields to the class and then add accessors for the fields.

Getting ready

First we will need to create a new project, so please refer to the recipes in *Chapter 1, Using NetBeans Projects*, for creating Java projects. To help follow this recipe, when creating a project, enter `CreatingProperties` as the project name and ensure that a main class called `com.davidsalter.cookbook.creatingproperties.CreatingProperties` is created.

How to do it...

To show how to create properties within a class, let's first create a class to represent a customer and then add some properties to the `Customer` class:

1. Right-click on the `CreatingProperties` project, and select **New** and **Java Class...**.
2. On the **New Java Class** dialog, type `Customer` as the **Class Name** field.
3. On the **Package** selection, click on the dropdown and select `com.davidsalter.cookbook.creatingproperties`.
4. Click on **Finish**.
5. A blank `Customer` class will now be created and opened in the NetBeans Java editor for editing.
6. Right-click on the body of the `Customer` class and click on **Insert Code...**.

7. On the pop-up **Generate** window, click on **Add Property…**. The **Add Property** dialog will now be displayed:

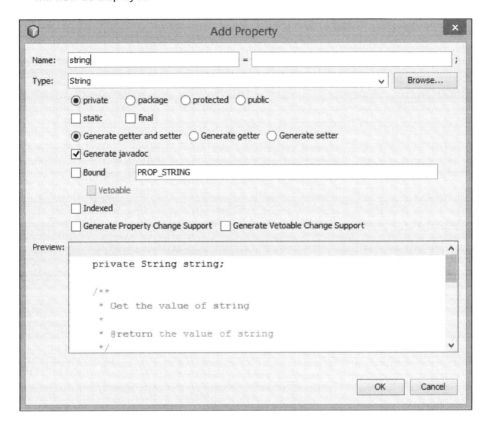

8. Enter id in the **Name** field and **long** in the **Type** field.

9. Ensure **Generate getter** is selected.

10. Click on **OK**.

The **Add Property** dialog will now close. Examine the generated code and you will see that an id property has been created with a public getter. The id field is marked as private.

Let's add a customer's name field to the class with the following steps:

1. Right-click on the body of the Customer class and click on **Insert Code…**.

2. On the pop-up **Generate** window, click on **Add Property…**. The **Add Property** dialog will now be displayed.

3. Enter name in the **Name** field and String in the **Type** field.

4. Ensure **Generate getter and setter** is selected.

5. Click on **OK**.

The **Add Property** dialog will now close. Examine the generated code again and you will see that a `name` property has been added with a `public` getter and setter. The `name` field is, again, marked as `private`.

How it works...

When specifying the details of the new property to be created, the **Add Property** dialog shows what the generated code will look like in a **Preview** section in the lower half of the dialog.

There's more...

When generating properties, the visibility can be set to either **private**, **package**, **protected**, or **public**. The default option is `private`.

The **Type** dropdown selection shows the basic Java types that properties may take (**String**, **int**, **float**, and so on). If you wish to create a property of any other type, click on the **Browse...** button and use the **Find Type** dialog to find the appropriate type.

The default value of any property can be set by specifying the value in the field to the right of = at the top of the dialog. If the property is intended to be an array, ensure the **Indexed** field is checked.

If you are creating a JavaBean property, you can use the **Bound** and **Generate Property Change Support** checkboxes as appropriate.

Overriding a method

Object-oriented development has been shown to be a good development practice. One of the principal aspects of object-oriented development is the ability to override classes. This is defining a method in a subclass that has the same signature as that in a superclass. In Java, all classes are derived from `java.lang.Object`.

In this recipe, we'll show how NetBeans provides tools to allow developers to easily override superclass methods within a subclass.

Getting ready

First we will need to create a new project, so please refer to the recipes in *Chapter 1, Using NetBeans Projects*, for creating Java projects. To help follow this recipe, when creating a project, enter `OverridingMethods` as the project name and ensure that a main class called `com.davidsalter.cookbook.overridigmethods.OverridingMethods` is created.

How to do it...

When the **Projects** explorer shows the `OverridingMethods` project, expand the `OverridingMethods` node of not yet expanded.

To show how NetBeans makes it easier to override methods, let's create a simple class that represents a book and then check if we have duplicate books with the following steps:

1. Right-click on the `OverridingMethods` project, and select **New** and **Java Class...**.

2. On the **New Java Class** dialog, type `Book` under the **Class Name** field.

3. On the **Package** selection, click on the dropdown and select `com.davidsalter.cookbook.overridingmethods`.

4. Click on **Finish**.

5. Change the implementation of the `Book.java` class as follows:

```
public class Book {
    public enum format {HARDBACK, PAPERBACK, EBOOK};
    private String title;
    private format bookFormat;

    public Book(String title, format bookFormat) {
        this.title = title;
        this.bookFormat = bookFormat;
    }
}
```

This class models a simple book, which has a title and a format (hardback, paperback, or e-book).

Now that we've modelled a book, let's create instances of some books and see if they are the same.

6. Double-click on the `OverridingMethods.java` file within the **Projects** explorer to open the file for editing.

7. Change the implementation of the `main` method to be as follows:

```
public static void main(String[] args) {
    Book book1 = new Book("NetBeans Cookbook",
    Book.format.PAPERBACK);
    Book book2 = new Book("Seam 2 Development",
    Book.format.EBOOK);
    Book book3 = new Book("Seam 2 Development",
    Book.format.PAPERBACK);

    System.out.println(
        "Book1 == book2 " +  book1.equals(book2));
```

```
    System.out.println(
        "Book2 == book3 " +  book2.equals(book3));
    System.out.println(
        "Book3 == book1 " +  book3.equals(book1));
}
```

8. Press *Shift + F6* to run the code.

When the code is executed, we can see that the output of all three comparisons between the books returns `false` telling us that we've got three different books. Is that what we'd expect? Well, it's probably not what we'd expect, but it's what we've written so far.

As we're comparing our books with the default `equals` method, Java is using the `equals` implementation from the `java.lang.Object` base class. This implementation basically says that if the two objects compared are the same, then return `true`, otherwise return `false`. In our example here, we have three distinct objects, so the base `equals()` comparison will always return `false`.

Fortunately, it's easy to fix our code and make it behave as expected. All we need to do is override the default `equals()` method with the following steps:

1. Double-click on the `Book.java` class within the **Projects** explorer to open the class for editing.

2. Right-click within the body of the class and select **Insert Code...**.

3. On the pop-up **Generate** window, select **Override Method...**. NetBeans will now display the **Generate Override Methods** dialog, as shown in the following screenshot:

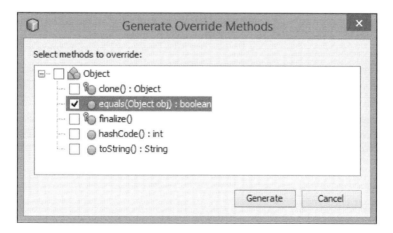

4. Ensure that the **equals(Object obj) : boolean** method is selected and all the other methods are unselected.

5. Click on **Generate**.

   The **Generate Override Methods** dialog will now close and a blank implementation for the `equals()` method will be added to the class.

6. Double-click on the `OverridingMethods.java` class within the **Projects** explorer to open it for editing.

7. Change the implementation of the generated `equals()` method to be as follows:

```
@Override
public boolean equals(Object obj) {
  if (obj instanceof Book) {
    return title.equalsIgnoreCase(((Book)obj).title);
  } else {
    return false;
  }
}
```

8. Press *Shift + F6* to run the application.

Running the application now shows that we have two distinct books made up from two paperbacks and one e-book.

How it works...

When using the wizard to override methods, NetBeans displays a list of all the methods within the class that can be overridden. If the class is not explicitly derived from any other class, then only the base methods on `java.lang.Object` that can be overridden are displayed. If the class, however, extends another class in your project, then any methods in your class hierarchy that can be overridden are also shown within the wizard.

Rename refactoring

Sometimes, when developing applications, a developer's first choice of a name for a package, class, or member, and so on, isn't the best choice. NetBeans allows developers to easily change the name of these objects using the **Rename** refactoring wizard. This wizard is clever enough to change both the name of the selected object and any references to it throughout the project's code base.

Getting ready

First we will need to create a new project, so please refer to the recipes in *Chapter 1,
Using NetBeans Projects*, for creating Java projects. We will use the same project for all the
refactoring recipes in this chapter. When naming the project, enter `Refactoring` in the
Project Name field and ensure that a main class called `refactoring.Refactoring`
is created. When the **Projects** explorer shows the `Refactoring` project, expand the
`Refactoring` node if not yet expanded.

How to do it...

First off, we will rename the initial package that was created with the project using the
following steps:

1. Expand the **Source Packages** node (if not yet expanded).

2. Right-click on `refactoring`.

3. Select **Refactor** and then **Rename...**.

4. In the **Rename** refactoring dialog, enter `com.davidsalter.cookbook.refactor`
   in the **New Name** field.

5. Click on **Refactor**.

A progress bar will briefly be shown on the **Rename** refactoring dialog showing the progress
of the refactoring and then the dialog will automatically close when the refactoring has
completed. When the refactoring has been completed, you will note that the **Source
Packages** node in the **Projects** explorer now shows that the package name has been
changed to `com.davidsalter.cookbook.refactor` as specified in step 4. If you
edit the `Refactoring.java` file within this project, you can see that the package name
of this class has also been modified accordingly.

Now, let's add some code to the `Refactoring` class and then show how we can rename it
with the following steps:

1. Open the `Refactoring.java` file for editing by double-clicking on it within the
   Projects explorer (if the file is not already open).

2. We are going to use this class for printing out environment variables, so
   `Refactoring` probably isn't the best name for the class. Right-click on the class
   name `Refactoring` on the line where the class is defined (that is, on the line that
   starts `public class Refactoring`).

3. Select **Refactor** and then **Rename…**.

4. On the **Rename Class Refactoring** dialog, enter `EnvironmentPrinter` in the **New Name** field.

5. Click on **Refactor**.

6. Notice how both the filename and the class name have been updated with this new name.

7. Edit the `EnvironmentPrinter.java` class so that it looks like this:

```java
public class EnvironmentPrinter {
  public static void main(String[] args) {
    EnvironmentPrinter ep = new EnvironmentPrinter();
    ep.print("JAVA_HOME");
  }

  public void print(String env) {
    String envVariableValue = System.getenv(env);
    System.out.println(envVariableValue);
  }
}
```

8. Press *Shift + F6* to run the file and note that the value of the `JAVA_HOME` environment variable is displayed within the **Output** window.

The code we have written works as expected and prints out the environment variable `JAVA_HOME` in the **Output** window. We're still not entirely happy with the code, however, as the name of the parameter to the `print()` method should probably be a bit more descriptive. Let's change it to `environmentVariableName` with the following steps:

1. Right-click on the parameter name `env` within the line `public void print(String env)`.

2. Select **Refactor** and then **Rename…**.

3. On the **Rename env** dialog, enter `environmentVariableName` in the **New Name** field.

4. Click on **Refactor**.

The parameter name is now refactored to `environmentVariableName`. You can see that the use of this variable within the method has also been updated to use the new name. The new `print()` method should look like the following code:

```java
public void print(String environmentVariableName) {
  String envVariableValue =
  System.getenv(environmentVariableName);
  System.out.println(envVariableValue);
}
```

How it works...

When refactoring, NetBeans has the ability to change variable, class, interface, and package names using a simple wizard. The power of refactoring, however, comes with the ability to change references to refactored objects as well as the original object. We saw that in the previous example, where we changed the name of a parameter in a method and saw that the references to the parameter within the method also changed.

NetBeans can not only perform **Rename** refactoring at a class level, but throughout an entire project. So for example, if you rename a class, every reference to the class throughout the project is also changed.

There's more...

To shortcut **Rename** refactoring, simply click on the object to rename (class, variable, package, and so on) within the editor window and press *Ctrl + R*. If the scope of the object being renamed is local and cannot affect any other object in the project (for example, renaming a local variable), then an in-place editor will be displayed on the screen rather than the **Rename** refactor wizard. All the local instances of the object will be renamed as the new name is typed in.

If the scope of an object being renamed can possibly affect other parts of a project, then the **Rename** refactor wizard is displayed. As renaming an object of this type can have repercussions across the whole of a project, the **Preview** button allows the developer to see a preview of all the files that would be changed if the refactoring was performed. This can be particularly useful when renaming affects large parts of a project.

 In general, when refactoring a file (using any type of refactoring, not just **Rename** refactoring), it's a good practice to ensure that the entire project can be compiled before proceeding with the refactoring. If the project cannot be compiled, then unexpected results may occur when refactoring.

If a file has been modified and you start to refactor some of the contents of the file, then the file will be saved before the **Rename** refactoring dialog is displayed.

Move refactoring

In the previous recipe, we saw how it's possible to rename various artifacts of a Java project. Sometimes, however, we've named our objects correctly, but we've put them in the wrong place! NetBeans allows developers to perform a **Move** refactor where class members can be moved to different classes or classes can be moved to different projects and/or packages.

Getting ready

First we will need a Java project to perform some **Move** refactoring. We will use the same project from the preceding recipe, *Rename refactoring*, and so ensure that you have the project open from the end of that recipe. If you have not followed that recipe, the project is available from the code download bundle under the `MoveRefactor` folder in `Chapter 3`. When the **Projects** explorer shows the `Refactoring` project, expand the `Refactoring` node if not yet expanded.

How to do it...

1. Open the `EnvironmentPrinter.java` file for editing from the **Projects** explorer by double-clicking on the filename.
2. When we look at this file, we can see that there is a `main()` method in the class. This probably should be placed in its own file, so let's create a file for the `main` method and then move it in there.
3. Right-click on the `com.davidsalter.cookbook.refactor` package in the `Refactoring` project, and select **New** and **Java Class...**.
4. On the **New Java Class** window, type `Main` under the **Class Name** field.
5. On the **Package** selection, ensure that `com.davidsalter.cookbook.refactor` is chosen as the new **Package** name.
6. Click on **Finish**.

A new class called `Main.java` has now been created within the `com.davidsalter.cookbook.refactor` package. We will now use the **Move** refactoring to move the `public static void main()` method into the new class created with the following steps:

1. Open the `EnvironmentPrinter.java` file from the **Projects** explorer by double-clicking on the Java source file.
2. Right-click within the `main` keyword that declares the `main()` method on the class and select **Refactor** and then select **Move...**.
3. The **Move Members** window is now displayed as shown in the following screenshot:

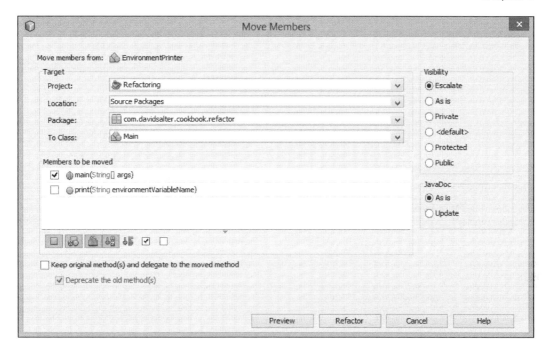

4. In the **To Class** section, select **Main** as the class we are going to move members to.

5. In the **Members to be moved** section, ensure that only the **main(String[] args)** method is selected.

6. Click on the **Refactor** button.

7. The **Move Members** refactor window will now close and the refactoring will be completed.

After the refactoring has been completed, you can see that the `Main.java` file has the `main()` method in it and the `EnvironmentPrinter.java` file only has a `print()` method within it.

There's more...

When moving members, the visibility of the moved members can be altered by specifying the **Visibility** section on the **Move Members** dialog. This allows, for example, `public` methods to be moved to a different class and automatically made `private`.

Javadoc can be modified to reference new class names when moving members to a different class. This is achieved by ensuring the **Update** option is selected under the **JavaDoc** section on the **Move Members** dialog.

If required, the original implementation of a method can be left, delegating functionality to a new class method. In this case, the new method is called from the old method, with both the new and old methods existing. Here, the method has been moved, but the original method still exists to call the new one. This technique is accomplished by selecting the **Keep original method(s) and delegate to the moved method** option. With this option, the original method can be marked as deprecated by checking the **Deprecate the old method(s)** option.

When performing a **Move** refactor on classes from one package to another, a shortcut is to simply drag the class from its source package in the **Projects** explorer to the destination package. Upon dropping the class in the destination package, the **Move Class** refactoring dialog will be displayed allowing the refactor to be completed.

Copy refactoring

Occasionally when writing code, you may want to copy a class from one package to another. The NetBeans **Copy** refactoring wizard allows this to be easily achieved.

Getting ready

First we will need a Java project to perform some **Copy** refactoring. We will use the same project from the earlier recipe, *Rename refactoring,* and so ensure that you have the project open from the end of that recipe. If you have not followed that recipe, the project is available from the code download bundle under the `MoveRefactor` folder in `Chapter 3`. When the **Projects** explorer shows the `Refactoring` project, expand the `Refactoring` node if not yet expanded.

How to do it...

To perform a **Copy** refactor, we need to have a destination package into which we can copy a class. First we will create an empty package and then we will make a copy of a class into this package. To create an empty package, perform the following steps:

1. Right-click on the `com.davidsalter.cookbook.refactor` package in the **Projects** explorer and select **New** and then **Java Package...**.
2. Enter `com.davidsalter.cookbook.refactor.copiedclasses` in the **Package Name** field.
3. Click on **Finish**.

We have now created a blank package, so let's use the NetBeans **Copy** refactoring tool to copy the `Main.java` class into this package with the following steps:

1. Double-click on the `Main.java` file in the **Projects** explorer to open the file for editing.
2. Right-click within the body of the class and select **Refactor** and then **Copy...**.

3. The **Copy Class** refactoring dialog is now shown. Enter `CopyOfMain` in the **New Name** field.

4. From the **To Package** section, select `com.davidsalter.cookbook.refactor.copiedclasses`.

5. Click on **Refactor**.

6. The **Copy Class** refactor dialog will now close and the **Copy** refactoring will be completed.

After the **Copy Class** refactoring dialog has closed, notice that the new `CopyOfMain` class has been created inside the `com.davidsalter.cookbook.refactor.copiedclasses` package. The original class (`com.davidsalter.cookbook.refactor.Main`) has not been modified.

There's more...

Apart from copying classes to different packages, the **Copy Class** refactor also allows classes to be copied to different projects. This is achieved by selecting a different project in the **Copy Class** dialog. The current project is always selected as the default destination project in this dialog.

Classes can also be copied to different locations within a project. For example, a class could be copied from the **Source Packages** node of a project into the **Test Packages** location.

When performing a **Copy** refactor on classes from one package to another, a shortcut is to simply drag the class from its source package in the **Projects** explorer to the destination package while holding down the *Ctrl* key. Upon dropping the class in the destination package, the **Copy Class** refactoring dialog will be displayed allowing the refactor to be completed.

One final shortcut for **Copy** refactoring is to right-click on a class within the **Projects** explorer and select the **Copy** menu option. Right-clicking on a subsequent package provides the **Paste** and **Refactor Copy...** menu items.

Delete refactoring

After writing code for a while, it's a common practice to review what you've written. At that point, you may decide that you want to delete some of the code as it's no longer needed. Deleting code, however, can be dangerous, especially on larger projects, as you don't always know how many references you have to the code to delete and where they are.

Fortunately, NetBeans provides a **Safely Delete** refactor.

Getting ready

First we will need a Java project to perform some safe delete refactoring. We will use the same project from the earlier recipe, *Rename refactoring*, and so ensure that you have the project open from the end of that recipe. If you have not followed that recipe, the project is available from the code download bundle under the `MoveRefactor` folder in `Chapter 3`. When the **Projects** explorer shows the `Refactoring` project, expand the `Refactoring` node if not yet expanded.

How to do it...

To show an example of safely deleting, we're going to create an interface and then implement the interface. When we subsequently attempt to delete the interface, NetBeans will warn us that the interface is still in use. We will perform the following steps:

1. Right-click on the `com.davidsalter.cookbook.refactoring` package in the **Projects** explorer and select **New** and then **Java Package...**.

2. Enter `com.davidsalter.cookbook.refactor.safedelete` in the **Package Name** field.

3. Click on **Finish**.

4. Right-click on the `com.davidsalter.cookbook.refactor.safedelete` package and select **New** and then **Java Interface...**.

5. Enter `Vehicle` in the **Class Name** field.

6. From the **Package** section, select `com.davidsalter.cookbook.refactor.safedelete`.

7. The `Vehicle.java` file will now be opened for editing. Change the definition of the interface to be:

```
public interface Vehicle {
  void drive();
}
```

8. A hint (displayed as a light bulb, 💡) will now be displayed in the margin next to the definition of the `Vehicle` interface. Click on the light bulb and from the pop-up hint, select **Implement Interface**.

9. On the **Implement Interface** dialog, enter `Car` in the **Class Name** field and leave the **Package Name** field as the default setting of `com.davidsalter.cookbook.refactor.safedelete`.

10. Click on **OK**.

We've now created an interface and a class that implements the interface. Let's see how NetBeans will warn us when we try to delete something that's in use elsewhere with the following steps:

1. Right-click on the `Vehicle.java` file within the `com.davidsalter.cookbook.refactor.safedelete` package and select **Refactor** and then **Safely Delete....**

2. The **Safely Delete** dialog will be displayed. Click on the **Refactor** button.

3. After a few moments, a list of errors will be shown in the **Safely Delete** dialog showing that there are references to the selected element elsewhere in the project.

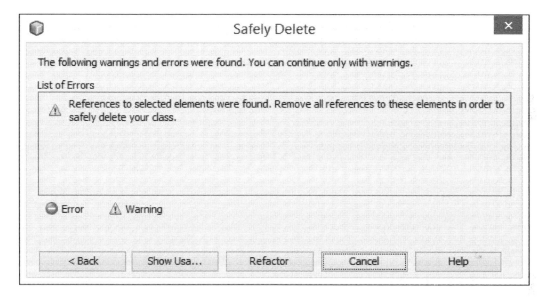

4. Click on the **Show Usages** button to see a list of all places within the project where the `Vehicle` interface is used.

How it works...

When performing the **Safely Delete** refactor, NetBeans checks through all the source files within the project to see if the selected element exists. If it does not exist, then the delete refactoring can continue and the selected element will be deleted.

If references to the selected element are found, they are shown within the **Usages** window where the developer is given the opportunity to rerun the **Safely Delete** refactor if they are happy that none of the uses are important. We can see the **Rerun Safely Delete** option in the following screenshot:

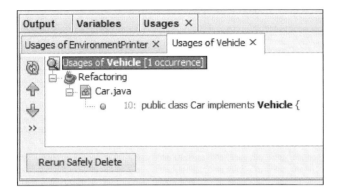

There's more...

The Safely Delete refactor can also be made to search through comments in the code by selecting **Search In Comments** on the first page of the **Safely Delete** dialog.

The keyboard shortcut for performing a safe delete is *Alt + Delete*.

Change parameters refactoring

Suppose we've written a method and we want to change the signature of it. Perhaps, we didn't originally envision what parameters we would need to pass into a method, or perhaps we're passing too many parameters and want to change the method signature to take a class that will represent all our parameters instead. The NetBeans **Change Method Parameters...** refactor helps us in these situations.

Getting ready

First we will need a Java project so that we can change the parameters of a method. We will use the same project from the earlier recipe, *Rename refactoring*, and so ensure that you have the project open from the end of that recipe. If you have not followed that recipe, the project is available from the code download bundle under the `MoveRefactor` folder in `Chapter 3`. When the **Projects** explorer shows the `Refactoring` project, expand the `Refactoring` node if not yet expanded.

How to do it...

To show an example of changing the parameters of a method, we're going to create a method with a specified signature and then use the NetBeans refactoring tools to change the method signature with the following steps:

1. Right-click on the `com.davidsalter.cookbook.refactor` package in the **Projects** explorer and select **New** and then **Java Package...**.

2. Enter `com.davidsalter.cookbook.refactor.parameters` in the **Package Name** field.

3. Click on **Finish**.

4. Right-click on the `com.davidsalter.cookbook.refactor.parameters` package and select **New** and then **Java Class...**.

5. Enter `Audit` in the **Class Name** field.

6. From the **Package** dropdown, select `com.davidsalter.cookbook.refactor.parameters`.

7. Click on **Finish**.

8. Edit the contents of the `Audit.java` file, changing the class to be defined as follows:

```
public class Audit {
   private void auditLogin(String loginName) {
     // Audit a login to the database.
   }
}
```

We've now created a class that could form the basics of auditing user logins to a system. What if we decide we want to audit the IP address that a user logs in from? We've also noticed that the auditing method is `private` so external classes can't call it—we really need the method to be `public`. Let's now use the method parameters refactoring to fix these issues with the following steps:

1. Right-click on the `auditLogin` method and click on **Refactor** and the **Change Method Parameters...**.

2. The **Change Method Parameters** dialog will now be shown:

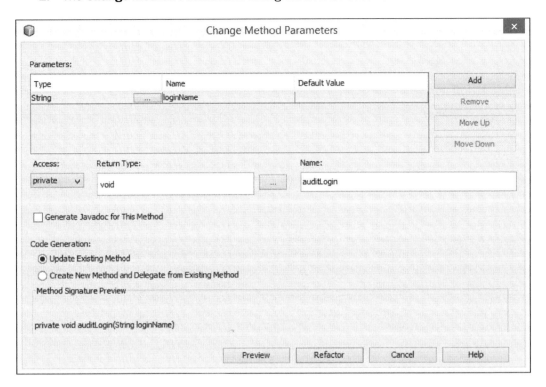

3. Click on the **Add** button to add a new parameter to the method.
4. Enter `String` as the new **Type** parameter.
5. Enter `ipAddress` as the new **Name** parameter.
6. Enter `null` as the new **Default Value** parameter.
7. On the **Access** selection, change the value from **private** to **public**.
8. Click on **Refactor**.

The **Change Method Parameters** dialog will now close. Inspecting the `Audit.java` class shows that the method signature has been changed so that the `auditLogin()` method is now `public` and takes two parameters, `loginName` and `ipAddress`.

The **Change Method Parameters** refactoring is useful when your code is more complex and the method being changed is called from multiple places within your code base. When you change method parameters, they are changed wherever the method is called within your code, with any new parameters taking a default value as specified within the **Change Method Parameters** dialog.

There's more

In addition to changing method parameters, the **Return Type** and **Name** fields of the method can also be changed.

Selecting the **Generate Javadoc for This Method** option will cause basic Javadoc information to be added to the method showing the parameters and return types for the method. If Javadoc already exists for the method, then the **Update Existing Javadoc of This Method** option is offered.

This refactoring also offers the ability to leave the existing method as it is and create a new method that is called from the original. To achieve this, ensure that the **Create New Method and Delegate from Existing Method** option is checked.

Pull up / push down refactoring

Pull up and push down refactoring relates to the ability to move methods and members of a class up into a superclass, or down into a subclass.

Getting ready

First we will need a Java project so that we can perform some pull up / push down refactoring. We will use the same project from the earlier recipe, *Rename refactoring*, and so ensure that you have the project open from the end of that recipe. If you have not followed that recipe, the project is available from the code download bundle under the `MoveRefactor` folder in `Chapter 3`. When the **Projects** explorer shows the `Refactoring` project, expand the `Refactoring` node if not yet expanded.

How to do it...

Let's consider we have a class to represent a `Vehicle` and a derived class that represents a sports car. We'll model those two classes in Java and show how to move properties between the two classes with the following steps:

1. Right-click on the `com.davidsalter.cookbook.refactor` package in the **Projects** explorer and select **New** and then **Java Class...**.
2. Enter `Vehicle` in the **Class Name** field.
3. From the **Package** selection, ensure `com.davidsalter.cookbook.refactor.pullup` is selected.

4. The `Vehicle` class will now be created and opened for editing. Change the contents of the class to be as follows:

```
public class Vehicle {
    protected float milesPerGallon;
    protected Boolean sportsMode;
}
```

5. Right-click on the `com.davidsalter.cookbook.refactor.pullup` package in the **Projects** explorer and select **New** and then **Java Class...**.

6. Enter `SportsCar` in the **Class Name** field.

7. From the **Package** selection, ensure `com.davidsalter.cookbook.refactor.pullup` is selected.

8. The `SportsCar` class will now be created and opened for editing. Change the `SportsCar` implementation so that it extends the `Vehicle` class.

We have now written an outline for a `SportsCar` class that extends the `Vehicle` class with the `extends` keyword. The `Vehicle` base class has a `sportsMode` field within it. This doesn't really make sense as `SportsMode` should be a property of the `SportsCar` class and not of a generic `Vehicle` class. Let's fix that now with the following steps:

1. Double-click on the `Vehicle.java` file within the **Projects** explorer to open it up for editing.

2. Right-click on the `sportsMode` field and select **Refactor** and then **Push Down...**.

3. The **Push Down** dialog will now be shown, which lists all the members in the current class that can be pushed down to any subclasses.

4. Ensure that the **sportsMode : Boolean** option is checked.

5. Click on **Refactor**.

6. The **Push Down** refactoring dialog will now close and the refactoring will be completed.

How it works...

After pushing down the `sportsMode` field, we can examine the source code for the `Vehicle` and `SportsCar` classes. We can see that `sportsMode` has been pushed down into the `SportsCar` class where it belongs, and has been removed from the base `Vehicle` class.

There's more...

If we have more than one subclass when we are pushing members, clicking on the **Refactor** button will move the selected members into all of the subclasses. If we only want to move the member into certain subclasses, click on the **Preview** button before clicking on **Refactor**. This will then show a hierarchy of all the subclasses that the members will be pushed to from which you can choose to only push to certain subclasses and not all.

Pull up refactoring

Pull up refactoring follows the same procedure as push down refactoring except that members are pulled up from subclasses into the superclass. To perform pull up refactoring, right-click on the member to pull up and click on **Refactor** and then **Pull Up...**. The **Pull Up** refactoring dialog allows a choice of members to be pulled up together with a **Destination Supertype** field—the destination that the members are pulled to.

Extract interface refactoring

Extracting an interface from a class is a useful technique when you have many objects that have similar behavior and you want to impose a contract on your objects stating that they must all implement the same set of methods.

If you have a class and wish to extract an interface from it, NetBeans **Extract Interface** refactoring allows this to be easily achieved.

Getting ready

First we will need a Java project so that we can extract an interface from a class. We will use the same project from the earlier recipe, *Rename refactoring*, and so ensure that you have the project open from the end of that recipe. If you have not followed that recipe, the project is available from the code download bundle under the `MoveRefactor` folder in `Chapter 3`. When the **Projects** explorer shows the `Refactoring` project, expand the `Refactoring` node if not yet expanded.

How to do it...

Let's assume that we have a set of classes for loading and drawing different types of raster images: `.png`, `.bmp`, `.jpg`, and so on. Each of our classes has the ability to load/save the file and draw the file. Looking at these methods, it would seem that the ability to load and save images would be required for all file types and would make a good candidate for an interface. Drawing different file types would also be a good candidate for a different interface.

Let's create the outline of the `PngImage` class and extract some interfaces from it with the following steps:

1. Right-click on the `com.davidsalter.cookbook.refactor` package and select **New** and then **Java Class...**.

2. Enter `PngImage` in the **Class Name** field.

3. Enter `com.davidsalter.cookbook.refactor.extractinterface` in the **Package** field.

4. The `PngImage` class will now be created and opened for editing. Change the contents of the class to be as follows:

```
public class PngImage {

  public boolean load(String file) {
    return true;
  }

  public boolean save(String file) {
    return true;
  }

  public boolean draw(int width, int height) {
    return true;
  }
}
```

We've now created a class, so let's proceed and extract both `Persistable` and `Drawable` interfaces from it with the following steps:

1. Right-click on the body of the `PngImage.java` class and select `Refactor` and then **Extract Interface...**.

2. The **Extract Interface** dialog will now be shown:

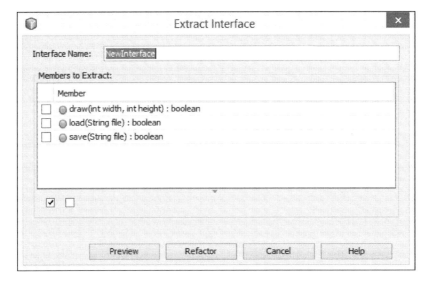

3. Enter `Persistable` in the **Interface Name** field.

4. Check the **load(String file) : boolean** method.

5. Check the **save(String file) : boolean** method.

6. Click on **Refactor**.

A new `com.davidsalter.cookbook.refactor.extractinterface.Persistable` interface will now be created, which the `PngImage` class will implement. Let's now complete the refactoring and create a `Drawable` interface. To do this, perform the following steps:

1. Double-click on the `PngImage.java` file in the **Projects** explorer to open the file for editing.

2. Right-click on the body of the `PngImage.java` class and select **Refactor** and then **Extract Interface...**.

3. The **Extract Interface** dialog will now be shown again.

4. Enter `Drawable` in the **Interface Name** field.

5. Check the **draw(int width, int height) : boolean** method.

6. Click on **Refactor**.

A new `com.davidsalter.cookbook.refactor.extractinterface.Drawable` interface will now be created. The `PngImage` class will now implement both of the interfaces we've just created.

There's more...

When extracting interfaces from classes, NetBeans offers the ability to preview the changes that will be made to our source code before the refactoring is completed. To perform this, click on the **Preview** button instead of the **Refactor** button.

Extracting superclasses

In addition to extracting interfaces from classes, NetBeans provides the ability to extract superclasses from the existing classes. This refactoring is achieved by right-clicking within the body of a class and selecting **Refactor** and then **Extract Superclass...**.

Extracting a superclass operates in a similar fashion to extracting an interface. The difference with this refactoring is that when extracting a superclass, the original class will be changed to extend the superclass using the `extends` keyword. When extracting an interface, the original class will be changed to implement the interface by using the `implements` keyword.

When defining a superclass, the refactoring wizard gives us the ability to define classes as `abstract` or not, giving full control over the methods that are created in the superclass. We can see the **Extract Superclass** dialog in the following screenshot:

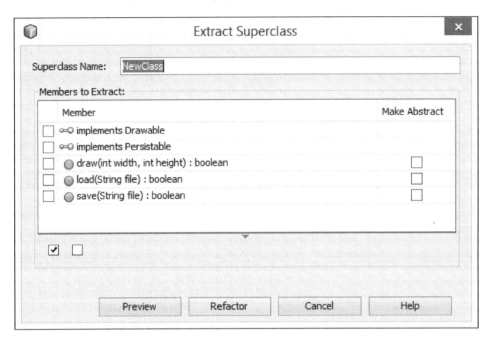

Encapsulate fields refactoring

Encapsulation provides a way of hiding members of a class, and restricting their access, so that potentially an object's members can only be manipulated by the object itself. Encapsulation is one of the keystones of object-oriented development.

Getting ready

First we will need a Java project so that we can encapsulate some fields within a class. We will use the same project from the earlier recipe, *Rename refactoring*, and so ensure that you have the project open from the end of that recipe. If you have not followed that recipe, the project is available from the code download bundle under the `MoveRefactor` folder in `Chapter 3`. When the **Projects** explorer shows the `Refactoring` project, expand the `Refactoring` node if not yet expanded.

How to do it...

Let's assume we're modelling an application in a mobile application store. We might want to model an application that would have name, author, and cost properties. Our application object may also have a list of reviews. First, let's create a Java class that implements all of these fields with the following steps:

1. Right-click on the `com.davidsalter.cookbook.refactor` package and select **New** and then **Java Class...**.

2. Enter `Application` in the **Class Name** field.

3. Enter `com.davidsalter.cookbook.refactor.encapsulation` in the **Package** field.

4. Click on **Finish**.

5. The Java class, `Application.java`, is now created and is opened within NetBeans for editing. Change the contents of this class to read:

```
package com.davidsalter.cookbook.refactor.encapsulation;

import java.util.ArrayList;
import java.util.List;

public class Application {

    public String name;
    public String author;
    public List<String> reviews = new ArrayList<String>();
    public float cost;
}
```

This basic class fulfils all our requirements described earlier, but isn't a very good implementation. Any other class within the system can change the `Application` class's properties—clearly we don't want this.

6. Right-click on the body of the `Application.java` file and select **Refactor** and then **Encapsulate Fields....** The **Encapsulate Fields** dialog will be displayed:

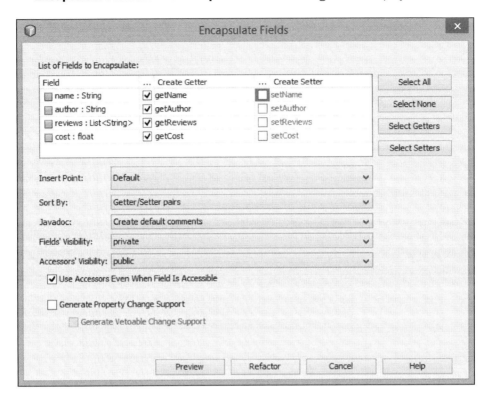

7. Check the **Create Getter** options, **getName**, **getAuthor**, **getReviews**, and **getCost**.

8. Do not check any of the **Create Setter** options as these will be set by the class's constructor.

9. Click on **Refactor**.

10. Right-click on the body of the class, select **Insert Code...**, and on the pop-up **Generate** dialog, click on **Constructor....**

11. On the **Create Constructor** dialog, check **name : String**, **author : String**, and **cost : float**.

12. Click on **Generate**.

Our class is nearly complete now. It allows the name, author, and cost properties to be set only during the constructor (arguably, we should add methods to allow the name and cost to be changed, but we will ignore that for this example). We've also implemented getters for all of the class's properties. All we need to do now is add a method to add a review.

Adding a review is a different process from setting other properties such as name or cost because the reviews are stored in an array. If we allowed callers to set the `reviews` property directly, they could add or remove the reviews list and we wouldn't have any good encapsulation for the reviews themselves. To overcome this problem, we need to add a single method that adds a review into the `reviews` list. We can achieve this with the following step:

1. Modify the `Application.java` class and add the following method to the bottom of the class:

```
public void addReview(String review) {
   this.reviews.add(review);
}
```

How it works...

The NetBeans **Encapsulate Fields** refactoring allows the developer to add getters and setters to any or all of the properties within a class. As has been seen in this recipe, encapsulating a field allows developers to write more robust code; however, care must be taken. Encapsulating arrays or objects within a class must be considered carefully before being implemented. Remember to ensure that the array or object itself can't be modified, but what it represents can be.

There's more...

When creating accessors, the **Insert Point** dropdown specifies where in the code the accessors are added. This can be as **First Method** or **Last Method** or after/before any other accessors. Accessors can be sorted in pairs, in alphabetic order, or with getters before setters. Check out the **Sort By** field to perform this.

The visibility of fields can be changed by setting the **Fields' Visibility** dropdown to **private**, **protected**, or **public**. Similarly, the accessors' visibility can be set by modifying the **Accessors' Visibility** dropdown.

The field encapsulation refactoring can also generate Javadoc for the accessors. Default comments can be generated or the Javadoc from the fields themselves can be copied over into the accessors.

Replacing a constructor with the Factory pattern

A good development practice can be to use factory methods instead of class constructors. Factory methods can be more descriptive than constructors and can perform additional functionality over constructors such as returning immutable objects or objects that implement a certain interface.

Getting ready

First we will need a Java project so that we can replace a class constructor with a factory method. We will use the same project from the earlier recipe, *Rename refactoring*, and so ensure that you have the project open from the end of that recipe. If you have not followed that recipe, the project is available from the code download bundle under the `MoveRefactor` folder in `Chapter 3`. When the **Projects** explorer shows the `Refactoring` project, expand the `Refactoring` node if not yet expanded.

How to do it...

Suppose we are writing a game and want to implement different levels. Increasing levels of the game could be more complex than the previous levels but each level offers a constant set of challenges and objectives. We could easily represent this with a basic model of a `GameLevel` class, which takes an integer difficulty as a constructor parameter. We could then refactor to replace the constructor with a factory to make the code more robust. In fact, let's do just that!

1. Right-click on the `com.davidsalter.cookbook.refactor` package and select **New** and then **Java Class...**.

2. Enter `GameLevel` in the **Class Name** field.

3. In the **Package** selection, enter `com.davidsalter.cookbook.refactor.factory`.

4. Click on **Finish**.

5. The `GameLevel` class will now be created and opened for editing. Change the contents of the class to be as follows:

```
public class GameLevel {
  private int difficulty;

  public GameLevel(int difficulty) {
    this.difficulty = difficulty;
  }
}
```

This simple class now represents a game level that has differing degrees of difficulty. Let's now change the constructor to use the Factory pattern with the following steps:

1. Right-click on the body of the constructor in the `GameLevel.java` class and select **Refactor** and then **Replace Constructor with Factory...**.

2. The **Replace Constructor With Factory** dialog will now be displayed:

3. Enter `levelWithDifficulty` in the **Factory Method Name** field.
4. Click on **Refactor**.
5. The **Replace Constructor With Factory** dialog will now close and the refactoring will be applied to the `GameLevel.java` class.

How it works...

Upon refactoring a constructor into a factory, the new factory method is created that instantiates the `GameLevel` class and returns it to the caller. The original constructor for the class is marked as `private` to stop callers directly instantiating the `GameLevel` class. The updated code of the `GameLevel` class is:

```
public class GameLevel {

    public static GameLevel levelWithDifficulty(int difficulty) {
        return new GameLevel(difficulty);
    }
    private int difficulty;

    private GameLevel(int difficulty) {
        this.difficulty = difficulty;
    }
}
```

Looking at this code, we can immediately see that the name of the factory method is a lot more meaningful than the name of the constructor with its single parameter.

You can also imagine how it would be easy to create a cached lookup of all the levels available within the game and return a level from cache within the factory method rather than instantiating a new `GameLevel` each time the factory method is called. In a real game, it would be easy to believe that constructing `GameLevel` could be an expensive task in terms of CPU performance and time. Since `GameLevel` is essentially immutable, there's no need to instantiate a new one each time it is requested. Returning `GameLevel` from cache would be a much more optimized task.

There's more...

Sometimes the Factory pattern is not the best way to instantiate an object—we may wish to user the Builder pattern instead.

Replacing constructors with the Builder pattern

If a constructor becomes more complex than a few parameters, or multiple operations are required to create an object, then the Builder pattern can be used to create objects instead of the Factory pattern.

NetBeans can apply the Builder pattern to classes enabling constructors to be replaced with a Builder pattern implementation. To replace a constructor with a Builder pattern, right-click on the body of a constructor and select **Refactor** and then **Replace Constructor with Builder...**. The **Replace Constructor With Builder** dialog will be displayed:

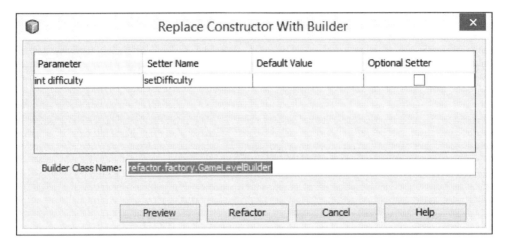

4

Developing Desktop Applications with NetBeans

In this chapter, we will cover the following recipes:

- ▸ Creating a Swing application
- ▸ Adding components to a form
- ▸ Creating menus
- ▸ Creating dialogs
- ▸ Creating toolbars
- ▸ Responding to events
- ▸ Building a distributable application from NetBeans

Introduction

The Java Swing API is a complete GUI toolkit that provides many different classes that allow developers to build complex user interfaces. Swing is based on the **Model-View-Controller** (**MVC**) pattern, which allows data to be decoupled from GUI controls and therefore encourages developers to write more maintainable code.

This may all sound very complicated to developers who are new to Swing, but fortunately, one of the greatest strengths of NetBeans is the powerful Swing GUI builder, also known as **Matisse**. Matisse hides a lot of the complexity of Swing development as it writes a lot of the Swing plumbing code for you.

For a comprehensive overview of Swing, check out the article, *A Swing Architecture Overview*, at `http://www.oracle.com/technetwork/java/architecture-142923.html`.

NetBeans uses Java's Swing as the default framework and with it, it's possible to:

- Create and design complex GUI applications
- Drag-and-drop components from a **Palette** component
- Design beautiful-looking applications
- Preview the changes before compiling
- Bind data straight from the database to your component

And it's possible to do much more.

Besides being totally free, the Swing GUI builder lets the developer concentrate on coding.

In the previous chapters, we learned how to create projects and how to become productive in developing Java applications with NetBeans. In this chapter, we'll start with the basics by creating a simple Java Swing desktop application. We'll then build on that by adding controls and toolbars and other GUI components.

If you have used previous versions of NetBeans, you may have seen references to the **Swing Application Framework** (a simple Swing framework that defined common infrastructure for desktop applications). As of NetBeans 7.1, support for the Swing Application Framework was dropped from the NetBeans IDE as the framework was withdrawn by the JCP. In this chapter, we will be concentrating purely on developing Swing applications with NetBeans.

Instead of the Swing Application Framework, developers can now use the NetBeans Platform (`https://netbeans.org/features/platform`) to develop **Rich Client Platform** (**RCP**) applications. To learn more about RCP development using the NetBeans Platform, check out the book at `https://www.packtpub.com/application-development/netbeans-platform-69-developers-guide`.

Within this chapter, we'll see how to develop a simple desktop GUI application to view the contents of `.jar` files. The final product will look like the following screenshot:

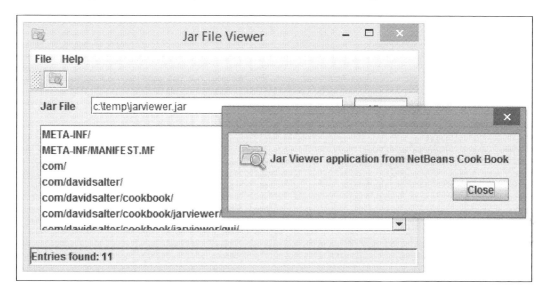

Creating a Swing application

With NetBeans 8.0, creating a desktop application is very similar to creating a standard console application as shown in *Chapter 1, Using NetBeans Projects*. To create a Swing application, we need to first create a blank Java application and then add a `JFrame` derived class to the application that will act as the main frame for the application. Once we've created a frame, we can set its title and give it an icon and we will get a basic Java desktop application.

Let's see how that can be achieved.

 For more information about JFrames and how to use top-level containers, check out `http://docs.oracle.com/javase/tutorial/uiswing/components/toplevel.html`.

Getting ready

To complete this recipe, we'll be using the Java SE NetBeans IDE download bundle. The Java EE or All bundles could also be used, but we will not be using any of their features in this recipe.

You need not have any projects open to start this recipe.

How to do it...

First off, we'll create a blank Java application that we can add our frame into with the following steps:

1. Click on **File** and then **New Project...**.
2. On the resultant dialog, select the **Java** category and **Java Application** as the project.
3. Click on **Next**.
4. Enter the **Project Name** field as `JarViewer`.
5. Enter the **Project Location** field. (The default location will most likely be correct.)
6. Ensure **Create Main Class** is checked and enter `com.davidsalter.cookbook.jarviewer.Main` as the **Main Class** name, as shown in the following screenshot:

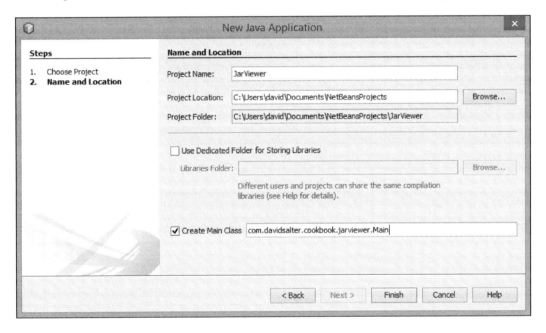

7. Click on **Finish**.

NetBeans has now created a blank application with a single main class in it.

Let's create a GUI frame for our application and open it when the application is launched with the following steps:

1. Right-click on the **Source Packages** node in the **Projects** explorer and select **New** and then **JFrame Form...**.
2. Enter the **Class Name** field as `MainFrame`.

3. Enter the **Package** field as com.davidsalter.cookbook.jarviewer.gui, as shown in the following screenshot:

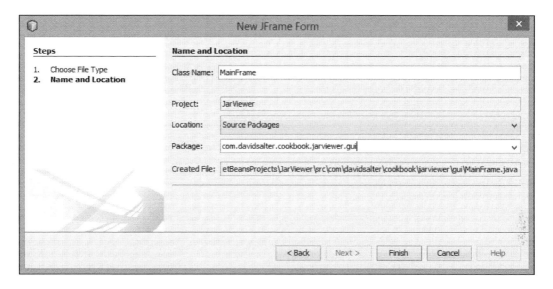

4. Click on **Finish**.

NetBeans will now create a MainFrame class for us and open it for GUI editing as shown in the following screenshot:

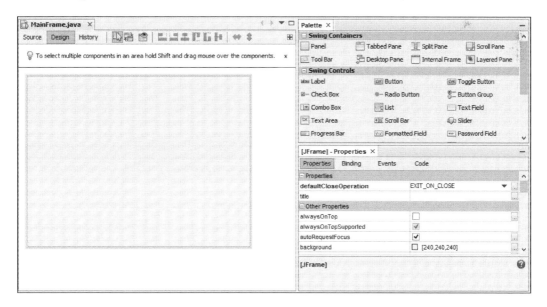

In the center of the screen, we can see that a blank form has been created with no components on it. To design GUIs, we drag components from the **Palette** section at the right-hand side of the main window onto the form, laying them out in the design we want.

We'll look at adding controls to a form in a later recipe. For now, let's set our application's title and give it an icon so that it starts to look like a proper GUI application, using the following steps:

1. Click on the `MainFrame.java` design surface in the center of the NetBeans IDE window. The **[JFrame] - Properties** explorer should now be displayed.

2. Locate the **title** property and enter `Jar File Viewer`, as shown in the following screenshot:

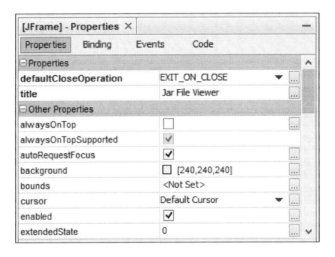

3. From the `assets` folder of the code download bundle for this chapter, locate the `folder_explore.png` file and drag it onto the `com.davidsalter.cookbook.jarviewer.gui` package in the **Projects** explorer. This will add the file into the NetBeans project so that we can reference it from within our application. The **Projects** explorer for our project is shown in the following screenshot:

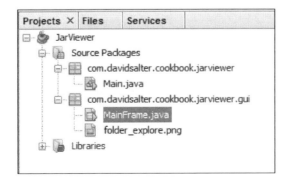

4. Click on the design surface for the `MainFrame.java` class again and locate the **iconImage** property.

5. Click on the **...** button (⬜) for the **iconImage** property to open up the property editor window.

6. Select the **Set Form's iconImage property using** field as **Custom code**.

7. Enter the custom code within the **Form.setIconImage** edit as:

    ```
    new javax.swing.ImageIcon(getClass().getResource
    ("/com/davidsalter/cookbook/jarviewer/gui/
    folder_explore.png" )).getImage()
    ```

    The **[JFrame] - iconImage** window is shown in the following screenshot:

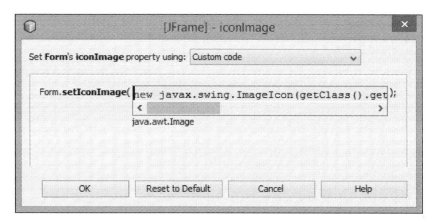

8. Click on the **OK** button to set the **iconImage** property.

    We've now created the basics for our desktop application. The final step is to wire up the `Main` class to instantiate the frame when the application is executed.

9. Double-click on `Main.java` within the **Projects** explorer to open it for editing.

10. Change the `main` method within `Main.java` to read:

    ```
    public static void main(String[] args) {
        java.awt.EventQueue.invokeLater(new Runnable() {
            public void run() {
                new MainFrame().setVisible(true);
            }
        });
    }
    ```

11. Press *F6* to run the application.

When creating a `JFrame` class, NetBeans actually creates a `main` method within the `JFrame` class; so, there is no need to create a separate Java class to implement the `main` method. We have created a separate `Main` class within this recipe to show how to display a `JFrame` within an application.

How it works...

In this recipe, we've created the first of our Swing components—a `MainFrame.java` class that extends `JFrame`.

When this file is opened within NetBeans, it has three views:

- ▶ **Source**
- ▶ **Design**
- ▶ **History**

These three views are displayed in the following screenshot:

The **Source** view allows us to see the Java source code that the class is composed of. This code is a mixture of automatically generated code and custom code that has been added by the developer.

The NetBeans GUI designer creates all the code for us to instantiate a form and initialize all the components on it, including their layout, size, and other properties. Code to use the basic properties that we entered within the **Properties** window (such as the frame's title) is also automatically generated for us. Any custom code that we enter for properties (such as the frame's **iconImage** property) is automatically added into the generated code.

When we look at the code for a GUI component, we can see that sections of the code are in editor folds that have a grey background. These sections of code are the ones that are automatically generated by NetBeans and cannot be edited within the Java editor. It's very important not to try to edit these sections of code in an editor external to NetBeans as this will almost always stop NetBeans from subsequently being able to edit the GUI component graphically.

If you want to edit the custom code that you have added as a component's property, then you need to select the custom code editor from the **Properties** window rather than attempting to edit the source code directly. NetBeans will not allow the custom code to be directly edited within the Java editor.

The **Design** view shows the layout of all the components on the frame. We will see more of this in the next recipe. For now, we'll just note that this is the area where we drag controls to build up our GUI.

The **History** view shows all the changes that we have made to the component, similar to the history we may see when viewing the history of a file within a source code control system such as Git or Subversion. Using the **History** view, we can revert to the earlier changes we made to the design of a form.

There's more...

When creating a `JFrame` form within a project, NetBeans automatically adds a `main` method into the new class. If your application only has one `JFrame` within it and you're not likely to do any other processing at application startup, then this can be a convenient way to automatically create a `main()` method for your application.

For each Java GUI class created by NetBeans, a corresponding XML file will be created that has the `.form` extension. In this recipe, we created a Java class called `MainFrame.java`. NetBeans automatically created a file called `MainFrame.form` in the same directory on disk to go along with this file. NetBeans stores all of its internal data within this `.form` file; so, it's very important not to delete or edit these files manually. Don't worry though, when you distribute an application, these `.form` files do not need to be distributed with the application. They are only required while developing within NetBeans.

Adding components to a form

In the previous recipe, we saw how to make a desktop GUI application. In this recipe, we'll see how we can add components onto a form and how we can preview the form at the design time.

For more information on using different Swing components, check out `http://docs.oracle.com/javase/tutorial/uiswing/components/index.html`.

Getting ready

To complete this recipe, we need to have the `JarViewer` project that was created in the *Creating a Swing application* recipe. If you have not completed this recipe, the source code is available with the code download bundle for this chapter.

How to do it...

1. Ensure that the `JarViewer` project is open in NetBeans and double-click on the `MainFrame.java` class to open it for editing.

2. From the **Palette** section, drag a **Label** component onto the form's design surface snapping it to the top-left side of the form. When dragging the label onto the form, you will see a horizontal and vertical dotted line when the label is at the preferred distance from the top corner. Drop the label at this point as shown in the following screenshot:

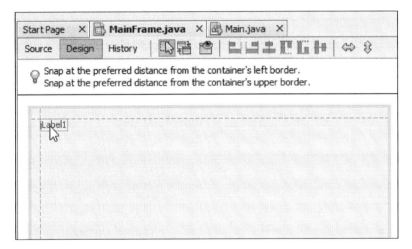

3. Right-click on the dropped label on the design surface and select **Change Variable Name...**.

4. Enter the **New Name** field as `jarLabel`.

Some developers like to use Hungarian notation for control names in GUIs to help distinguish the types of components that are being added to a form, for example, `lblJarLabel`. Throughout this book however, I've not used Hungarian notation to distinguish variable types as the compiler can do this for me. For more information, about Hungarian notation, check out `http://en.wikipedia.org/wiki/Hungarian_notation`.

5. Locate the **text** property within the **jarLabel [JLabel] – Properties** window. Set the property value to be `Jar File`.

6. The text displayed for the label on the form will now change to read **Jar File**.

7. From the **Palette** section, drop a **Button** component onto the form at the top right. Just like when dropping the **Label** component in step 2, the guidelines will be displayed on the form indicating that the button has been snapped to the top-right side of the form.

8. Right-click on the dropped button on the design surface and select **Change Variable Name...**.

9. Enter the **New Name** field as `viewButton`.

10. Right-click on the button once more and select **Edit Text**.

11. The text displayed on the button will become editable. Enter the text `View` and press the *Return* key.

12. From the **Palette** section, drag a **Panel** component onto the form, snapping it to the left and bottom of the form. Drag the panel to the right to additionally snap it to the right-hand side of the form as well.

13. Drag the height of the panel to be `16`.

14. Right-click on the panel and select **Change Variable Name...**.

15. Enter the **New Name** field as `statusPanel`.

16. Locate the **border** property for the panel within the **statusPanel [JPanel] – Properties** window.

17. Click on the **...** button (⬚) to open the border property window.

18. Select **Bevel Border** from the **Available Borders** section.

19. Select **Lowered** as the **Type** field, as shown in the following screenshot:

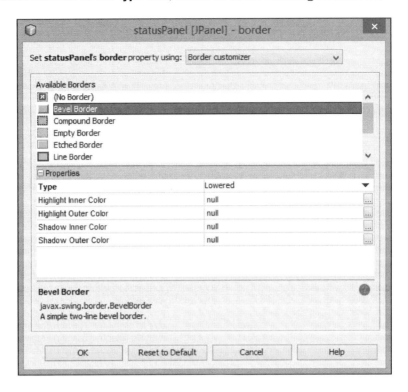

20. Click on **OK**.

21. From the **Palette** section, drag a **Label** component onto statusPanel aligning it with the bottom-left side of the panel.

22. Right-click on the label and select **Change Variable Name...**.

23. Enter the **New Name** field as statusLabel.

24. Locate the **text** property within the **statusLabel [JLabel] – Properties** window and delete the property value so that no value is set.

25. From the **Palette** section, drag a **Text Field** component onto the form's design surface. Snap the **Text Field** component to the top of the form and the right-hand side of the jarLabel label.

26. Drag the **Text Field** component to the right and snap it to the left-hand side of the viewButton component.

27. Right-click on the text field and select **Change Variable Name...**.

28. Enter the **New Name** field as `jarName`.

29. Locate the **text** property within the **jarName [JTextField] – Properties** window and delete the property value so that no value is set.

30. From the **Palette** section, drag a **List** control onto the form, snapping it to the left-hand side of the form and to the bottom of the `jarLabel` component.

31. Drag the **List** control to the right and snap it to the right-hand size of the form.

32. Drag the **List** control to the bottom and snap it to the top of the `statusPanel` component.

33. Right-click on the **List** control and select **Change Variable Name...**.

34. Enter the **New Name** field as `jarEntries`.

    We have now completed the design of our form. The completed form should look like the following screenshot:

    We could now run our application to see what it looks like; however, NetBeans provides an excellent design-time tool that allows us to preview the form without running the application.

 On a small application, there isn't much benefit in previewing forms at design time, but as your application grows, this ability can rapidly increase your productivity.

35. Click on the **Preview Design** button at the top of the design surface. NetBeans will open a preview version of the form. Resize the form and note that all of the controls on the form correctly resize with the form, as shown in the following screenshot:

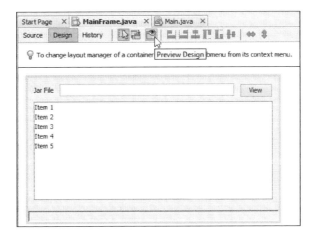

How it works...

When designing forms within NetBeans, there is a vast array of components that are available within the **Palette** section that can be simply dragged-and-dropped onto the design surface.

We can add controls (such as labels, buttons and lists, and so on), Swing fillers, Swing menus, or even other Swing windows (file choosers and color choosers, and so on). We can even add AWT components or our own custom-defined Beans. We can see the **Palette** window in the following screenshot:

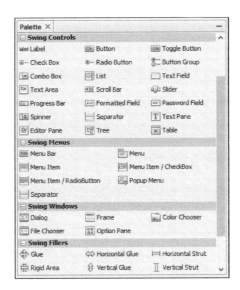

With each control we add, we can choose to either add it at a given size on the form, or snap it to other controls/edges of the form thus providing the ability for controls to properly resize when the form is resized.

Not only can we add controls onto a form, but we can also add controls into other controls. We saw how to add `JPanel` and then drop `JLabel` inside it to make a more complicated control.

For each control that we add to the form, there's a corresponding set of properties that can be set for the control. As we've seen previously, these properties can be set at the design time as simple values, or can be implemented as custom code snippets.

There's more...

We can also write custom code that can be triggered at different times during a component's lifecycle. On the **Code** tab of a component's **Properties** window, we can specify a lifecycle event (such as **Pre-Creation Code** or **Post-Creation Code**) together with the custom code to run. This can be very useful if we wish, for example, to initialize components on a form when they are created.

Using the **Binding** tab, we can also bind component properties with other JavaBeans components, so, for example, we could automatically update a progress bar based upon some external action.

If you look at many desktop applications, you'll see that many components such as buttons have a shortcut assigned—these are generally referred to as a mnemonic. For example, a button labelled **Close** will invariably be displayed as **<u>C</u>lose** (note the underlined **C**) indicating that pressing *Alt + C* will have the same effect as clicking on the button. We can easily define these keyboard mnemonics in NetBeans by setting the **mnemonic** property of a component.

In this recipe, we created a `JLabel` that described another component (we created the `JLabel` with the text `Jar File`, which described `JTextField` next to it). To aid accessibility, it's a good practice to set the `labelFor` property on a `JLabel` to describe which component it is the label for. This can greatly enhance the performance of screen readers and other accessibility software.

Wait, what if we want to add more complex components such as toolbars or menus to our application?

Fortunately, this is a simple procedure when using NetBeans.

In the next recipe, we'll take a look at adding menus into our application. In subsequent recipes, we'll show how to add toolbars and then see how to use events to wire up all of these components.

If you want to see some more examples of GUI forms within NetBeans, check out the provided sample applications. When creating a new project, select **Samples** and then **Java** from the **Categories** list. The three sample projects, **Anagram Game**, **GUI Form Examples**, and **Client Editor**, provide further examples of using the NetBeans GUI editor.

Creating menus

Now that we've created a basic GUI for our application, let's add a menu structure so that we can close the application easily and view the application's **About** box.

Getting ready

To complete this recipe, we need to have the `JarViewer` project that was created in the *Adding components to a form* recipe. If you have not completed this recipe, the source code is available with the code download bundle for this chapter.

How to do it...

To add a menu to an application, we need to have the main form of the application open for editing in the design view. We then drag-and-drop a menu bar and menu items from the **Palette** section onto the form. Let's see how that can be achieved with the following steps:

1. Double-click on the `MainFrame.java` file within the **Projects** explorer to open it for editing. Ensure the **Design** tab is selected for editing the design surface of the class.

2. From the **Palette** section, drag a **Menu Bar** control anywhere onto the dialog's surface, as shown in the following screenshot:

Note that the **File** and **Edit** menus have been added to the dialog now, but they have no menu items in them. In our application, we want a **File** menu and a **Help** menu so that we can add the options, **File | Exit** and **Help | About**. Let's now delete the **Edit** menu and add the required menu items with the following steps:

1. Right-click on the **Edit** menu in the `MainFrame.java` class and select **Delete**.

2. Right-click on the **File** menu and select **Change Variable Name...**.

3. Enter the **New Name** field as `fileMenu`.

4. From the **Palette** section, drag a **Menu** control onto the existing **Menu Bar** component. The new menu will initially have the name `jMenu1`.

5. Right-click on the `jMenu1` menu and select **Edit Text**.

6. In the in-place editor, type the new menu name as `Help` and press the *Return* key.

7. Right-click on the **Help** menu and select **Change Variable Name...**.

8. Enter the **New Name** field as `helpMenu`.

9. From the **Palette** section, drag a **Menu Item** control and drop it onto the **File** menu. The new menu item will initially have the name `jMenuItem1`.

10. Right-click on the menu item `jMenuItem1` and select **Edit Text**.

11. In the in-place editor, type the new menu name as `Exit` and press the *Return* key.

12. Right-click on the **Exit** menu item and select **Change Variable Name...**.

13. Enter the **New Name** field as `exitMenuItem`.

14. From the **Palette** section, drag a **Menu Item** control and drop it onto the **Help** menu. The new menu item will initially have the name `jMenuItem1`.

15. Right-click on the menu item `jMenuItem1` and select **Edit Text**.

16. In the in-place editor, type the new menu name as `About` and press the *Return* key.

17. Right-click on the **About** menu item and select **Change Variable Name...**.

18. Enter the **New Name** field as `aboutMenuItem`.

Now that we've added all of the menu items onto our form, we just need to set the accelerator key for the **Exit** menu. The accelerator key is the keyboard combination that will act as a shortcut for the menu item. Typically, in Windows, *Alt + F4* is use to close an application. On a Macintosh, the keyboard shortcut is usually *cmd + Q*. Let's perform the following steps:

1. Click on the **Exit** menu item.

2. In the **exitMenuItem [JMenuItem] – Properties** window, click on the **...** button next to the **accelerator** property.

3. In the **exitMenuItem [JMenuItem] – accelerator** dialog, click in the **Key Stroke** textbox and then press *F4*.

4. Select the **Alt** button.

 If you're using a Mac, make sure that you select *cmd + Q* as your accelerator key instead of *Alt + F4*.

The accelerator definition dialog is shown in the following screenshot:

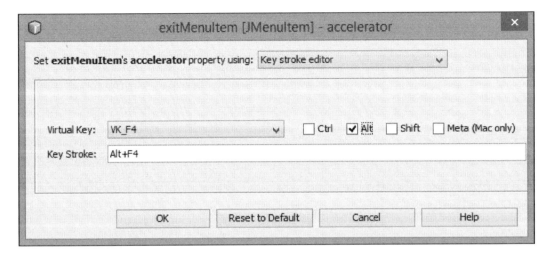

5. Click on **OK** to set the accelerator key and close the dialog.
6. Click on the **Preview Design** button to see how the menu will look when the application is executed.

There's more...

Using the NetBeans GUI editor, we've seen how we can easily create menu structures by dragging the appropriate entries from the **Palette** section onto a form.

In addition to setting menu item accelerator keys, we can also set graphics for menu items that will appear to the left of the menu text. This can be achieved by setting the **icon** property.

We can also set tooltips for menu items by setting the **toolTipText** property. Menu item tool tips are then displayed when the mouse is hovered over a menu item.

If you run the application now, you may spot that clicking on the menus does nothing at the moment. In the recipe, *Responding to events*, we'll see how to make the menu items work fully.

Creating dialogs

In the previous recipe, we saw how to add menus to a form. We added a menu that will allow us to display an **About** box for our application. So far, we've not created any dialogs though.

In this recipe, we'll see how to create dialogs.

Getting ready

To complete this recipe, we need to have the `JarViewer` project that was created in the *Creating menus* recipe. If you have not completed this recipe, the source code is available with the code download bundle for this chapter.

How to do it...

1. Right-click on the `com.davidsalter.cookbook.jarviewer.gui` package in the **Projects** explorer and select **New** and then **Other...**.

2. In the **New File** dialog, select **Swing GUI Forms** under **Categories** and **OK / Cancel Dialog Sample Form** from the **File Types** section.

3. Click on **Next**.

4. Enter the **Class Name** field as `AboutDialog` and ensure the **Package** section is set to `com.davidsalter.cookbook.jarviewer.gui`.

5. Click on **Finish**.

A new blank dialog will now be created with **OK** and **Cancel** buttons on it as shown in the following screenshot:

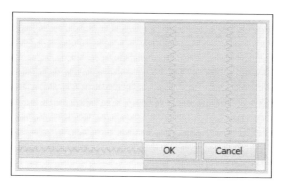

We don't want the **OK** button, so let's delete that and then add some information to the dialog with the following steps:

1. Right-click on the **OK** button and select **Delete**.

2. Locate the **text** property for the **Cancel** button and set it to read `Close`.

3. Using the techniques we learned in the *Adding components to a form* recipe, change the design of the form to look like the following screenshot:

> To create an image and text on the dialog, simply drop a **Label** control and set its icon and text properties.

4. Since we're creating a dialog, we want to give it a fixed size. Click on the dialog's background and then ensure the **resizable** attribute is not checked on the **[JDialog] – Properties** window.

5. Preview the design of the dialog by clicking on the **Preview Design** button.

How it works...

When creating the dialog with the **New File** wizard, we selected to create simple JDialog with **OK** and **Cancel** buttons on it. Doing this, NetBeans automatically wired up the **OK** and **Cancel** buttons to close the dialog (although, we later deleted the **OK** button because we didn't want it).

> We could have just created a JDialog form, but then we wouldn't have automatically got **OK** and **Cancel** buttons added; so, we would have needed to do some extra work to add the required buttons.

When creating dialogs, NetBeans provides the opportunity to create different types of dialogs. These are all based upon the JDialog form, but with additional controls and layouts added onto them to save additional time. I recommend you to experiment with these different types of dialog so that you will know which one best suits your needs in the future.

Adding components onto a dialog is exactly the same procedure as adding components onto a main form. Check out the recipe, *Adding components to a form*, earlier in this chapter for more details.

There's more...

If you want to try out a dialog from a running executable code instead of previewing it from within NetBeans, you can simply right-click on the class within the **Projects** explorer and click on **Run File**. NetBeans adds a `main()` method into each `JDialog` class that it creates so that you can run the dialog independently from your application to get a good indication of how it will look when running.

We've now created a dialog, in the recipe, *Responding to events*, we'll see how we can invoke the dialog and display it on the screen.

Creating toolbars

The final stage of designing the GUI for our application is to add a toolbar with a button on it. Clicking on the button on the toolbar will cause the contents of selected `.jar` files to be displayed.

Getting ready

To complete this recipe, we need to have the `JarViewer` project that was created in the *Creating dialogs* recipe. If you have not completed this recipe, the source code is available with the code download bundle for this chapter.

How to do it...

Since we are adding a toolbar to the main form of our application, we need to make sure that the form is open and ready for designing. Double-click on the `MainFrame.java` file in the **Projects** explorer and ensure the **Design** surface is visible, and perform the following steps:

1. From the **Palette** section, drag a **Tool Bar** control onto the form and align it with the top-left side of the form just underneath the menu.

    The **Tool Bar** control is located in the **Swing Containers** section of the **Palette** window and as such allows us to drop other controls on top of it.

2. Right-click on the dropped toolbar and select **Change Variable Name...**.
3. Enter the **New Name** field as `toolBar`.
4. Click on **OK**.
5. From the **Palette** window, drag a **Button** control onto the `toolBar` control. The button will initially be called `jButton1`.

6. Right-click on `jButton1` and click on **Change Variable Name...**.

7. Enter the **New Name** field as `viewToolBarButton`.

8. Click on **OK**.

The layout of the toolbar doesn't look very good at the moment; so, let's remove the text from the button and add an image instead with the following steps:

1. Click on the `viewToolBarButton` component and locate the **text** property in the **viewToolBarButton [JButton] - Properties** window. Ensure the **text** property is not set to anything.

2. Within the **viewToolBarButton [JButton] - Properties** window, click on the **Code** button to enable custom code generation for the button.

3. Locate the **Custom Creation Code** option and click on the **...** button (⬚) to open the custom code creation dialog, as shown in the following screenshot:

4. Enter the **Custom Creation Code** dialog as:

```
new javax.swing.JButton(new javax.swing.ImageIcon(new
javax.swing.ImageIcon(getClass().getResource("/com/davidsal
ter/cookbook/jarviewer/gui/folder_explore.png")).getImage()
.getScaledInstance(16, 16, java.awt.Image.SCALE_SMOOTH)))
```

5. Click on **OK**.

6. Run the application by pressing *F6* to see the toolbar with its button, as shown in the following screenshot:

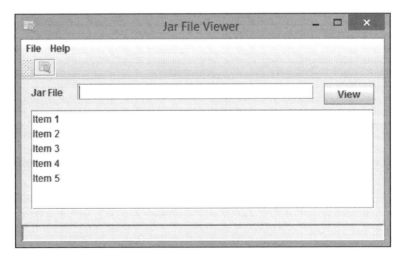

This is a good example of where clicking on the **Preview Dialog** button does not show an accurate representation of the form. Since we added the custom code to create the toolbar button, NetBeans does not know how to generate a preview of the button and so no toolbar button is displayed.

How it works...

A toolbar is simply a container (much like the main application frame) that can have additional components placed inside it. To create a toolbar, we added a button inside the container.

Typically, toolbars have no text but are represented by images. Since we had an image within out project, it made sense to use that.

The image that we have used previously however is too big to be used as a standard image for a toolbar button hence the custom creation code for the button.

This custom creation code loads the image file from the application's classpath and resizes it to a 16 x 16 image, which is then set into the button.

In the next recipe, *Responding to events*, we'll see how to make the button respond to click events.

Responding to events

So far, we've designed a Swing desktop application. We've added some controls onto a form, added a menu system, and added a toolbar. At the moment, there's no functionality behind the controls and menu items.

The next step after designing a Swing desktop application is to add behaviors to it.

In Swing, this is done by implementing **event listeners**. Firstly, we must register specific objects, the event listeners, onto Swing components in order to perform a determined task. When an event is triggered, the Swing component passes this to the listeners to handle the action according to what was implemented.

There are multiple kinds of events in Swing that include mouse, focus, key, and window events.

For a more detailed view of event listeners, visit
`http://download.oracle.com/javase/tutorial/uiswing/events/intro.html`.

Getting ready

To complete this recipe, we need to have the `JarViewer` project that was created in the *Creating toolbars* recipe. If you have not completed this recipe, the source code is available with the code download bundle for this chapter.

How to do it...

The first behavior that we'll add to our application is to make the controls on the form work correctly. That is, if we type in a valid `.jar` filename and click on the **View** button, we should see what the contents of the `.jar` file are. Perform the following steps to check this:

1. Double-click on the `MainFrame.java` class within the **Projects** explorer to open it up for editing. Ensure the **Design** tab is selected for editing the design surface of the class.

2. Click on the **View** button within the `MainFrame.java` designer. This will allow us to edit the events for the button.

3. Locate the **viewButton [JButton] – Properties** window and click on the **Events** button, as shown in the following screenshot:

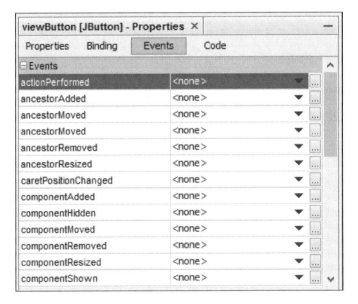

4. Click on the down arrow (▾) to the right of the **actionPerformed** event listener.

5. A pop-up tooltip will be displayed showing the default name for this event listener as `viewButtonActionPerformed`. Click on this tooltip to create the event handler, as shown in the following screenshot:

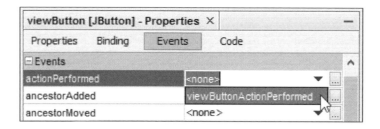

6. The design window for the form will now close and the Java source code window for `MainFram.java` will be opened at the newly created event handler, as shown in the following screenshot:

```
private void viewButtonActionPerformed(java.awt.event.ActionEvent evt) {
    // TODO add your handling code here:
}
```

7. Replace the body of the `viewButtonActionPerformed()` method with the following code:

```
statusLabel.setText("Parsing JAR file");
try {
  DefaultListModel model = new DefaultListModel();
  ZipInputStream zip = new ZipInputStream(
  new FileInputStream(jarName.getText()));
  for (ZipEntry entry = zip.getNextEntry();
  entry != null;
  entry = zip.getNextEntry()) {
    model.addElement(entry.getName());
  }
  jarEntries.setModel(model);
  statusLabel.setText("Entries found: " + model.size());
} catch (IOException ioe) {
  statusLabel.setText("Entries found: 0");
  JOptionPane.showMessageDialog(this,
  ioe.getLocalizedMessage(),
  "Oops - an error occurred",
  JOptionPane.ERROR_MESSAGE);
}
```

We should really be closing the `ZipInputStream` class properly here if an exception occurs to avoid any `.jar` locking problems. For brevity, this has been omitted from this code.

This code takes the name of the `.jar` file we wish to view and opens a `ZipInputStream` instance for the file. A Swing `DefaultTableModel` instance is created and an entry is added to it for each `ZipEntry` instance within `ZipInputStream`.

The table model is then set on the `jarEntries` component.

If any errors occur during parsing the file, an error message box is displayed.

 For more information about Swing List and ListModel, check out The Java Tutorial, *How to Use Lists*, at `http://docs.oracle.com/javase/ tutorial/uiswing/components/list.html`.

The next stage in adding behaviors to our application is to respond to the menu options. In the *Creating menus* recipe, we added the menu options, **File | Exit** and **Help | About**. For adding behaviors to our application, perform the following steps:

1. In the **Navigator** window, click on the `exitMenuItem` node, which is shown in the following screenshot:

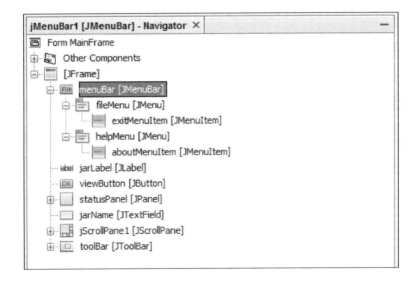

 When working with a user interface that has a lot of controls on it, the **Navigator** window can be invaluable in helping you to select individual controls for editing their properties. Sometimes, locating a control via the **Navigator** window can be a lot easier than clicking on the control within the main design surface, especially when a control has no text!

2. Click on the down arrow to the right of the **actionPerformed** event handler.

3. A pop-up tooltip will be displayed showing the default name for this event handler as `exitMenuItemActionPerformed`. Click on this tooltip to create the event handler.

4. Replace the body of the `exitMenuItemActionPerformed` method with the following line:

```
System.exit(0);
```

5. Click on the **Design** button to go back to the design surface for the class.

6. In the **Navigator** window, click on the `aboutMenuItem` node.

7. Click on the down arrow to the right of the **actionPerformed** event handler.

8. A pop-up tooltip will be displayed showing the default name for this event handler as `aboutMenuActionPerformed`. Click on this tooltip to create the event handler.

9. Replace the body of the `aboutMenuItemActionPerformed` method with the following lines:

```
AboutDialog dialog = new AboutDialog(this, true);
dialog.setVisible(true);
```

Finally, we need to add behavior to the toolbar button so that it performs the same action as the **View** button. To do this, perform the following steps:

1. Click on the **Design** button to go back to the design surface for the class.

2. In the **Navigator** window, click on the `viewToolBarButton` node.

3. Click on the down arrow to the right of the **actionPerformed** event handler in the **viewToolBarButton [JButton] – Properties** window.

4. A pop-up tooltip will be displayed showing the default name for this event handler as `viewToolBarButtonActionPerformed`. Click on the tooltip to create the event handler.

At this point, we've got a decision to make because both the toolbar button and the **View** button perform the same functionality. We obviously don't want to type the same code into both action handlers, so what should we do?

Let's refactor the code we added in the `viewButtonActionPerformed` handler out into a separate method called `parseJarFile()` and then call this method from both action handlers with the following steps:

1. Using the mouse, select all of the text inside the `viewButtonActionPerformed` method.

 Don't select the line with the method signature or the last line containing only } as these line are automatically generated by NetBeans and we won't be allowed to refactor these!

2. Right-click on the code and select **Refactor**, and then **Introduce** and then **Method...**.

3. In the **Introduce Method** dialog, enter the **Name** field as `parseJarFile`, as shown in the following screenshot:

4. Click on **Finish**.

5. Locate the `viewToolBarButtonActionPerformed` method and replace the body of the method with:

```
parseJarFile();
```

We've now added the functionality to our application to allow it to read .jar files and show us their contents. You can now run the application by pressing *F6*. Enter a valid .jar file into the **Jar File** field and click on the **View** button to see the contents of the .jar file, as shown in the following screenshot:

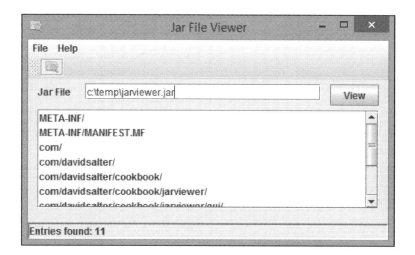

How it works...

When we clicked on the **actionPerformed** event within the **Properties** window for the **View** button, NetBeans created us an empty method called `viewButtonActionPerformed()` in which we placed our event handler.

What we didn't see is that NetBeans also automatically added an action listener to the `viewButton` component so that this method would be invoked at the correct time.

If we look at the source code for the `MainFrame.java` class, we can see that there is a method called `initComponents()` that is collapsed by default. NetBeans adds all component initialization within this method. This is an automatically generated method and cannot be edited directly within the Java editor; rather its contents are created based upon the properties, bindings, and events that we define at design time.

Digging into the `initComponents()` method, we can find the code that adds the action listener, as shown in the following screenshot:

```
52          viewButton.addActionListener(new java.awt.event.ActionListener() {
            public void actionPerformed(java.awt.event.ActionEvent evt) {
54              viewButtonActionPerformed(evt);
55          }
56      });
```

 When looking through the automatically generated code, we can see why it's a good idea to use a naming mechanism for controls and not just use the default names of `jList1`, `jButton1`, and so on.

NetBeans added similar code for the other event handlers that we added. If you expand the autogenerated code for the class, you will see action listeners have been created for all the events we've added in this recipe.

 In larger projects with more complex GUI forms and dialogs, it's a good practice to try to keep the amount of the custom code added into a form or a dialog to a minimum. By keeping the implementation of a form and the logic behind it separate, we can easily refactor, and change the forms appearance, without affecting major parts of our application.

There's more...

When we added the event handler for the **actionPerformed** event, we chose the default name for the handler as `viewButtonActionPerformed`. What if we don't want to choose the default name, but instead prefer something shorter like `viewButtonPressed`?

Clicking the **...** button to the right of each event opens up the **Handlers** window for the specific event. From within this window, we can create new handlers giving them the names that we want, we can remove the existing handlers, or we can rename the existing handlers. We can see the **Handlers** window in the following screenshot:

If you want to quickly access the code for an event handler, then click on the handler's name within the **Events** section of the **Properties** window. NetBeans will then open up the code editor for you at the correct place.

In addition to editing and creating events via the **Properties** window for a component, you can quickly create/edit event handlers by right-clicking on a component and selecting **Events** and then the event handler you wish to create/edit, as shown in the following screenshot:

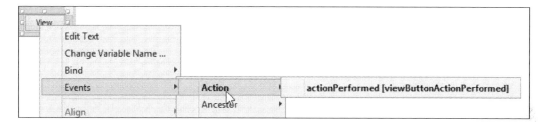

Building a distributable application from NetBeans

When we've developed our application, we want to get it out of the IDE and into our customer's hands as soon as possible. Fortunately, NetBeans makes it very easy to create an executable `.jar` file that we can distribute to our customers.

Getting started

To complete this recipe, we need to have the `JarViewer` project that was created in the *Responding to events* recipe. If you have not completed this recipe, the source code is available with the code download bundle for this chapter.

How to do it...

When NetBeans builds an executable `.jar` file for a desktop GUI application, it adds all the necessary references to any external libraries that are required and bundles those with the application. Since our `JarViewer` application doesn't use any third-party dependencies, let's add one on the assumption that our application does use it. We'll add the Java DB driver to our project, as it's possible to see that at some point in the future we may want to add database functionality to the application, with the following steps:

1. Right-click on the **Libraries** node for the project within the **Projects** explorer and click on **Add Library...**. The **Add Library** window is shown in the following screenshot:

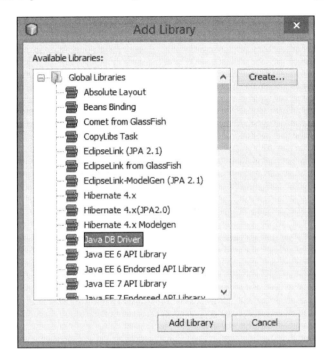

2. From the list of **Available Libraries**, click on **Java DB Driver**.

3. Click on **Add Library**.

The library has now been added to the `JarViewer` project and will be included in the project's distribution.

Let's now create that distribution with the following steps:

1. Right-click on the project's root node (`JarViewer`) in the **Projects** explorer and select **Clean and Build**.

2. The project will now get built. Examine the **Output** window and notice that NetBeans tells us how to run the application from the command line:

    ```
    To run this application from the command line without Ant, try:
    java -jar "C:\NetBeansProjects\JarViewer\dist\JarViewer.jar"
    ```

3. Open up the **Files** explorer and expand the `dist` node, as shown in the following screenshot:

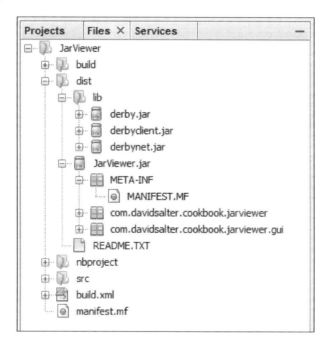

4. Note that the `.jar` file for our project is located underneath the `dist` folder.

5. Note also the `dist/lib` folder that includes all third-party libraries that we have referenced.

6. To distribute our application, we now only need to take a copy of everything underneath the `dist` folder and provide it to our customers.

How it works...

When building the application, NetBeans creates a `MANIFEST.MF` file within the `META-INF` folder of the archive. The `MANIFEST.MF` file for the application created in this recipe is shown in the following screenshot:

```
1   Manifest-Version: 1.0
2   Ant-Version: Apache Ant 1.9.2
3   Created-By: 1.7.0_51-b13 (Oracle Corporation)
4   Class-Path: lib/derby.jar lib/derbyclient.jar lib/derbynet.jar
5   X-COMMENT: Main-Class will be added automatically by build
6   Main-Class: com.davidsalter.cookbook.jarviewer.Main
7
```

This file contains all of the information required to run the `.jar` file from the command line. All of this information is automatically generated from the project properties:

- **Class-Path**: This references all of the third-party libraries that we need to use so that they can be located at runtime
- **Main-Class**: This specifies the main class to run when the archive is executed

There's more...

When creating a `.jar` archive, it's important to note that only `.jar` files are copied to the `dist/lib` folder. If you have other types of files on the classpath that are used by your application, for example, image files, these will not be copied into the `dist` folder and will not be available for deployed applications.

Does that mean the custom icon we specified for our application will not be available in the distribution?

Fortunately, our custom icon will be available within the distribution as we added the image file directly into the source folder of the application. You may remember that when we loaded the image, we loaded it from the classpath not from the filesystem.

If you want to make a `.exe` file for your application rather than distributing it as a `.jar` file, consider third-party products such as Launch4j. Launch4j is an open source product that wraps a `.jar` file with a `.exe` file giving control over the JRE settings used when launching the application. Check out `http://launch4j.sourceforge.net` for further details.

5
NetBeans Enterprise Application Development

In this chapter, we will cover the following recipes:

- ▶ Adding WildFly support to NetBeans
- ▶ Adding TomEE support to NetBeans
- ▶ Creating a web application
- ▶ Creating a web application with JSF support
- ▶ Adding JSF support to a web application
- ▶ Creating a JSF composite component
- ▶ Creating an EJB
- ▶ Creating a Message Driven EJB
- ▶ Creating a timer
- ▶ Creating a REST web service
- ▶ Using the Chrome Connector

Introduction

Java EE is a remarkable technology for all that it can accomplish, but in earlier versions, it was criticized for being overly complicated and verbose.

Much of this criticism was justified for the fact that Java EE relied heavily on XML-based configuration, requiring many interfaces and exceptions, and presenting developers with many hurdles to face when using it. Technologies such as Hibernate and Spring emerged, and gained much attraction simply because they sought to address those complexities.

With the introduction of Java EE 5, the core platform once again gained the upper hand, tying together the same formula that helped catapult Hibernate and Spring into developers' favor. Annotations were brought in to tone down the verbosity of code, along with the reduction of checked exceptions, POJO programming, introduction of JSF, enhancements in EJB QL and Application Container, and simplification of Session Beans.

Session Beans are Java objects that perform a multitude of operations but are mainly used for managing transactional data. With Java EE 7, Session Beans can be either Stateless, Stateful, or Singleton beans:

▸ **Stateful Session Beans** maintain a conversational state for the entire client session.

▸ **Stateless Session Beans** do not maintain a conversational state. These beans are maintained in memory for as long as the client request takes and after that, the state is no longer kept in memory.

▸ **Singleton Session Beans** are guaranteed to only have one instance within an application and exist for the entire life of the application.

The idea of simplifying development continues in Java EE 7. Java EE 7 has three main aims, as follows:

▸ Increase developer productivity by requiring less boilerplate code and using more annotations / less XML

▸ Provide better HTML 5 support with the likes of JSON processing, REST and Web Sockets

▸ Meet enterprise demands with the new batch, concurrency and simplified JMS APIs

In Java EE 7, some of the heavyweight, outdated technologies and APIs such as JAXR, EJB 2.x Entity Beans, and Java EE Application Deployment, have been marked as **pruned**, either for low usage by developers, or for not being entirely implemented by the vendors that chose to create the application containers. On top of that, performance enhancements for deployment and resources used, such as Java EE web profiles, were added so that developers who do not utilize the entire Java EE stack can deploy applications based only on what they use, enabling a much more lightweight application.

Adding WildFly support to NetBeans

Many years ago, **JBoss** released its first application server, the JBoss application server. The JBoss application server was developed as an open source software up until version 7, when it was redeveloped and renamed **WildFly 8**. WildFly 8 is one of the most used open source Java EE application servers available. Version 8 fully supports both the Java EE 7 full and web profiles making it one of the select few application servers that fully supports the Java EE 7 full platform.

WildFly is built on top of many open source projects such as Hibernate for persistence, Weld for contexts and dependency injection, and Mojarra for Java Server Faces.

WildFly provides both web-based and command-line-based management tools together with full Maven support for managing project deployments. These tools allow NetBeans to provide full control over WildFly when developing Java EE applications.

A standalone and a domain mode of WildFly are provided with the distribution. The standalone mode is most likely what developers will use during application development as it provides a single application server instance running within a single JVM. The domain mode allows WildFly to run across multiple JVMs while providing synchronization of applications and settings across different JVMs. In this recipe, we'll discuss the standalone mode of WildFly.

Before we see how to install WildFly support within NetBeans, let's first take a look at how to install WildFly and take a quick look around WildFly's application structure.

Installing WildFly is a very straightforward process. Simply download the distribution from the project's download site (`http://wildfly.org/downloads`) and unzip/untar it into a local directory.

For each release of WildFly, the full EE 7-certified application server, a minimalistic core distribution and the application server source code can be downloaded. Ensure that you download the full Java EE 7-certified server:

Downloads

Version	Date	Description	License	Size	Format
8.0.0 Final	2014-02-11	Java EE7 Certified Server	LGPL	148 MB	⬇ ZIP
				134 MB	⬇ TGZ
		Minimalistic Core Distribution	LGPL	15 MB	⬇ ZIP
		Application Server Source Code	LGPL	29 MB	⬇ ZIP
				17 MB	⬇ TGZ
		Release Notes			✏ Notes

WildFly is provided under the LGPL v2.1 license, so please ensure that you have read the license (`http://www.gnu.org/licenses/lgpl-2.1.html`) before using the software.

Once unzipped/untarred, the WildFly directory structure will look like the following screenshot:

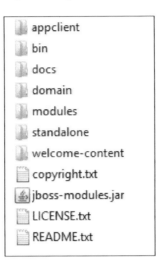

Let's take a look at what these different directories mean in WildFly:

Directory	Description
appclient	Configuration files used by the application client container
bin	Management scripts including those to start up the application server
docs	Example configuration files together with XML schema definitions
domain	Configuration files and deployments for the domain mode configuration
modules	Modules (additional `.jar` files) required by the application server, for example, database drivers or JSON providers
standalone	Configuration files and deployments for the standalone mode configuration
welcome-content	Contents for the default homepage for the application server

Once you've installed WildFly, you need to learn how to start the application server. To start WildFly, open a command prompt (or a terminal if running on Linux/Mac OS X), change the directory to the root installation of WildFly, and execute one of the following commands:

- If running on Windows, use this command: `bin\standalone.bat`
- If running on Linux/Mac OS X, use this command: `./bin/standalone.sh`

The following screenshot shows WildFly starting up in a Windows command shell:

To stop WildFly, press *Ctrl + C* within the command/terminal window. Now that we've had a brief overview of WildFly, let's see how to integrate it into NetBeans.

Getting ready

To add WildFly as an application server within NetBeans, it's preferable to be running the Java EE download bundle of NetBeans so that additional plugins other than WildFly do not need to be installed.

It's recommended to use the latest version of either Java 7 or Java 8 for both NetBeans and WildFly, so if you haven't got one of those installed yet, you can install either of them from

`http://www.oracle.com/technetwork/java/index.html`

How to do it ...

Perform the following steps:

1. Ensure that NetBeans is running, and then click on **Tools** and then **Plugins** from the main menu.

2. Click on the **Available Plugins** tab. Notice that the number in brackets at the end of the tab name shows the number of available plugins as shown in the following screenshot:

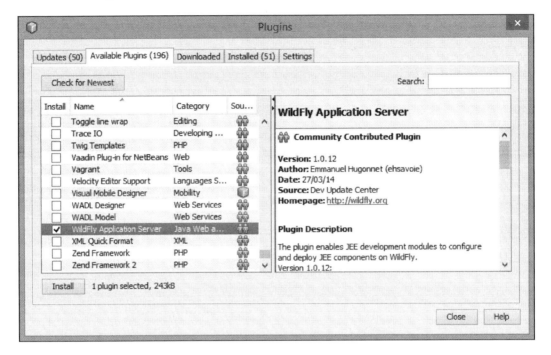

3. Locate the **WildFly Application Server** plugin and check the **Install** checkbox next to it.

4. Click on the **Install** button.

5. The NetBeans IDE plugin installer will now be displayed showing that the WildFly application server plugin is to be installed.

6. Click on **Next**, accept the license agreement, and then click on **Install**.

7. When prompted, select **Restart the IDE Now** to complete the installation of the plugin.

NetBeans will now restart with the WildFly plugin successfully installed. The final stage is to add a WildFly server instance into NetBeans so that we can start developing applications against it. Perform the following steps:

1. Click on **Tools** and then click on **Servers** from the main menu. The NetBeans **Servers** definition dialog will now be displayed:

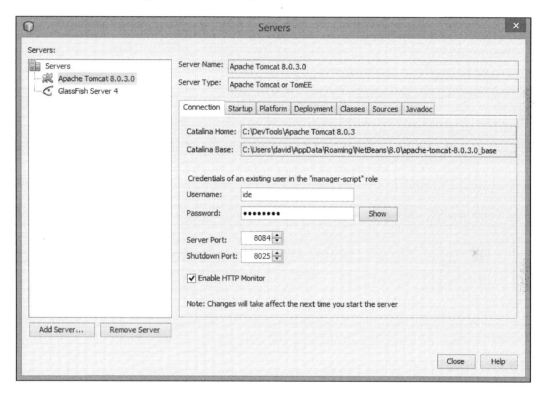

2. Click on the **Add Server** button.

3. On the **Add Server Instance** dialog, select **WildFly Application Server** as shown in the following screenshot:

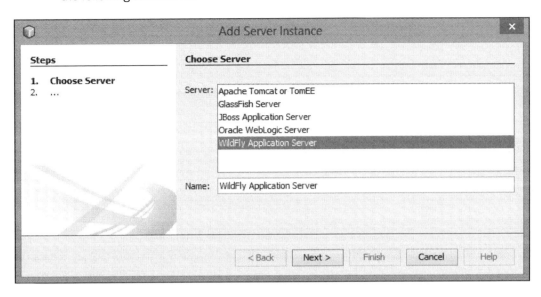

4. Click on **Next**.

5. Enter the **Server Location** field as the home directory where you previously installed WildFly.

 I always install my development software into a `c:\DevTools` folder, so for me, the **Server Location** field would be set to `c:\DevTools\WildFly-8.0.0.Final`.

6. Upon specifying **Server Location**, the **Server Configuration** field will be automatically set to the configuration file of the standalone WildFly instance within your distribution.

7. Click on **Next**.

8. The **Instance Properties** page will now be shown. Verify that the default **Host** value is `localhost` and **Port** is `8080`, and change them to the values for your environment if not.

9. Click on **Finish**.

10. You have now added an instance of the WildFly application server within NetBeans. Click on **Close** to exit the **Servers** dialog.

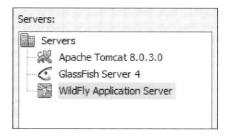

How it works...

We've now successfully added an instance of WildFly into NetBeans, but how do we control the server? If we locate the **Services** explorer, the **Servers** node displays a list of all application servers registered within NetBeans including our newly registered WildFly instance. Right-clicking on the server displays a context menu that allows the server to be started (in standard, debug or profiling modes), stopped, or restarted. We can view the server log, which displays the running WildFly console output into the NetBeans **Output** window. This can be especially useful for examining debug messages and WildFly log messages while debugging applications.

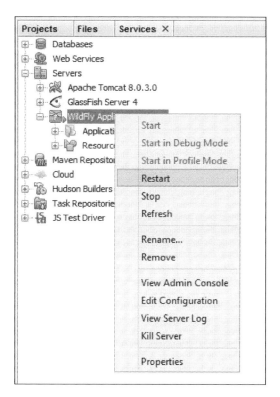

Located within the WildFly application server node on the **Services** explorer, we can also see what Enterprise Applications, EJBs, and web modules are deployed. From here, we can also stop and undeploy them.

We can also see what resources are deployed to the application server, whether they are data sources, JMS resources, or mail sessions. The current version of the NetBeans plugin allows us to view these resources, but not edit them.

Viewing the application server properties allows us to specify the configuration file that defines the application server instance (although, you'll probably never need to change that). We can also change the VM options that are used to start the application server. The default JVM settings (`-Xms128m -Xmx512m -XX:MaxPermSize=256m`) are probably sufficient for most small applications, but may need modifying for larger applications. JVM settings such as these will only take effect upon restarting the server.

Adding TomEE support to NetBeans

TomEE is a Java EE 6 web profile compatible application server based upon the Apache Tomcat servlet container.

TomEE started out being an integration between OpenEJB (a lightweight EJB container) and Tomcat, and has now grown to include all of the Java EE 6 web profile features such as CDI, EJB, and Bean validation. All of these features are provided within TomEE via different Apache products. For example, Apache OpenWebBeans provides the implementation of CDI, Apache OpenEJB provides the implementation for EJB, and Apache BVal provides the implementation of Bean validation.

NetBeans 8 provides native support for TomEE without the need for installing additional plugins. This functionality was not available with NetBeans 7.4 and earlier. Installing TomEE support into NetBeans, therefore, is a matter of registering a new server instance. Before we look at that, let's take a quick look at how to install a TomEE server.

Installing TomEE is very similar to installing WildFly as seen in the previous recipe, *Adding WildFly support to NetBeans*.

To install TomEE, download a distribution from `http://tomee.apache.org/downloads.html`, and unzip/untar it into your preferred location.

Apache TomEE 1.7.0 August 2014

Web Profile

Java EE6 Certified

Apache TomEE Web Profile delivers
Servlets, JSP, JSF, JTA, JPA, CDI,
Bean Validation and EJB Lite

Comparison »

- apache-tomee-1.7.0-webprofile.tar.gz
  (asc - md5)
- apache-tomee-1.7.0-webprofile.zip
  (asc - md5)

Once unzipped, the TomEE directory structure will look like the following screenshot:

If you've ever used Apache Tomcat, you'll instantly recognize this as the same directory
structure that Tomcat uses—TomEE is based upon Tomcat after all!

We'll not go over the installation/directory structure of TomEE any further here,
as it's very similar to Tomcat. For further details, check out the TomEE documentation
at `http://tomee.apache.org/documentation.html`.

Getting ready

To create a TomEE instance within NetBeans, it's preferable to be running the Java EE download bundle of NetBeans so that additional plugins do not need to be installed.

It's recommended to use the latest version of either Java 7 or Java 8 for both NetBeans and TomEE, so if you haven't got one of those installed yet, you can install either of them from:

`http://www.oracle.com/technetwork/java/index.html`

How to do it ...

Perform the following steps:

1. Click on the **Services** explorer and expand the **Servers** node:

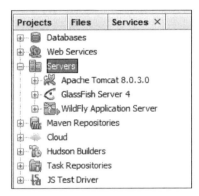

2. Right-click on the **Servers** node and select **Add Server** from the pop-up context menu.
3. On the **Add Server Instance** dialog, select **Server** as **Apache Tomcat or TomEE**:

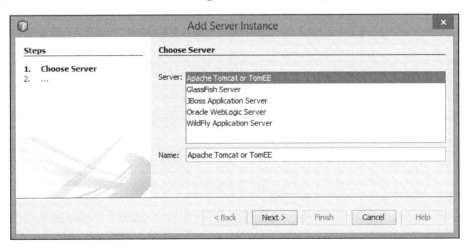

4. Click on **Next**.

5. On the **Add Server Instance** page, specify **Server Location** as the directory into which you unzipped/untarred the TomEE distribution.

 I always install my development software into a `c:\DevTools` folder, so for me, the **Server Location** field would be set to `c:\DevTools\Apache-TomEE-WebProfile-1.7.0`.

6. Enter **Username** as `admin`. This user will be created, if they do not exist, to perform management tasks against the TomEE server.

7. Enter a value for **Password**.

8. Click on **Finish**.

How it works ...

We've now successfully created a TomEE instance within NetBeans. Now, we can manage the server in a fashion similar to how we managed WildFly application servers as detailed in the previous recipe, *Adding WildFly support to NetBeans*.

Right-clicking on an Apache TomEE server within the **Services** explorer lets us manage the server properties.

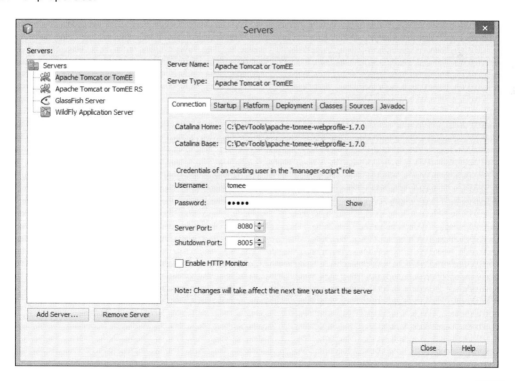

From here, we can change the management user credentials or change the ports that are used by the server. On the **Startup** tab, we can define **Debugger Transport** detailing how we can connect to the server to debug our applications.

We can define JVM options and deployment timeouts, which can be useful to change when deploying larger applications.

Creating a web application

In the previous recipes, *Adding WildFly support to NetBeans* and *Adding TomEE support to NetBeans*, we saw how to create and manage instances of WildFly and TomEE, respectively.

In this recipe, we'll see how to create web applications and deploy them against our chosen application server. For this recipe, we'll use TomEE.

> NetBeans supports both Ant and Maven for creating web applications. In this recipe, we'll create a project using NetBeans built-in Ant project support.

Getting ready

To complete this recipe, you need to have a valid installation of TomEE configured within NetBeans. If you do not have this, follow the earlier recipe, *Adding TomEE support to NetBeans*.

How to do it...

Perform the following steps:

1. Click on the **File** menu and select **New Project**.
2. On the **New Project** dialog, select **Java Web** from the **Categories** list and then **Web Application** from the **Projects** list.
3. Click on **Next**.
4. Enter the **Project Name** field as `FirstWebApp`.
5. Click on **Next**.
6. On the **Server and Settings** page of the **New Web Application** wizard, select your TomEE instance as **Server**.

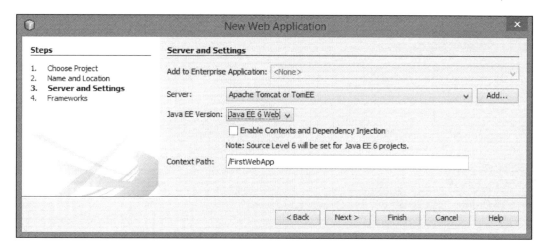

7. Click on the **Finish** button.

NetBeans has now created a blank web application with a single `index.jsp` file within it. Let's see how we can deploy and run the application, and then make changes to it:

1. Right-click on the **FirstWebApp** project within the **Projects** explorer and click on **Run**.

2. The application will now be deployed to TomEE with the application server being automatically started if it is not already running. The default system browser will be opened and the application will be run within it:

As seen in the previous step, NetBeans automatically deploys web applications when they are executed from within the IDE. In order to increase developer productivity, NetBeans will also automatically deploy the web application when we make changes to the files:

1. Ensure that the `index.jsp` file is open for editing.
2. Locate the `<h1>` tag and change its contents from `Hello World!` to `Hello from our first Web Application!`.
3. Press *Ctrl + S* (*Cmd + S* on Mac OS X) to save the file.
4. Refresh the browser and notice that the web page has been updated.

How it works ...

When deploying an application on TomEE, NetBeans creates a configuration descriptor file with the same name as the application and deploys it to TomEE.

```
INFO: Deploying configuration descriptor C:\DevTools\apache-tomee-
webprofile-1.7.0\conf\Catalina\localhost\FirstWebApp.xml
```

From this configuration descriptor, TomEE is able to deploy the web application as an exploded `.war` archive, which saves deployment time, especially for larger projects.

There's more

What if we want to see exactly what requests we've made to TomEE so that we can perform debugging or check out load performance? TomEE allows us to view all the HTTP requests made to the application server. This is disabled by default, but can be easily enabled by viewing the server properties and checking the **Enable HTTP Monitor** checkbox.

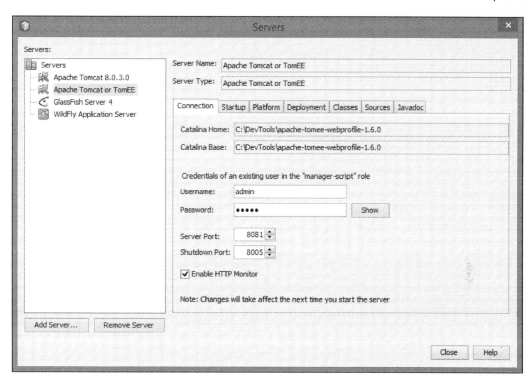

Once you've changed the server properties to enable the HTTP monitor, you'll need to restart TomEE for the changes to take effect. This can easily be achieved by right-clicking on the TomEE instance within the **Services** explorer and selecting the **Restart** option.

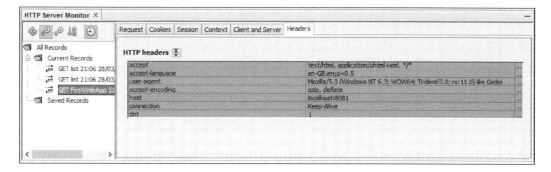

When running an application, NetBeans can be configured to open a specific browser. The default option is to open the operating system's default browser, which in many cases, will be the most suitable option. It is possible, however, to change the browser that is opened. This is achieved by editing the project properties and changing the **Browser** option under the **Run** category. Options are available to view using any browsers that you have installed on your computer or by using the NetBeans-embedded Webkit browser. For those doing mobile development, the choice is available to use an Android emulator or an Android device.

In addition to the HTTP Server Monitor that is provided with the Tomcat/TomEE support, NetBeans provides a **Network Monitor** that can be used in conjunction with the embedded Webkit browser.

The Network Monitor logs any failed web requests, including failed REST requests, and can therefore be useful when diagnosing AJAX applications to examine when requests fail.

Creating a web application with JSF support

In the *Creating a web application* recipe, we saw how to create a basic JSP web application and introduced the concepts behind creating, deploying, and running a web application.

In this recipe, we'll take things a little further and show how to create a **Java Server Faces** (**JSF**) web application and run it on the WildFly application server. This recipe isn't intended to be a thorough tutorial on JSF, although we will go through the basics.

We'll create a JSF application that asks for our name and then welcomes us to the application. We'll see how NetBeans helps us make the development easier.

Getting ready

To complete this recipe, we need to have a running instance of the NetBeans Java EE bundle, together with a local installation of the WildFly 8 application server. We need to have the WildFly 8 plugin installed into NetBeans. See the *Adding WildFly support to NetBeans* recipe for further details.

How to do it...

Perform the following steps:

1. Click on the **File** menu, select **New**, and then **New Project...**.
2. On the **New Project** dialog, select **Java Web** from the **Categories** list, and then **Web Application** from the **Projects** list.
3. Click on **Next**.
4. Enter the **Project Name** field as `HelloJSF`.
5. Click on **Next**.

6. On the **Server and Settings** page of the **New Web Application** wizard, select your WildFly instance as **Server** and ensure that **Java EE Version** is set to **Java EE 7 Web**.

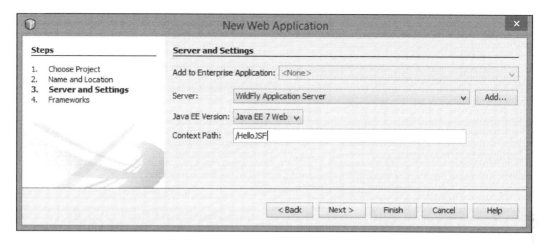

7. Click on the **Next** button.

8. On the **Frameworks** selection page, check **JavaServer Faces** as a selected framework.

9. Click on **Finish**.

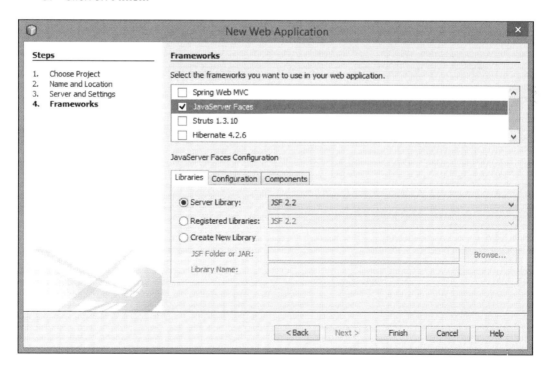

10. Double-click on the `index.xhtml` file within the **Projects** explorer to open it up within the HTML editing window.

11. Delete the default text, `Hello from Facelets`.

12. Right-click between the `<h:body>` and `<h:/body>` tags and select **Insert Code...** from the context menu.

13. On the **Generate** pop-up window, click on **JSF Form**. The contents of the `<h:body>` tag will now be updated to include a `<f:view>` tag containing a `<h:form>` tag as shown:

```
<h:body>
    <f:view>
        <h:form>
        </h:form>
    </f:view>
</h:body>
```

14. Insert the following markup between the `<h:form>` and `</h:form>` tags:

```
<h:panelGrid columns="3">
  <h:outputText value="Hello.  What is your name?"/>
  <h:inputText id="name" value="#{helloBean.name}"/>
  <h:commandButton action="#{helloBean.sayHello}"
        value="Hello"/>
</h:panelGrid>
```

We've now created a simple input JSF page that displays some output text, asks for some input, and then has a button that can be clicked to submit the input.

Let's now create an output page that can echo the input that the user types, as follows:

1. Right-click on the **Web Pages** node in the **Projects** explorer, click on **New**, and then click on **Other**.

2. In the **New File** dialog, select **JavaServer Faces** from the **Categories** list, and **JSF Page** from the list of **File Types**.

3. Click on **Next**.

4. Enter the **File Name** value as `hello`.

 It's tempting here to enter **File Name** as `hello.xhtml` instead of just `hello`. You must, however, omit adding the suffix to the filename as this is automatically added by NetBeans. Otherwise, NetBeans will create a file called `hello.xhtml.xhtml`.

5. Ensure that the option specifies **Facelets** instead of **JSP File**.

6. Click on **Finish**.

7. The new `hello.xhtml` file will now be opened for editing. Replace the default body of `Hello from Facelets` with:

   ```
   Hi, <h:outputText value="#{helloBean.name}"/>
   ```

We've now created all of the views for our JSF application, all we need to do now is create a **JSF backing bean** that can take our input and forward it on to the output page. Perform the following steps:

1. Right-click on the **Source Packages** node of the **HelloJSF** application and click on **New**, and then click on **Other**.

2. In the **New File** dialog, select **JavaServer Faces** from the **Categories** list and **JSF Managed Bean** from the list of **File Types**.

3. Click on **Next**.

4. Enter the **Class Name** value as `HelloBean` and the **Package** value as `com.davidsalter.hellojsf`.

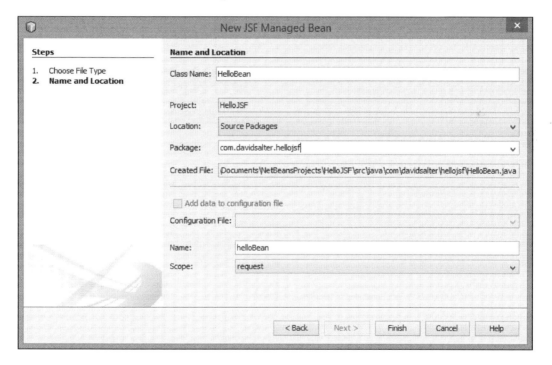

> Notice that the bean is created with a default **Name**, the same as **Class Name** (capitalized as **camelCase** however), and the default **Scope** of the bean is set to `request`.

5. Click on **Finish**.

6. The `HelloBean.java` file will now be opened for editing. Replace the body of the class with the following code:

```java
private String name;

public HelloBean() {
}

public String sayHello() {
    return "hello.xhtml";
}
public String getName() {
    return name;
}
public void setName(String name) {
    this.name = name;
}
```

The `HelloBean.java` class has one property, `name`, with corresponding getters and setters. There is one method, `sayHello()`, which is invoked when the button is clicked on our form. This method tells JSF to render the `hello.xhtml` view when it is called.

Let's now deploy and run our application and see how it runs. Right-click on the **Hello JSF** project within the **Projects** explorer and then click on **Run**.

When the application is first run, WildFly is started up if it is not already running. The application's `.war` file is then deployed to the running server. The initial page of the application is as shown in the following screenshot:

After entering your name and clicking on the **Hello** button, JSF says **"Hi"**:

 Now that the application is running, making any changes to the view files (the .xhtml files) or the JSF managed beans will automatically be hot deployed to WildFly when they are saved. The application does not need to be run again, all that is needed is a browser refresh to utilize the new content.

How it works...

When we created a JSF application, there were two aspects that we developed. We developed a couple of view pages (index.xhtml and hello.xhtml) and a managed JSF bean (HelloBean).

For the view pages, we used the **Facelets** technology. Facelets is the default view technology used with Java Server Faces 2 and has taken over from the use of JSP within Java Server Faces 1.x applications. JSP is now considered a legacy technology.

Facelets is a powerful templating system that allows developers to use any of the JSF components and create template-based web pages. Template-based web pages allow, for example, a layout page to be developed that has a header and a footer and a piece of content in between the two. With templating, we can use a layout page that defines all of the layout outside of the main content so that we can concentrate only on the main content. If we later decide that we wish to change the layout to add a sidebar, for example, we just need to change the template and not all of the pages we have developed.

Facelets allows the use of different component libraries. These libraries must be registered via a tag library in the `<html>` definition of a file. The two standard libraries for HTML and forms are provided with the JSF runtime. When we created a JSF page in this recipe, we told Facelets about these two libraries by defining the `h` and `f` tag libraries in the `<HTML>` definition, as follows:

```
<html xmlns="http://www.w3.org/1999/xhtml"
      xmlns:h="http://xmlns.jcp.org/jsf/html"
      xmlns:f="http://xmlns.jcp.org/jsf/core">
```

By referencing these tag libraries, we were able to reference any of the components within the `h` and `f` tag libraries (such as `<h:outputText />` and `<f:view />`).

For more information regarding Facelets, check out the Oracle documentation at:

`http://docs.oracle.com/javaee/7/tutorial/doc/jsf-facelets.htm`

To perform some processing, we created a JSF managed bean. This is simply a POJO with the `@ManagedBean` annotation applied to it. We also applied the `@RequestScoped` annotation to the bean so that the lifecycle of the bean is tied to an HTTP request. The bean is therefore initialized every time an HTTP request is made. Within the managed bean, we created a single member to hold the name entered by the user and a single method (`sayHello`) that returned the address of the Facelets page to render when the button was pressed on the form.

To link the view and the managed bean, we used expression language. Here we link the input box to the name property of the managed bean as follows:

```
<h:inputText id="name" value="#{helloBean.name}"/>
```

We also link the button action to the `sayHello` method in the bean as follows:

```
<h:commandButton action="#{helloBean.sayHello}" value="Hello"/>
```

There's more

How did JSF know what page to display first, and how did it know to use `.xhtml` as the file extension for Facelets views?

When we created the project, we used the NetBeans defaults and allowed NetBeans to create some default configuration within the `web.xml` file for the project.

The Faces servlet was defined with a URL pattern set to `/faces/*`:

```
<servlet>
    <servlet-name>Faces Servlet</servlet-name>
    <servlet-class>javax.faces.webapp.FacesServlet</servlet-class>
    <load-on-startup>1</load-on-startup>
</servlet>
<servlet-mapping>
    <servlet-name>Faces Servlet</servlet-name>
    <url-pattern>/faces/*</url-pattern>
</servlet-mapping>
```

All JSF requests go through the Faces servlet as this is what enables the lifecycle of Facelets components. Without this mapping, Facelets would just not work! This mapping states that any request to `/faces/*` will be executed via the Faces servlet. So for example, `/faces/index.xhtml` would cause the `index.xhtml` file to be processed as a JSF Facelets file.

NetBeans also configured the default page of the application to be `faces/index.xhtml`:

```
<welcome-file-list>
    <welcome-file>faces/index.xhtml</welcome-file>
</welcome-file-list>
```

This specifies the default page that will be opened when the root URL of the application is accessed.

What if I wanted to use a CDI bean or an EJB instead of the JSF managed bean. Could I do that?

Yes, it's entirely possible to use a different type of a managed bean as the backing bean for JSF pages. With Java EE 7, CDI beans are very common and can be used interchangeably with JSF managed beans. EJBs can also be used as backing beans if required, but they provide a greater overhead as they are considered more heavyweight (even though they are still essentially POJOs) than JSF backing beans or CDI beans.

A good rule of thumb it to use the lightest bean possible for a required situation and only move to the next higher level of bean when required.

So, for a simple application, a JSF Managed bean is sufficient. It allows us to receive data from the web page and then update the web page with some results. We don't really need anything more complex.

If we find that we need to start injecting beans into other resources, then a CDI managed bean makes sense. We can inject EJBs into CDI beans if we need to perform any processing within the bean.

If we find that we need to make our backing beans transactional (one of the key aspects of EJBs), then we could consider using an EJB as a backing bean.

Start with the simplest possible type of bean and only increase complexity when needed.

What if I want to perform validation on input fields? Does JSF allow that? It certainly does. We can either use the Bean Validation API to perform validation within our model, or we can perform JSF validation within the view.

To output error messages to the view, we can use the `<h:message />` tag to output a message for a single element, or the `<h:messages />` tag to output a list of all the error messages within the form:

```
<h:inputText value="#{cc.attrs.editValue}" id="inputText" />
<h:message for="inputText" />
```

Using the Bean Validation API, we can add annotations onto fields that will be validated before being accepted by the JSF runtime. Bean Validation provides many annotations to perform validation, and even allows custom validators to be written. Some of the more common validations are as follows:

- `@NotNull`: The specified field value must not be null
- `@Min`: The specified field value must be at least that specified by the constraint
- `@Max`: The specified field value must be at most that specified by the constraint
- `@Past`: The specified field value date must be a date in the past
- `@Pattern`: The specified field value must match that specified by a regular expression
- `@Size`: The size of the field value must be between the specified limits

For more information on Bean Validation, check out the website `http://beanvalidation.org`.

With JSF validation, we can perform a similar task to Bean Validation, but instead using JSF tags. Validation is performed within the Validation phase of a JSF component's lifecycle. As with bean validation, JSF allows custom validators to be written. Some of the standard JSF validators are:

- `<f:validateLength />`: The size of the field value must be between the specified limits
- `<f:validateLongRange />`: The range of a long integer must be between the specified limits
- `<f:validateDoubleRange />`: The range of a double must be between the specified limits

Adding JSF support to a web application

If you've created a web application and later decide that you wish to add JSF support to it, NetBeans provides the facility to easily add JSF support together with support for popular JSF component libraries.

In this recipe, we'll show how to add JSF support to a basic web application and how to add support for the **PrimeFaces** component library.

Getting ready

To complete this recipe, we will need to have a Java EE web application that has not previously been configured with JSF support. That is to say, we've not referenced any JSF support in the application's `web.xml`, and the default view technology for the application is something other than Facelets.

If you are unsure on how to create such an application, follow the *Creating a web application* recipe earlier in this chapter. When creating the application, ensure that the project name is **AddingJSF** and that WildFly is selected as **Server**.

How to do it...

Perform the following steps:

1. Right-click on the **AddingJSF** project node within the **Projects** explorer and click on **Properties**.
2. Click on **Frameworks** from within the **Categories** list to show all the frameworks used by the application. At present, this list is empty.
3. Click on the **Add...** button to display the **Add a Framework** dialog as shown in the following screenshot:

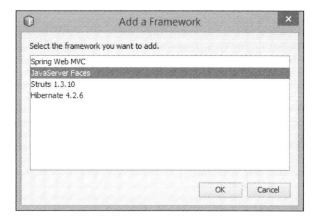

4. Click on **JavaServer Faces** to select it as the framework to add and then click on the **OK** button.

5. The **Add a Framework** dialog will now close and **JavaServer Faces** will be listed within **Used Frameworks**.

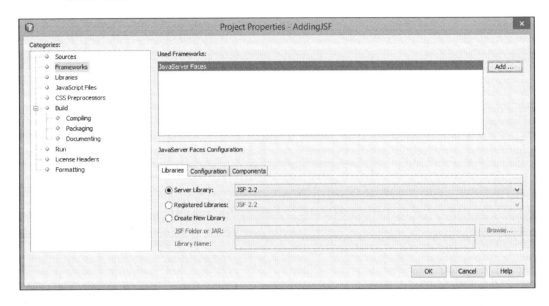

The default JSF URL mapping with NetBeans generated projects is to render the `.xhtml` files at the URL of `/faces/*.xhtml`. If you don't like this mapping, it can be easily changed. Another popular mapping URL, for example, is `*.jsf`.

Let's now change the configuration so that JSF pages are served via the `*.jsf` URL mapping and then add the PrimeFaces component library to our application. Perform the following steps:

1. Click on the **Configuration** tab within **JavaServer Faces Configuration**.

2. Change **JSF Servlet URL Pattern** from `/faces/*` to `*.jsf`.

If you enter an invalid URL pattern here, such as `*`, then NetBeans will warn you that the pattern is invalid.

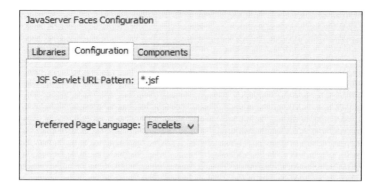

3. Click on the **Components** tab to show the list of JSF component libraries that can be added to the project:

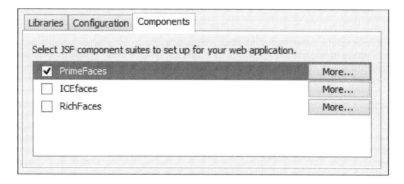

4. Check the **PrimeFaces** component entry.

 If this is the first time that you have used PrimeFaces within NetBeans, you may encounter an error message stating **JSF library PrimeFaces not set up properly: Searching valid PrimeFaces library. Please wait....** This error message indicates that a NetBeans library for PrimeFaces has not yet been created. PrimeFaces is, however, distributed with NetBeans, so NetBeans is clever enough to know this and will create the library for you. You just need to wait a few seconds for the library to be created before this error message disappears.

5. Click on the **OK** button to complete adding JSF support, together with the PrimeFaces component library, into the application.

6. Right-click on the **AddingJSF** project within the **Projects** explorer and select **Run** to deploy and execute the application.

The application will now launch in your default browser. Notice the link on the page to PrimeFaces—click on it to see a demonstration of what PrimeFaces can do.

How it works ...

When we add JSF support to the application, NetBeans will automatically add some XML configuration to the project's `web.xml` file.

The Faces servlet was added and configured to serve JSF pages via the `*.jsf` pattern, as follows:

```
<servlet>
    <servlet-name>Faces Servlet</servlet-name>
    <servlet-class>javax.faces.webapp.FacesServlet</servlet-class>
    <load-on-startup>1</load-on-startup>
</servlet>
<servlet-mapping>
    <servlet-name>Faces Servlet</servlet-name>
    <url-pattern>*.jsf</url-pattern>
</servlet-mapping>
```

Additionally, JSF was configured into the development mode in order to help us while developing:

```
<context-param>
    <param-name>javax.faces.PROJECT_STAGE</param-name>
    <param-value>Development</param-value>
</context-param>
```

Finally, the welcome file for the application was configured to be `index.jsf`:

```
<welcome-file-list>
    <welcome-file>index.jsf</welcome-file>
</welcome-file-list>
```

To demonstrate PrimeFaces, NetBeans added a new page, `welcomePrimefaces.xhtml` to the project. This page shows how to reference the `PrimeFaces` namespace within the Facelets file and shows some of the different layout features available within PrimeFaces along with links to PrimeFaces demonstration and documentation.

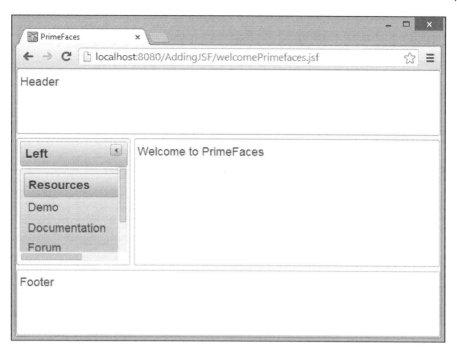

There's more

When adding JSF component libraries, we had the option of adding PrimeFaces, ICEfaces, or RichFaces. NetBeans only distributes the PrimeFaces library, so if you wish to use either ICEfaces or RichFaces, you will need to download the relevant distribution for the library. Once downloaded, click on the **More...** button on the components configuration screen, next to your selected library, to create the library and configure it within your projects.

What if I want to use a different JSF component library? Well, that can be achieved in NetBeans also. Simply download the component library you wish to use, create a NetBeans library for it and then add the library to the project. See the *Creating a library* recipe in *Chapter 1, Using NetBeans Projects*, for further details on how to achieve this.

What if I want to use a different version of JSF than is supplied with my application server, or my application server doesn't bundle JSF with it? On the **Libraries** tab within the JSF configuration, we can select to use a version of JSF that is shipped with the application server, use one of the NetBeans registered JSF libraries, or we can create a new JSF library and use that.

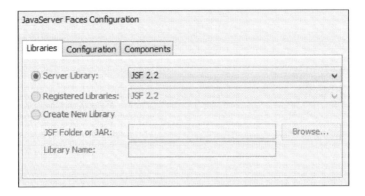

When adding JSF support to a web application, you need to think carefully about what version of JSF to use. Most often, unless there are specific reasons, the version provided with the application server will be the best choice. Some application servers allow you to choose the version of JSF to use, whereas others force you to use the provided version. Once you've specified a version of JSF to use, you can't change it without removing the JSF support and then adding it again.

Creating a JSF composite component

JSF is a rich component-based framework, which provides many components that developers can use to enrich their applications. We saw in a previous recipe how different vendors provide additional JSF toolkits such as PrimeFaces, RichFaces, and Icefaces that all provide additional components above those that are provided with the base JSF components.

JSF 2 also allows composite components to be easily created, which can then be inserted into other JSF pages in a similar way to any other JSF components such as buttons and labels.

In this recipe, we'll see how to create a custom component that displays an input label and asks for corresponding input. If the input is not validated by the JSF runtime, we'll show an error message. The component is going to look like this:

Forename		size must be between 1 and 25

The custom component is built up from three different standard JSF components. On the left, we have a `<h:outputText/>` component that displays the label. Next, we have a `<h:inputText />` component. Finally, we have a `<h:message />` component. Putting these three components together like this is a very useful pattern when designing input forms within JSF.

Getting ready

To complete this recipe, you will need to have a working installation of WildFly that has been configured within NetBeans. If you are unsure how to achieve this, check the *Adding WildFly support to NetBeans* recipe earlier in this chapter.

We will be using the Enterprise download bundle of NetBeans as this includes all of the tools we need to complete the recipe without having to download any additional plugins.

How to do it ...

First of all, we need to create a web application and then create a JSF composite component within it. Perform the following steps:

1. Click on **File** and then **New Project...**.
2. Select **Java Web** from the list of **Categories** and **Web Application** form the list of **Projects**.
3. Click on **Next**.
4. Enter the **Project Name** value as `CompositeComp`.
5. Click on **Next**.
6. Ensure that **Add to Enterprise Application** is set to **<None>**, **Server** is set to **WildFly Application Server**, **Java EE Version** is set to **Java EE 7 Web**, and **Context Path** is set to `/CompositeComp`.
7. Click on **Next**.
8. Click on the checkbox next to **JavaServer Faces** as we are using this framework for this recipe.
9. All of the default JSF configurations are correct, so click on the **Finish** button to create the project.
10. Right-click on the **CompositeComp** project within the **Projects** explorer and click on **New** and then **Other...**.
11. In the **New File** dialog, select **JavaServer Faces** from the list of **Categories** and **JSF Composite Component** from the list of **File Types**.
12. Click on **Next**.

13. On the **New JSF Composite Component** dialog, enter the **File Name** value as `inputWithLabel` and change the folder to `resources\cookbook`.

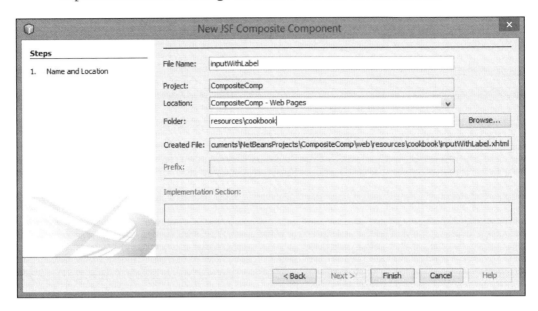

14. Click on **Finish** to create the custom component.

In JSF, custom components are created as Facelets files that are stored within the `resources` folder of the web application. Within the `resources` folder, multiple subfolders can exist, each representing a namespace of a custom component. Within each namespace folder, individual custom components are stored with filenames that match the composite component names.

We have just created a composite component within the `cookbook` namespace called `inputWithLabel`.

Within each composite component file, there are two sections: an interface and an implementation. The interface lists all of the attributes that are required by the composite component and the implementation provides the XHTML code to represent the component.

Let's now define our component by specifying the interface and the implementation. Perform the following steps:

1. The `inputWithLabel.xhtml` file should be open for editing. If not, double–click on it within the **Projects** explorer to open it.

2. For our composite component, we need two attributes to be passed into the component. We need the text for the label and the expression language to bind the input box to. Change the interface section of the file to read:

```
<cc:interface>
    <cc:attribute name="labelValue" />
    <cc:attribute name="editValue" />
</cc:interface>
```

3. To render the component, we need to instantiate a `<h:outputText />` tag to display the label, a `<h:inputText />` tag to receive the input from the user, and a `<h:message />` tag to display any errors that are entered for the input field. Change the implementation section of the file to read:

```
<cc:implementation>
    <style>
    .outputText{width: 100px; }
    .inputText{width: 100px; }
    .errorText{width: 200px; color: red; }
    </style>
    <h:panelGrid id="panel" columns="3" columnClasses="outputText,
inputText, errorText">
        <h:outputText value="#{cc.attrs.labelValue}" />
        <h:inputText value="#{cc.attrs.editValue}" id="inputText"
/>
        <h:message for="inputText" />
    </h:panelGrid>
</cc:implementation>
```

4. Click on the lightbulb on the left-hand side of the editor window and accept the fix to add the `h=http://xmlns.jcp.org/jsf/html` namespace.

We've now successfully created a composite component. Let's now create an input page that uses this component to ask for some information from the user. Perform the following steps:

1. Double-click on the `index.xhtml` page within the **Projects** explorer to open the application's home page for editing.

2. We need to add a reference to the composite component's name space within the `<html />` section of the file so that the JSF components can be used correctly. Change the `<html>` definition to read:

```
<html xmlns="http://www.w3.org/1999/xhtml"
    xmlns:h="http://xmlns.jcp.org/jsf/html"
    xmlns:cookbook ="http://xmlns.jcp.org/jsf/composite/cookbook">
```

3. We can now reference the composite component from within the Facelets page. Add the following code inside the `<h:body>` code on the page:

```
<h:form id="inputForm">
    <cookbook:inputWithLabel labelValue="Forename"
editValue="#{personController.person.foreName}"/>
    <cookbook:inputWithLabel labelValue="Last Name"
editValue="#{personController.person.lastName}"/>
    <h:commandButton type="submit" value="Submit"
action="#{personController.submit}"/>
</h:form>
```

This code instantiates two instances of our `inputWithLabel` composite control and binds them to `personController`. We haven't got one of those yet, so let's create one and a class to represent a person. Perform the following steps:

1. Create a new Java class within the project. Enter **Class Name** as `Person` and **Package** as `com.davidsalter.cookbook.compositecomp`.

2. Click on **Finish**.

3. Add members to the class to represent `foreName` and `lastName`:

```
private String foreName;
private String lastName;
```

4. Use the **Encapsulate Fields** refactoring to generate getters and setters for these members.

5. To allow error messages to be displayed if the `foreName` and `lastName` values are inputted incorrectly, we will add some Bean Validation annotations to the attributes of the class. Annotate the `foreName` member of the class as follows:

```
@NotNull
@Size(min=1, max=25)
private String foreName;
```

6. Annotate the `lastName` member of the class as follows:

```
@NotNull
@Size(min=1, max=50)
private String lastName;
```

7. Use the *Fix Imports* tool to add the required imports for the Bean Validation annotations.

8. Create a new Java class within the project. Enter **Class Name** as `PersonController` and **Package** as `com.davidsalter.cookbook.compositecomp`.

9. Click on **Finish**.

10. We need to make the `PersonController` class an `@Named` bean so that it can be referenced via expression language from within JSF pages.

11. Annotate the `PersonController` class as follows:

```
@Named
@RequestScoped
public class PersonController {
```

12. We need to add a `Person` instance into `PersonController` that will be used to transfer data from the JSF page to the named bean. We will also need to add a method onto the bean that will redirect JSF to an output page after the names have been entered.

13. Add the following to the `PersonController` class:

```
private Person person = new Person();

public Person getPerson() {
    return person;
}

public void setPerson(Person person) {
    this.person = person;
}

public String submit() {
    return "results.xhtml";
}
```

14. The final task before completing our application is to add a results page so we can see what input the user entered. This output page will simply display the values of `foreName` and `lastName` that have been entered.

15. Create a new JSF page called `results` that uses the Facelets syntax.

16. Change the `<h:body>` tag of this page to read:

```
<h:body>
    You Entered:
    <h:outputText value="#{personController.person.foreName}"
/> 
    <h:outputText value="#{personController.person.lastName}" />
</h:body>
```

The application is now complete. Deploy and run the application by right-clicking on the project within the **Projects** explorer and selecting **Run**.

Note that two instances of the composite component have been created and displayed within the browser.

Click on the **Submit** button without entering any information and note how the error messages are displayed:

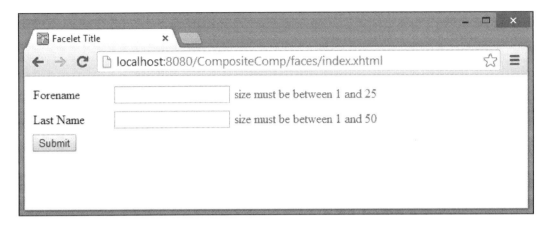

Enter some valid information and click on **Submit**, and note how the information entered is echoed back on a second page.

How it works...

Creating composite components was a new feature added to JSF 2. Creating JSF components was a very tedious job in JSF 1.x, and the designers of JSF 2 thought that the majority of custom components created in JSF could probably be built by adding different existing components together. As it is seen in this recipe, we've added together three different existing JSF components and made a very useful composite component.

It's useful to distinguish between custom components and composite components. Custom components are entirely new components that did not exist before. They are created entirely in Java code and build into frameworks such as PrimeFaces and RichFaces. Composite components are built from existing components and their graphical view is designed in the .xhtml files.

There's more

When creating composite components, it may be necessary to specify attributes. The default option is that the attributes are not mandatory when creating a custom component. They can, however, be made mandatory by adding the `required="true"` attribute to their definition, as follows:

```
<cc:attribute name="labelValue" required="true" />
```

If an attribute is specified as required, but is not present, a JSF error will be produced, as follows:

```
/index.xhtml @11,88 <cookbook:inputWithLabel> The following
attribute(s) are required, but no values have been supplied for them:
labelValue.
```

Sometimes, it can be useful to specify a default value for an attribute. This is achieved by adding the `default="..."` attribute to their definition:

```
<cc:attribute name="labelValue" default="Please enter a value" />
```

Creating an EJB

Enterprise Java Beans (**EJBs**) are server-side managed classes intended to provide business functionality to applications. Since Java EE 5, EJBs have been made much simpler and more lightweight.

EJBs no longer have to be defined by XML descriptors, but are defined using Java annotations instead. This allows EJBs to be developed more quickly and probably more importantly, to be fully testable outside of the application server.

In Java EE 7, there are four types of EJB. They are **Stateless**, **Stateful**, **Singleton**, and **Message Driven** EJBs. J2EE also had Entity beans used for modeling data, but these have been deprecated since Java EE 5 to be replaced with **POJOs** and **JPA**.

Stateless EJBs, as their name suggest, maintain no state. When a request is made from a client to obtain an EJB, the application server returns one from a pool of EJBs. The client may or may not get the same EJB on subsequent requests.

A Stateful EJB on the other hand, maintains its state, so every time a request is made for an EJB of a particular type, the same EJB is supplied to the client. Stateful EJBs are therefore useful when a client needs to remember information between invocations. The classic example of using Stateful EJBs is to implement a shopping cart. In a web application, the HTTP protocol maintains no state so Stateful EJBs can be used to maintain information within the application server between HTTP requests.

A Singleton EJB has global state shared across the entire JVM. The application server guarantees that there is only one instance of a Singleton bean within the JVM and can provide a thread safe access to its data.

Message Driven Beans are built on top of the **Java Message Service** (**JMS**) API and listen for events to occur before being triggered. They are typically used for processing long-running asynchronous events or for sending data to multiple clients where each client can be listening to a JMS queue or topic.

For more information on Java EE 7 EJBs, check out the Oracle Java EE 7 Enterprise Beans Tutorial at `http://docs.oracle.com/javaee/7/tutorial/doc/ejb-intro.htm`.

In this recipe, we're going to show how to create Stateless and Stateful EJBs and show how to invoke them. In the next recipe, *Creating a Message Driven EJB*, we'll see how to create Message Driven EJBs.

Getting ready

For this recipe, we will use the WildFly application server together with the Enterprise download bundle of NetBeans. Ensure that you have a working installation of WildFly configured within NetBeans before starting this recipe. If you need to configure WildFly within NetBeans, check out the *Adding WildFly support to NetBeans* recipe earlier in this chapter.

How to do it...

To deploy EJBs to the application server, we need to create a NetBeans project that will host the EJBs. EJBs can be deployed either within an **Enterprise Archive** (**EAR**) file, or within a **Web application Archive** (**WAR**) file. For this recipe, we'll be deploying our EJBs in a `.war` file together with a Servlet, which will act as the client by invoking the EJB.

For a lot of application types, the `.war` archive is a good choice for deployment as any included EJBs are co-located with web resources such as Servlets or JSF pages. For more flexibility, EJBs can be separated from the web application code and deployed as a Java archive within an `.ear` file. The `.ear` files can contain multiple standard Java archives as well as multiple `.war` files. This therefore enables greater flexibility for deployment, but comes at the cost of greater complexity.

Perform the following steps:

1. Click on **File** and then **New Project...**
2. Select **Java Web** from the list of **Categories** and **Web Application** from the list of **Projects**.
3. Click on **Next**.

4. Enter **Project Name** as EJBQuote.

5. Click on **Next**.

6. Ensure **Add to Enterprise Application** is unselected, **Server** is set to **WildFly Application Server**, **Java EE Version** is set to **Java EE 7 Web**, and **Context Path** is set to /EJBQuote.

7. Click on **Finish**.

We've now created an empty web project. Let's add an EJB to the project that will provide us with random quotes. Perform the following steps:

1. Right-click on the **Source Packages** node for the **EJBQuote** project within the **Projects** explorer and click on **New**, and then click on **Other...**.

2. In the **New File** dialog, select **Enterprise JavaBeans** from the list of **Categories** and **Session Bean** from the list of **File Types**.

3. Click on **Next**.

4. Enter **EJB Name** as QuoteBean.

5. Enter the **Package** name as com.davidsalter.cookbook.quote.

6. Select **Session Type** as **Singleton**.

7. Check the **Local** tick-box as shown in the following screenshot:

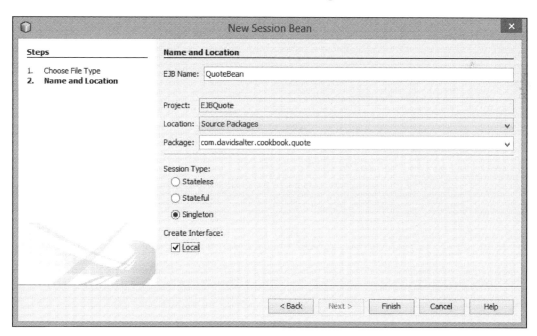

8. Click on **Finish**.

The **New Session Bean** dialog will now close and NetBeans will create a new Singleton Session Bean along with a local interface for the bean.

We now need to add business logic to our bean to return a quote to callers. Perform the following steps:

1. Ensure that the `QuoteBean.java` file is open for editing and right-click within the body of the class and select **Insert Code...**.

2. On the **Generate** pop-up window, click on **Add Business Method...**.

3. The **Add Business Method** dialog will now open, where we can define method signatures for business methods within EJBs.

4. Enter **Name** as `getQuote` and **Return Type** as `java.lang.String`.

5. Since we're using a local interface to implement our EJB, ensure that the **Use in Interface** option is set to **Local** as shown in the following screenshot:

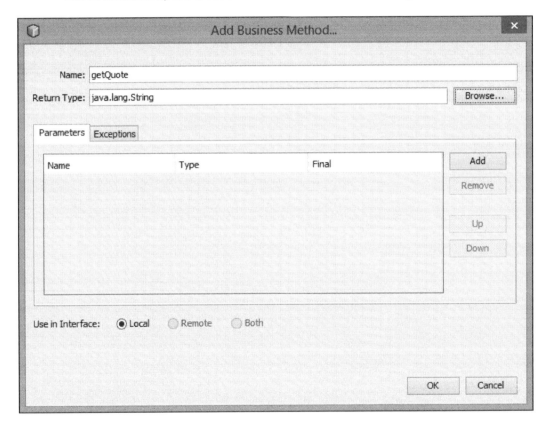

6. Click on **OK**.

The `getQuote` business method is now created within the `QuoteBean.java` class. Let's now implement the method. Perform the following steps:

1. Ensure that the `QuoteBean.java` file is open for editing.

2. Our `QuoteBean` class is going to maintain a list of quotes and return a random one to callers. We therefore need to initialize the list of quotes within the bean. Add the `@Startup` annotation to the class definition so that the EJB will be started up as soon as it is deployed. The class definition should now look like:

```
@Startup
@Singleton
public class QuoteBean implements QuoteBeanLocal {
```

3. We now need to add a private member to the class to maintain a list of quotes, and initialize it after the bean is constructed. Add the following code into the `QuoteBean.java` class:

```
private List<String> quotes;

@PostConstruct
void initialize() {
    quotes = new ArrayList<String>();
    quotes.add("Always catch exceptions.");
    quotes.add("Did you make that field final?");
    quotes.add("Remember to implement a toString() method.");
}
```

4. Finally, we need to implement the `getQuote()` method that returns a random quote to the caller. Change the `getQuote()` method to read:

```
@Override
public String getQuote() {
    Random rand = new Random();
    return quotes.get(rand.nextInt(quotes.size()));
}
```

5. Add the required imports to the class so that the entire class reads as follows:

```
package com.davidsalter.cookbook.quote;

import java.util.ArrayList;
import java.util.List;
import java.util.Random;
import javax.annotation.PostConstruct;
import javax.ejb.Singleton;
import javax.ejb.Startup;
```

```
@Startup
@Singleton
public class QuoteBean implements QuoteBeanLocal {

    private List<String> quotes;

    @PostConstruct
    void initialize() {
        quotes = new ArrayList<String>();
        quotes.add("Always catch exceptions.");
        quotes.add("Did you make that field final?");
        quotes.add("Remember to implement a toString() method.");
    }

    @Override
    public String getQuote() {
        Random rand = new Random();
        return quotes.get(rand.nextInt(quotes.size()));
    }
}
```

Now that we've created an EJB, let's create a servlet that can invoke the EJB and return random quotes to us. Perform the following steps:

1. Right-click on the **EJBQuote** node within the **Projects** explorer and select **New** and then **Other...**.

2. In the **New File** dialog, select **Web** from the **Categories** list and **Servlet** from the list of **File Types**.

3. Click on **Next**.

4. Enter **Class Name** as `QuoteServlet` and **Package** as `com.davidsalter.cookbook.quote`.

5. Click on **Next**.

6. Ensure that **Add information to deployment descriptor (web.xml)** is checked and click on **Finish**.

7. The servlet class will now be created and opened for editing. Add a reference to the EJB's local interface at the top of the class:

```
@EJB
private QuoteBeanLocal quoteBean;
```

8. Locate the line within the class that begins with `out.println("<h1>Servlet QuoteServlet`... and replace it with:

    ```
    out.println(quoteBean.getQuote());
    ```

9. Fix any imports with the class so that the `javax.ejb.EJB` package is included.

We've now completed the application, so deploy and run the application by right clicking on the `QuoteServlet.java` file in the **Source Packages** node of the **Projects** explorer and selecting the **Run** option. NetBeans will ask for confirmation of any query parameters. Since there are none, click on **OK** to launch your default browser and run the servlet.

Refresh your browser a few times to get some good advice.

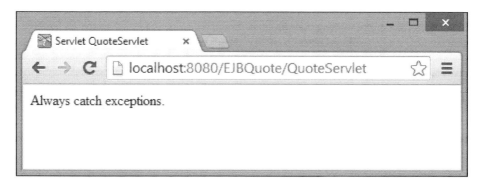

How it works...

In this recipe, we first created an EJB that implemented a local interface. We don't have to implement interfaces to define EJBs, but its good practice to do so.

To define a Singleton EJB, we annotated a POJO class with the `@Singleton` annotation. We also added the `@Startup` annotation to cause the EJB to start as soon as it was deployed.

Since we're using a local interface for the bean, the bean class must implement the local interface. The basic definition of our Singleton bean was therefore:

```
@Startup
@Singleton
public class QuoteBean implements QuoteBeanLocal {
```

In EJB 3, a local interface is just a plain old interface, but it must be annotated with the `@Local` annotation. This is what differentiates a local interface from a remote interface (which is annotated with `@Remote`):

```
@Local
public interface QuoteBeanLocal {
```

To add business logic to the EJB, we used the insert code option within the NetBeans editor window. When adding business logic to an EJB, this wizard creates both the new method that we are creating and its interface definition. That is to say, both the interface and the EJB class are updated. Even though we're using interfaces, we don't need to edit two files as this is all taken care of for us by NetBeans.

To allow us to perform some initialization on the EJB, we annotated a method with the `@PostConstruct` annotation. This method is called after the EJB is injected into clients, so is used as a place to perform initialization.

Since we created an EJB with only a local interface, it's only possible to access it from within the local JVM, hence making a call to it from within a servlet that is also running inside the same JVM. If we'd created the EJB to implement a `@Remote` interface, then we would have been able to access the EJB from outside of the application server, from a standalone client, or from a different application server.

In the servlet, we referenced the local interface for the EJB using the `@EJB` annotation. This injects the EJB into the servlet class and allows us to use it without having to create a `new` instance of the class when we want to use it.

When we created the servlet, we allowed NetBeans to add information to the deployment descriptor file so that we could see the type of information added to this file. This is old-school servlet creation as the servlet is registered with the application server via XML instead of via annotations:

```
<servlet>
    <servlet-name>QuoteServlet</servlet-name>
    <servlet-class>com.davidsalter.cookbook.quote.QuoteServlet</
servlet-class>
</servlet>
<servlet-mapping>
    <servlet-name>QuoteServlet</servlet-name>
    <url-pattern>/QuoteServlet</url-pattern>
</servlet-mapping>
```

In the next recipe, *Creating a Message Driven EJB*, we'll see how to define a servlet using annotations instead of XML.

There's more

In this recipe, we saw how to create a Singleton session bean. What if we wanted to create a Stateful session bean, or a Stateless session bean? Well, the procedure for creating those is exactly the same as that outlined within this recipe except that on the **New Session Bean** dialog, we need to choose either **Stateless** or **Stateful** instead of **Singleton**.

What EJBs are deployed?

After EJBs are deployed to WildFly, we can get a list of what has been deployed via the **Servers** node within the **Services** explorer.

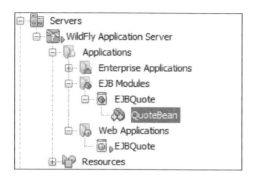

This view lists all of the EJB modules that are deployed and all of the EJBs that are deployed within each module.

Creating a Message Driven EJB

A **Message Driven EJB** is a special type of EJB that is responsible for listening to messages sent to **JMS** queues and acting upon them. Message Driven EJBs provide an easy way of interfacing with JMS queues and make full use of Java annotations to define queue settings.

In this recipe, we'll see how we can send a message to a JMS queue hosted on WildFly, and then how a Message Driven Bean will respond to the message.

Getting ready

In order to complete this recipe, we need to have an instance of WildFly installed locally and configured within NetBeans. We will be using the Enterprise download bundle of NetBeans as this provides all of the necessary plugins required to work with EJBs.

To send messages to a JMS queue, we first need to create the queue within WildFly.

Since the WildFly plugin for NetBeans can't currently create message queues, we'll need to create a message queue using the WildFly command-line interface.

Start WildFly from NetBeans within the **Services** explorer.

The WildFly CLI is located within the `WildFly\bin` folder, so open a command prompt (or terminal), change to the `WildFly\bin` folder of your local distribution and start the CLI: `jboss-cli.bat` (for Windows users) or `./jboss-cli.sh` (for Mac OS X and Linux users).

Once the CLI has started, you need to connect to the running instance of WildFly. This is achieved with the `connect` command with the CLI:

```
[disconnected /] connect
```

Now that we're connected to WildFly, execute the following command to create a message queue called `cookbookQueue`:

```
[standalone@localhost:9990 /] jms-queue add –queue-address=cookbookQueue
–entries=java:/jms/queue/cookbookQueue
```

Once the queue has been added via the CLI, we can verify that it has been deployed correctly by opening up the **JMS Destinations** node within the **WildFly Application Server** node in the **Services** explorer:

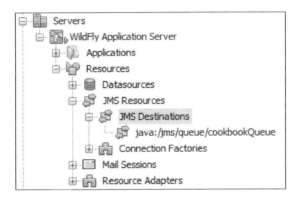

How to do it...

Perform the following steps:

1. Click on **File** and then **New Project...**.

2. In the **New Project** dialog, select **Java Web** from the list of **Categories**, and **Web Application** from the list of **Projects**.

3. Click on **Next**.

4. Enter **Project Name** as `MessageBeans`.

5. Click on **Next**.

6. Ensure that **Add to Enterprise Application** is not set, and that the **Server** is set to **WildFly Application Server**, **Java EE Version** is set to `Java EE 7 Web`, and the **Context Path** is set to `/MessageBeans`.

7. Click on **Finish**.

8. Right-click on the **MessageBeans** project within the **Projects** explorer and click on **New** and then **Other...**.

9. In the **New File** dialog, select **Enterprise JavaBeans** from the list of **Categories** and **Message-Driven Bean** from the list of **File Types**.

10. Click on **Next**.

11. In the **New Message-Driven Bean** dialog, specify **EJB Name** as `CookbookQueueListenerBean` and the **Package** name as `com.davidsalter.cookbook.messagebeans`.

12. Select the **cookbookQueue** queue from the dropdown by the **Server Destinations** radio button.

13. Click on the **Next** button.

14. The **Activation Config Properties** dialog will now be shown. Since we don't need to change any of the defaults here, click on **Finish**.

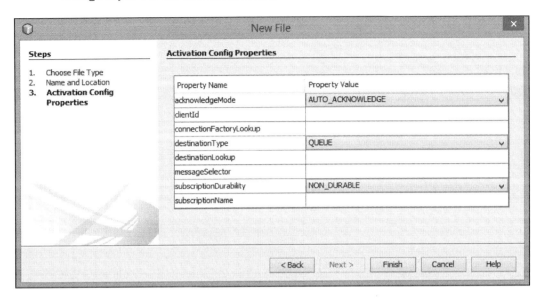

A basic Message Driven Bean has now been created by NetBeans. Let's add some basic logging to the bean so that we can see what messages are sent to it. Perform the following steps:

Ensure that the `CookbookQueueListenerBean.java` file is open for editing, and change the `onMessage()` method to the following:

```java
@Override
public void onMessage(Message message) {
    try {
        if (message instanceof TextMessage) {
            TextMessage txtMessage = (TextMessage) message;
            System.out.println("I've got a message:" + txtMessage.getText());
        }
    } catch (JMSException e) {
        throw new RuntimeException(e);
    }
}
```

This is a very simplistic implementation of what to do when a Message Driven Bean receives a message, but it does show how to get the text contents out of `TextMessage` and that we need to be catching `JMSExceptions` just in case of any runtime errors.

That's all we need to do to define a Message Driven Bean. Let's now create a servlet that will post messages to the bean. Perform the following steps:

1. Right-click on the **MessageBeans** project within the **Projects** explorer and select **New** and then **Other...**.

2. In the **New File** dialog, select **Web** from the **Categories** list and **Servlet** from the list of **File Types**.

3. Click on **Next**.

4. In **Class Name**, enter `SendMessageServlet` and in the **Package** name, enter `com.davidsalter.cookbook.messagebeans`.

5. Click on **Next**.

6. In this recipe, we are not going to define the servlet via the `web.xml` file, so click on **Finish**. NetBeans will register the servlet via annotations instead of XML.

A servlet called `SendMessageServlet` has now been created and opened within NetBeans for editing. Let's change the servlet so that it sends a message to our message queue when the servlet is invoked. Perform the following steps:

1. Inject a reference to `JMSContext` and the message queue into the servlet by adding the following code to the beginning of the `SendMessageServlet` class:

```
@Inject
private JMSContext context;

@Resource(mappedName="java:/jms/queue/cookbookQueue")
private Queue queue;
```

2. Send a message to the message queue by changing the `processRequest()` method body to read:

```
response.setContentType("text/html;charset=UTF-8");

String message = "Message sent at: " + new Date();
context.createProducer().send(queue, message);

try (PrintWriter out = response.getWriter()) {
    out.println("<!DOCTYPE html>");
    out.println("<html>");
    out.println("<head>");
```

```
out.println("<title>Servlet SendMessageServlet</title>");
out.println("</head>");
out.println("<body>");
out.println("<p>" + message + "</p>");
out.println("</body>");
out.println("</html>");
}
```

As we are using **Contexts and Dependency Injection** (**CDI**), we need to add a `beans.xml` file into our project; otherwise, `@Inject` will not resolve correctly and the context variable will be set to `null`. Perform the following steps:

1. Right-click on the **MessageBeans** project within the **Projects** explorer and click on **New** and then **Other...**.

2. Select **Contexts and Dependency Injection** from the list of **Categories** and **beans. xml (CDI Configuration File)** from the list of **File Types**.

3. Click on **Next**.

4. Click on **Finish** to create the file.

The application is now complete, so we can run it and test it out. Right-click on the `SendMessageServlet.java` file in the **Projects** explorer and then select **Run File**. As we have no request parameters to add to the URL, click on **OK** to launch your default browser and invoke the servlet.

The default browser will now open. Open the `http://localhost:8080/MessageBeans/SendMessageServlet` URL to access the servlet and send a message to the message queue.

The date and time of the message will be displayed in the browser, as shown in the following screenshot:

The date and time of the message will also be shown in the WildFly Application Server Output window, as shown in the following screenshot:

```
Output ×
WildFly Application Server ×   MessageBeans (run-deploy) ×
|
20:51:24,725 INFO  [stdout] (Thread-13 (HornetQ-client-global-threads-2012667705)) I've got a message:Message sent at: Fri Apr 04 20:51:24 BST 2014
```

How it works...

The first task in this recipe was to create a Message Driven Bean. In Java EE 7, a Message Driven Bean is simply a POJO that is annotated with the `@MessageDriven` annotation. Our Message Driven Bean was annotated as follows:

```
@MessageDriven(activationConfig = {
  @ActivationConfigProperty(propertyName = "destinationLookup",
                            propertyValue = "cookbookQueue"),
  @ActivationConfigProperty(propertyName = "destinationType",
                            propertyValue = "javax.jms.Queue")
})
```

These annotations declare the Message Driven Bean as well as stating that the bean will listen to a `javax.jms.Queue` and that the `cookbookQueue` queue will be called.

If we'd wanted to listen to a topic instead, we would simply have specified `destinationType` as `javax.jms.Topic`.

A message sent to a JMS queue will be received by only one listener. Only one Message Driven Bean can receive a message sent to a queue. A topic, on the other hand, works more like a publish/subscribe model where a message sent to a topic can be received by zero or more listeners.

Within Message Driven Beans, messages are delivered to the `onMessage()` method. In our implementation, we checked to see if the message was of the type `TextMessage` (we had foreknowledge that it would always be of this type!) and if it was, we cast the received message into `TextMessage` and then extracted the message using the `.getText()` method.

To send a message to the Message Driven Bean, we used CDI to make things a lot easier. We injected a `JMSContext` into a servlet. We injected a reference to our queue into the servlet as well using the `@Resource` annotation to specify the queue we wanted to use. Finally, we sent a text message by calling the `context.createProoducer().send()` method.

There's more

What if we wanted to send more than a simple text to a message queue? Is that possible? It certainly is. The `send()` method of the `JMSProducer` class allows us to send a `Map`, a `Message`, a `Serializable`, or a `byte[]` as well as sending a `String`. If we are to send objects of these types to the Message Driven Bean, then we must remember that the type of message received by the `OnMessage()` method will be either `BytesMessage`, `MapMessage`, `ObjectMessage`, or `StreamMessage`. For further information about sending different types of messages, check out the Oracle Message documentation at `http://docs.oracle.com/javaee/7/api/javax/jms/Message.html`.

Manually injecting `JMSContext` and `Queue` involved too much typing! Can NetBeans make this any easier? It certainly can. Right-clicking within the body of a class (for example in a session bean) and selecting the **Insert code...** menu item provides the option to **Send JMS Message...**. From this dialog, we can specify queues and topics to send messages to and then automatically generate the required code.

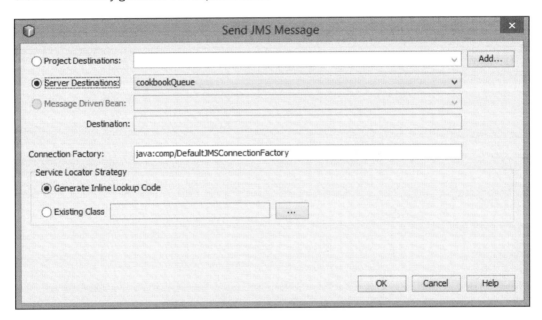

Creating a timer

When developing Enterprise applications, it can be useful to perform operations at specific times of the day, or at specific regular intervals, for example, every 12 hours, or the last day of every month.

In the Unix world, this is analogous to the **cron** concept where system administrators can define tasks that run under a given schedule.

In Java EE 7, we have the concept of timers that can run Java code at predefined intervals.

Getting ready

To complete this recipe, we need to have a valid instance of WildFly installed and configured within NetBeans. We will be using the Enterprise download bundle of NetBeans as this provides all the features we need to complete this recipe without having to download any additional plugins.

How to do it...

Perform the following steps:

1. Click on **File** and then **New Project**.

2. In the **New Project** dialog, select **Java Web** from the list of **Categories** and **Web Application** from the list of **Projects**.

3. Click on **Next**.

4. Enter **Project Name** as `Timers`.

5. Click on **Next**.

6. Ensure that **Add to Enterprise Application** is set to **<None>**, **Server** is set to **WildFly Application Server**, **Java EE Version** is set to `Java EE 7 Web`, and **Context Path** is set to `/Timers`.

7. Click on **Finish**.

8. Right-click on the **Timers** project in the **Projects** explorer and click on **New** and then click on **Other...**.

9. On the **New File** dialog, select **Enterprise Java Beans** from the list of **Categories** and **Timer Session Bean** from the list of **File Types**.

10. Click on **Next**.

11. Enter **EJB Name** as `TimerBean` and the **Package** name as `com.davidsalter.cookbook.timers`.

12. Change **Method schedule** to the following:

    ```
    dayOfWeek = "*", month = "*", hour = "*", dayOfMonth = "*", year =
    "*", minute = "*", second = "*/10", persistent = false
    ```

13. Click on **Finish**.

That's all is there for creating a timer. Right-click on the **Timers** project within the **Projects** explorer and select **Deploy**. Watch in the WildFly Application Server Output Window and note that a timer message is executed every 10 seconds as defined within our timer schedule.

```
Output ×
  WildFly Application Server ×   Timers (run-deploy) ×
    21:41:04,662 INFO  [org.jboss.as.server] (management-handler-thread - 8) JBAS018562: Redeployed "Timers.war"
    21:41:10,003 INFO  [stdout] (EJB default - 5) Timer event: Fri Apr 04 21:41:10 BST 2014

    21:41:20,003 INFO  [stdout] (EJB default - 6) Timer event: Fri Apr 04 21:41:20 BST 2014

    21:41:30,001 INFO  [stdout] (EJB default - 7) Timer event: Fri Apr 04 21:41:30 BST 2014

    21:41:40,002 INFO  [stdout] (EJB default - 8) Timer event: Fri Apr 04 21:41:40 BST 2014

    21:41:50,001 INFO  [stdout] (EJB default - 9) Timer event: Fri Apr 04 21:41:50 BST 2014
```

How it works...

Creating a timer is as simple as creating a session bean and adding an `@Schedule` annotation to a method in the bean:

```
@Schedule(dayOfWeek = "*", month = "*", hour = "*", dayOfMonth = "*",
year = "*", minute = "*", second = "*/10", persistent = false)
```

A timer can be created as a session bean or a singleton bean, but as a singleton bean has only one instance within the JVM, it may be a better choice for a timer as it's guaranteed to only run one instance of the timer at the given schedule.

The schedule for a timer takes several parameters to define the schedule as seen in the `TimerBean.java` class:

`second`	The number of seconds in the range 0 through 59
`minute`	The number of minutes in the range 0 through 59
`hour`	The number of hours in the range 0 through 23
`dayOfWeek`	The day of the week in the range 0 through 7, or the values Sun, Mon, Tue, Wed, Thu, Fri, Sat
`dayOfMonth`	The day of the month in the range 1 through 31 and -1 through -31. The special case Last means the last day of the month and negative numbers mean days before the end of the month.
`month`	The month in the range 1 through 12, or the values Jan, Feb, Mar, Apr, May, Jun, Jul, Aug, Sep, Oct, Nov, Dec
`year`	The year in the format yyyy
`info`	Any custom information to be sent to the schedule, for example a schedule name

There's more

What if I want to execute a method at multiple schedules? Do I need to create multiple timers? No, not at all.

To run a method at multiple schedules, annotate the method with the `@Schedules` annotation instead of the `@Schedule` annotation. Then, simply define multiple `@Schedule` annotations within, for example:

```
@Schedules({
    @Schedule(…),
    @Schedule(…)  })
```

What if I want my timer to be persistent across reboots of the application server? This can be achieved by setting the persistent parameter of the `@Schedule` annotation to be `true`.

> Be careful when setting a timer to be persistent. As the timer state is persisted when the server is offline, it is mandated to run any missed iterations of the schedule when the application is brought back on line. If this is not what you require, don't set your timers to be persistent.

Creating a REST web service

With the advent of modern web application development, **REST**-based web services have become a popular method of sending data from application servers to clients. Many **JavaScript** frameworks, such as **AngularJS**, have been developed that make calling REST-web services a simple and convenient way of getting data.

REST web services use different HTTP methods (`GET`, `PUT`, `DELETE` for example) to perform different operations. `GET` is typically used for retrieving data, whereas `PUT` is used for storing data.

Well-designed REST web services are modeled such that "reading the URL" explains what the request is for. For example, a `GET` request to the `http://localhost/Travel/busroute/1` URL would return information about bus route number 1, whereas a `PUT` request to the same URL would indicate that bus route 1 is to be stored within the application server via the data uploaded to the server with the request.

To retrieve information about all of the bus routes, a `GET` request would be made to the `http://localhost/Travel/busroute/all` URL.

In this recipe, we'll see how NetBeans can help us to develop REST-based web services like these.

Getting ready

To complete this recipe, you will need to have a valid installation of WildFly correctly configured within NetBeans. If you are unsure how to achieve this, please refer to the *Adding WildFly support to NetBeans* recipe earlier in this chapter.

We will be using the Enterprise download bundle of NetBeans as this includes all of the necessary tools to complete the recipe without having to download any additional plugins.

In this recipe, we will create a web service that returns information about books. We will implement a web service to get information about a single book and another web service to get information about all the books.

How to do it...

Perform the following steps:

1. Click on **File** and then click on **New Project...**.

2. In the **New Project** dialog, select **Java Web** from the **Categories** list and **Web Application** from the list of **Projects**.

3. Click on **Next**.

4. Enter **Project Name** as `BookService`.

5. Click on **Next**.

6. Ensure that the **AddTo Enterprise Application** option is set to **<None>**, **Server** is set to **WildFly Application Server**, **Java EE Version** is set to `Java EE 7 Web`, and **Context Path** is set to `/BookService`.

7. Click on **Finish**.

8. Right-click on the **BookService** node within the **Projects** explorer and click on **New** and then click on **Other...**.

9. Select **Web Services** from the list of **Categories** and **RESTful Web Service from Patterns** in the list of **File Types**.

10. Click on **Next**.

11. Ensure that **Simple Root Resource** is selected as **RESTful web service design pattern**.

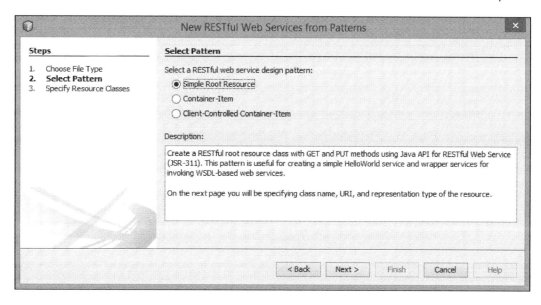

12. Click on **Next**.

13. On the **Specify Resource Classes** page, enter **Resource Packages** as
    `com.davidsalter.cookbook.bookservice`.

14. Enter **Path** as `book`.

15. Enter **Class Name** as `BookResource`.

16. Select `application/json` as **MIME Type**.

17. Click on **Finish**.

We've now created the basic structure for our web service; let's now create a class to represent a book and implement the web service so that it can return details about the book to clients. Perform the following steps:

1. Right-click on the **Source Packages** node within the **BookService** project and click on **New** and then click on **Other...**.

2. On the **New File** dialog, select **Java** from the **Categories** list and **Java Class** from the list of **File Types**.

3. Click on **Next**.

4. Enter `Book` as **Class Name**.

5. Enter `com.davidsalter.cookbook.bookservice` as the **Package** name.

6. Click on **Finish**.

7. In our representation of a book, a book has attributes ISBN, name, and author, all of which are strings. Add the following code to the `Book.java` class to define these attributes:

```
private String name;
private String author;
private String isbn;
```

8. Use the **Encapsulate Fields** refactoring to create getters and setters for both the attributes. If you are unsure on how to perform this refactoring, check out the *Encapsulate fields refactoring* recipe in *Chapter 3, NetBeans Productivity*.

9. Use the generate constructor code generation to create a constructor that takes a name, an author, and an ISBN number as parameters. If you are unsure how to perform this refactoring, check out the *Creating a constructor* recipe in *Chapter 3, NetBeans Productivity*.

10. Once complete, the `Book.java` class should look like:

```java
public class Book {

    private String name;
    private String author;
    private String isbn;

    public Book(String name, String author, String isbn) {
        this.name = name;
        this.author = author;
        this.isbn = isbn;
    }

    public String getName() {
        return name;
    }

    public void setName(String name) {
        this.name = name;
    }

    public String getAuthor() {
        return author;
    }

    public void setAuthor(String author) {
        this.author = author;
    }
    public String getIsbn() {
```

```
        return isbn;
    }

    public void setIsbn(String isbn) {
        this.isbn = isbn;
    }

}
```

11. Double-click on the `BookResource.java` file from within the **Projects** explorer to open it up for editing.

12. Define a list in the `BookResource.java` class that will hold a list of all our books (normally, we would get our list of books form a database, but in this instance, we're holding a list of books in memory). Add the following to the `BookResource` class:

```
    private List<Book> books;
```

13. Change the constructor of the `BookResource` class to initialize the list of books by amending the constructor to the following:

```
    public BookResource() {
        books = new ArrayList<Book>();
        books.add(new Book("Moby Dick", "Herman Melville", "1"));
        books.add(new Book("A Princess of Mars", "Edgar Rice
Burroughs", "2"));
    }
```

14. Add a method to return a book based upon its ISBN number, as follows:

```
    @GET
    @Path("{isbn}")
    @Produces("application/json")
    public Book getBook(@PathParam("isbn") String isbn) {
        for (Book book : books) {
            if (book.getIsbn().equals(isbn))
                return book;
        }
        throw new WebApplicationException(404);
    }
```

15. Add a method to return all of the books in the catalog, as follows:

```
    @GET
    @Produces("application/json")
    @Path("all")
    public List<Book> getBooks() {
        return books;
    }
```

Finally, we want to change the URL of our web service so it is mapped to `/BookService/ Catalog/book`. The default implementation generated by NetBeans is at `/BookService/ webresources/book`. Perform the following steps:

1. Double-click on the `ApplicationConfig.java` class within the **BookService** project.

2. Amend the `@javax.ws.rs.ApplicationPath` annotation to read:

    ```
    @javax.ws.rs.ApplicationPath("Catalog")
    ```

The application is now complete. Deploy and run the application by right-clicking on the **BookService** project within the **Projects** explorer, and then clicking on **Run**.

Browse `http://localhost:8080/BookService/Catalog/book/all` and you will see all of the books that we defined earlier listed in the JSON format.

Browse `http://localhost:8080/BookService/Calalog/book/1` and you will see **"Moby Dick"** listed in the JSON format.

Finally, browse an invalid ISBN reference at `http://localhost:8080/BookService/ Catalog/book/3` and you will see the **HTTP 404 error** page indicating that the book was not found.

For developers on Windows, I'd recommend using a browser other than Internet Explorer for debugging JSON returned from web services as Internet Explorer doesn't display JSON correctly. I recommend using Google Chrome with the **JSONView** plugin installed, as this allows JSON to be viewed in a readable format with the ability to expand and close nodes within a JSON document.

How it works...

When we created our `BookResource` class for serving information about books, NetBeans automatically annotated the class with the `@Path("book")` annotation:

```
@Path("book")
public class BookResource {
```

This annotation declared the last part of the URL for our book service as `/BookService/Catalog/book`. Any attempts to access this URL are then passed to the `BookResource` class for handling.

We annotated the `getBook()` method with an `@Path` annotation and also annotated one of the parameters of the method with the `@PathParam("isbn")` annotation, as follows:

```
@GET
@Path("{isbn}")
@Produces("application/json")
public Book getBook(@PathParam("isbn") String isbn) {
```

The `@Path` annotation identifies the class as being able to handle URLs with an additional parameter at the end called `isbn`. Therefore, when we access a URL of the `/BookService/Catalog/book/isbn` pattern, the `isbn` parameter is mapped to any parameters within the `getBook()` method that has a matching `@PathParam` annotation. Given our code, this last parameter in the URL is mapped to the `isbn` parameter of the `getBook()` method.

In a similar fashion, we annotated the `getBooks()` method with the `@Path("all")` annotation, as follows:

```
@GET
@Produces("application/json")
@Path("all")
public List<Book> getBooks() {
```

This annotation has no parameters (there is nothing inside { } brackets) so all requests to `/BookService/Catalog/book/all` will be handled by this method.

When we searched for a book and did not find it, we returned `WebApplicationException(404)` to the client. This returns a **HTTP 404—Not Found** error message. This is the standard error message that is returned to browsers when a resource is not found. Typically, it is returned to browsers when a page cannot be found, but is also used within RESTful web services to indicate that an entity could not be found.

There's more

What if I want to return something other than JSON from my web services? When we created the RESTful web service, NetBeans gave us an option to specify the MIME Type of the response. We chose `application/json` as that is what is commonly used when developing websites.

If, however, you're developing RESTful web services that perhaps aren't going to be consumed by a website or the website technology you're using requires a different format, then NetBeans can be configured to send replies in a different format.

When creating the web service, 4 different MIME types are available; they are as follows:

- `application/xml`
- `application/json`
- `text/plain`
- `text/html`

Individual methods within a REST class can be configured to respond with different MIME types by adding the `@Produces` annotation to a method and specifying the MIME Type to return. For example:

```
@GET
@Produces("application/xml")
@Path("all")
public List<Book> getBooks() {
```

What if I want to create a RESTful web service for existing entities that I have? Is there a way to achieve this? Certainly! When creating a RESTful web service, select the option **RESTful Web Services** from entity classes. This provides you with a list of entities within your application (classes annotated with `@Entity`) from which NetBeans can create web services.

Can I easily see what RESTful web services I've created? Within NetBeans, projects that have RESTful web services within them have an additional node, **RESTful Web Services** within the **Projects** explorer. Expanding this node give a preview of all the RESTful services available within the project.

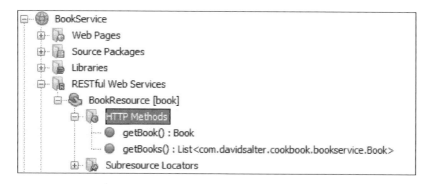

Using the Chrome Connector

The **Chrome Connector** allows an additional level of integration between NetBeans and the Google Chrome browser.

Two way DOM querying is provided such that if a DOM element is clicked within the browser, it is shown within NetBeans and in the same way if the user clicks on a DOM element in NetBeans, that element is selected within the browser.

The Chrome Connector can change the size of the browser window to help developers when writing applications for multiple platforms. For example, the browser can be set to the size of a tablet or a smartphone so that the layout of a web application can be examined for different devices.

For HTML 5 projects, the Chrome Connector allows changes to be automatically updated within the browser so whenever changes are made and saved within NetBeans, they are automatically updated in the browser. Unfortunately, this functionality is not present for JSF pages.

Getting ready

To complete this recipe, we need to have a valid installation of WildFly configured within NetBeans. We will be using the Java EE download bundle of NetBeans as this provides all of the tools necessary to complete this recipe.

Finally, since we're going to be investigating the Chrome Connector, we will use a sample application that is provided with the download bundle for this book. This will allow us to see some of the features of the Connector.

How to do it...

Perform the following steps:

1. From the download bundle for this book, locate the project `Chapter 5\Todo`. Click on **File** and then click on **Open Project**. Browse the `Chapter 5` folder of the download bundle and open the **Todo** project.

> The Todo project is a simple Todo list that shows many of the features of a Java EE 7 application. We're not too worried about the features here, but about how the project will interact with the Chrome Connector. The Todo application uses JSF as its view technology with Twitter Bootstrap providing the styling for the application.

2. To run the application using the Chrome Connector, click on the down arrow next to the globe (●▾) within the toolbar.

3. From the **Browser** selection window, click on **Chrome** within the **With NetBeans Connector** category.

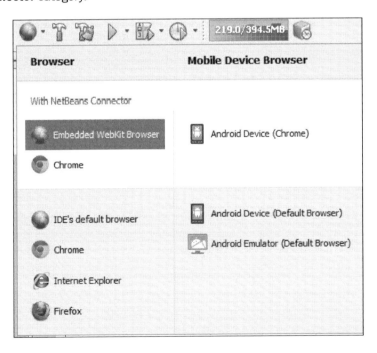

4. NetBeans is now configured to run the application using the Chrome Connector. Right-click on the **Todo** application within the **Projects** explorer and click on **Run...**.

5. Since we have yet to install the Chrome Connector, NetBeans will show a warning dialog stating that we need to go to the Chrome store and install the plugin into the Chrome browser.

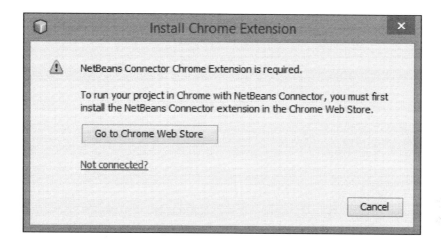

6. Click on the **Go to Chrome Web Store** button to launch the store:

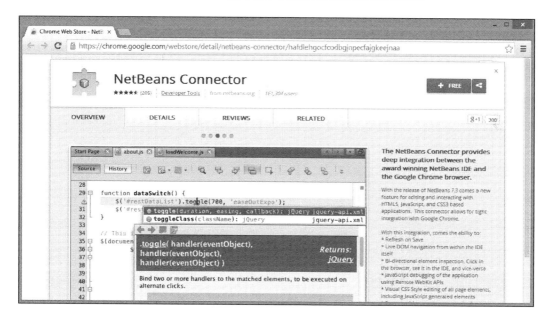

7. In Chrome, click on the add button (+ FREE) to install the Chrome Connector.

8. In the **Confirm New Extension** dialog, click on the **Add** button to allow the extension to be added to Chrome.

9. Go back to NetBeans and click on the **Re-Run Project** button to launch the project with the Chrome Connector enabled:

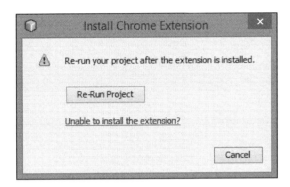

10. The **Todo** application will now be opened within Chrome. A notification message indicates that **"NetBeans Connector" is debugging this tab**. At the top-right of the address bar, the NetBeans logo is displayed indicating that integration with NetBeans is enabled. Do not close this tab during debugging, or the NetBeans Connector will shut down and you will need to start the debugging procedure again.

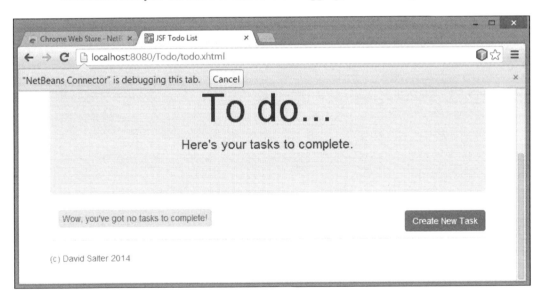

Now that we've got the connector installed, let's see how we can change the size of the browser window to mimic that of different devices. Perform the following steps:

1. Click on the NetBeans logo at the top right of the browser window. In the pop-up dialog, click on **Smartphone Portrait**. Note how the browser window changes the size to 320 x 480 pixels:

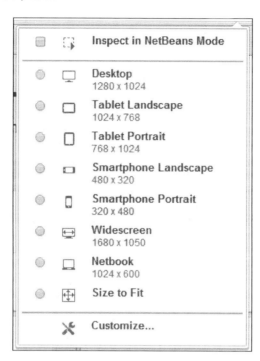

2. Not only can the Chrome Connector change the browser window size to match that of different devices, it also provides two-way DOM querying.

3. Click on the NetBeans logo within the browser address bar.

4. On the resulting dialog, click on **Inspect in NetBeans Mode**.

5. Hover the mouse over the **Create New Task** button and note how the DOM information for the object is displayed:

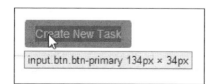

6. Click on the **Create New Task** button within Chrome and note how the button is selected within the Browser DOM within NetBeans:

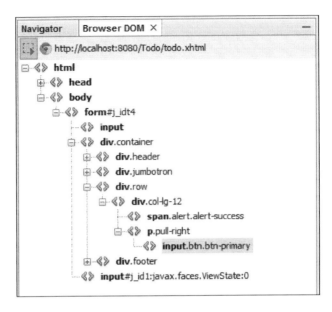

7. Hover the mouse cursor over the **div.jumbotron** element within the Browser DOM explorer in NetBeans and note how the corresponding element is highlighted within Chrome.

There's more

When running an HTML 5 project, changes made to HTML pages are automatically updated within the browser when the page is saved. The browser does not need to be refreshed to display updated content, all that is required is for the page to be saved within NetBeans. The Chrome Connector then automatically forces the browser to refresh the page.

In addition to the Chrome Connector, the Chrome Developer Tools provided within Chrome itself provide excellent debugging and diagnostic tools. This allows the DOM to be queried, custom JavaScript to be executed, and can show all network traffic that is performed while allowing the developer to investigate what is sent and received on each request. The Chrome Developer Tools can also be used for performance monitoring showing the time taken for resources to download. The combination of the Chrome Connector and the Chrome Developer Tools is an excellent tool for enterprise and web developers.

6
Managing Databases with NetBeans

In this chapter, we will cover the following recipes:

- ▶ Connecting to Java DB
- ▶ Registering and managing a MySQL Server
- ▶ Connecting to Microsoft SQL Server and Oracle
- ▶ Connecting to PostgreSQL
- ▶ Managing a SQL database
- ▶ Connecting to MongoDB

Introduction

Databases can be one of the most fundamental parts of applications, whether they are large or small. They can also, unfortunately, be forgotten and thought of as unimportant parts of systems.

Fortunately, NetBeans provides excellent tooling for connecting to databases allowing developers to create tables and views and run SQL statements against a wide variety of databases.

In this chapter, we'll take a look at how to connect to some open source databases and even some proprietary ones.

We'll look at making connections to Java DB (also known as Apache DB) as well as MySQL and PostgreSQL. From the commercial world, we'll look at how to make connections to Microsoft SQL Server and Oracle—two of the main heavyweight contenders in enterprise data technologies.

When we've seen how to connect to these databases, we'll see how NetBeans can help a Java developer to write and execute SQL.

Finally, we'll take a look at the world of NoSQL databases. We'll see how we can connect to MongoDB from within NetBeans.

Connecting to Java DB

Java DB is a distribution of the Apache Derby database provided by Oracle Corporation. It provides a fully ANSI-compliant SQL database that can be run as either an embedded database or a network server.

Java DB has a small footprint (approximately 2.6 MB) yet provides advanced features such as transactions, stored procedures, and XA (two-phase commit) transactions.

Due to the fact that Java DB is small, it is provided with the JDK and that it can be executed as an embedded database, it is ideal for use within an application that does not need the power of larger databases such as Oracle or Microsoft SQL Server. It is also ideal to use as a database for integration testing of code modules.

From Java 7 onwards, Java DB has been supplied as standard with the JDK; so, no additional downloads are required.

For further information about Java DB, visit the Oracle site at:

```
http://www.oracle.com/technetwork/java/javadb/overview/index.html
```

For further information on Apache Derby, visit the Apache DB site at:

```
http://db.apache.org/derby/
```

Getting ready

If you are using Java 7 onwards, Java DB is supplied with your installation of the JDK.

If you have installed GlassFish within NetBeans, or are using the Enterprise download bundle of NetBeans, then Java DB will already be configured to run as a network server. If not, then everything that is required to connect NetBeans to Java DB is included with your JDK installation.

How to do it...

1. Right-click on the **Java DB** node within the **Databases** node in the **Services** explorer and select **Properties**.

2. In the **Java DB Properties** window, enter the location of the Java DB executable files under the **Java DB Installation** field. Unless you have downloaded Apache DB separately, the Java DB installation folder will be the db folder underneath your JDK's home folder.

3. In the **Database Location** field, enter the path to a location where the database files and settings will be held, as shown in the following screenshot:

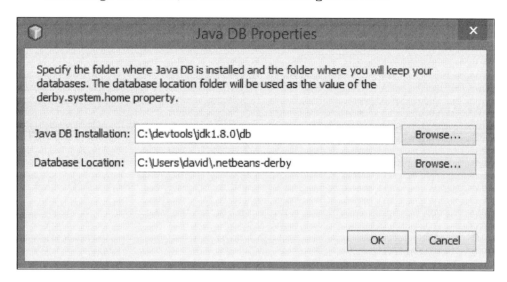

4. Click on **OK** to complete the configuration.

How it works...

Specifying the location of the Java DB installation and the location in which to store database configuration files provides NetBeans with all the information required to run the Java DB as a network server. To start the server, right-click on the **Java DB** node within the **Services** explorer and select **Start Server**. NetBeans will start the server and provide the following confirmation to the **Output** window that the server has started:

```
Tue Apr 22 20:41:05 BST 2014 : Apache Derby Network Server - 10.10.1.2 -
(1495037) started and ready to accept connections on port 1527
```

To stop the server, right-click on the **Java DB** node within the **Services** explorer and select **Stop Server**.

There's more...

In addition to registering a Java DB server within NetBeans, we can also create new databases that can then be connected to via JDBC.

To create a database, right-click on the **Java DB** node within the **Services** explorer and select the **Create Database...** option. Enter a database name, along with a username and password, to create a new database, as shown in the following screenshot:

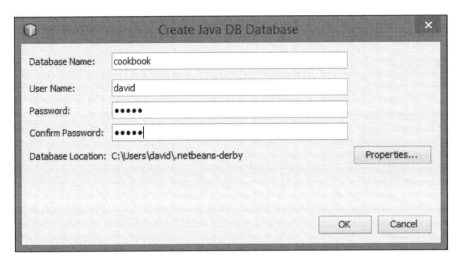

Once a database has been created, NetBeans connects to it and fetches the schema from the server. A new database connection is placed within the **Databases** node of the **Services** explorer.

Registering and managing a MySQL Server

MySQL is an Oracle Corporation product, which was previously a Sun Microsystems product, and a MySQL Abs product before that. It is one of the most famous open source relational database management systems, RDBMS, in the world. The code is available under the GPL license.

It is used by many companies, such as Nokia, Facebook, and Google, for its robustness and for being free for use.

Getting ready

For this recipe, we will use MySQL version 5.6.17 and MySQL GUI Tools.

Installation and configuration of MySQL Server and components onto the operating system is beyond the scope of this recipe. What we will learn here is how to configure MySQL with NetBeans so that the integration between database and IDE can be achieved.

In this recipe, we will assume that the database is installed locally and the password is chosen by the user.

> For more information and downloads, visit the following link for the database: `http://dev.mysql.com/downloads/`
> And for MySQL Workbench, visit `http://dev.mysql.com/downloads/tools/workbench/`.

How to do it...

With the IDE open, perform the following steps:

1. Navigate to the **Services** explorer window and expand the **Databases** section.

2. Right-click on **Databases** and select **Register MySQL Server...**, as shown in the following screenshot:

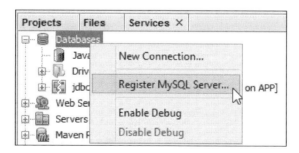

3. Under **Basic Properties**, NetBeans, by default, enters `localhost` as the **Server Host Name** field and `3306` as the **Server Port Number** field. If your MySQL instance is not running with these defaults, change them here.

4. Ensure that the **Administration User Name** and **Administration Password** fields that you configured for your MySQL instance are entered correctly.

The **MySQL Server Properties** window should look more or less like the following screenshot:

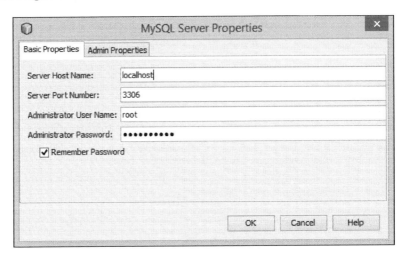

5. Click on the **Admin Properties** tab.

6. Enter the path to the MySQL administration tool (to manage MySQL graphically, enter the path to the MySQL Workbench) under the **Path/URL to admin tool** field.

7. Enter the paths to the MySQL start and stop commands under the **Path to start command** and **Path to stop command** fields, as shown in the following screenshot:

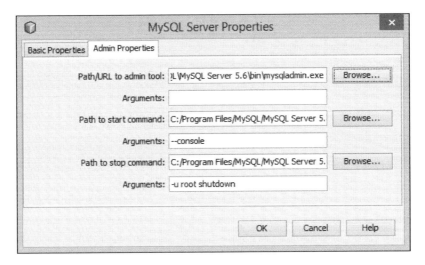

8. Click on **OK**.

9. A **MySQL Server** node is added underneath the **Databases** node within the **Services** explorer.

How it works...

The **Basic Properties** tab contains the minimum information required to connect to a MySQL Server. This is all that is needed for the connection to work. The information required to better control the MySQL Server is on the **Admin Properties** tab. The **Start** and **Stop** commands and path for the MySQL-related tools are also included in the submenu, which can be accessed by right-clicking on the **MySQL Server** node.

Upon registration, there are two ways of checking whether the MySQL Server is connected or not:

- If the **MySQL Server** node cannot be expanded, it means that it is not connected
- If the **MySQL Server** node displays **(disconnected)**, it means that it is not connected

Once the **MySQL Server** node is expanded, NetBeans will show a list of all databases created within the server. Right-clicking on a database and selecting **Connect...** adds a database connection within the **Databases** node that allows database tables, views, and so on to be managed.

There's more...

Want to create databases and run the administration tool from within NetBeans? You've come to the right place.

Creating databases

To create databases on a registered **MySQL Server** instance, simply:

1. Right-click on the **MySQL Server** node and select **Create Database...**.

2. A **Create MySQL Database** window will ask for **New Database Name** and provides the **Grant Full Access To** option to grant full access to a specified user. Enter the appropriate name for a new database and click on **OK**.

3. A new database will be created and a new JDBC connection will be added to the **Databases** node, as shown in the following screenshot:

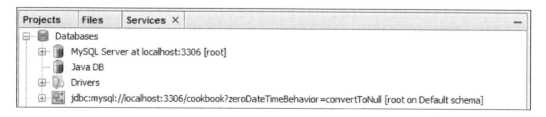

Running the administration tool

To run the MySQL administration tool, it is necessary to configure NetBeans with the correct path. If unsure how to do this, refer to the beginning of this recipe, under **MySQL Server Properties**, in the **Admin Properties** tab.

For graphical management of MySQL, the MySQL Workbench can be configured here as the MySQL administration tool. MySQL Workbench is included with downloads for MySQL Server, or can be downloaded as an additional option.

With the configuration in place, perform the following steps:

1. Navigate to the **Services** explorer and expand the **Databases** node.

2. Right-click on the **MySQL Server** node.

3. Click on **Run Administration Tool**.

The techniques described in this recipe apply equally to MariaDB, which is a drop-in replacement for MySQL. More information on MariaDB can be found at https://mariadb.org.

Connecting to Microsoft SQL Server and Oracle

Now that we've looked at some open source databases, let's take a look at some of the commercial databases that we can connect to and manage from within NetBeans.

First, let's look at Microsoft SQL Server.

It may seem strange talking about Microsoft products when we're integrating with NetBeans; however, Microsoft SQL Server is one of the more popular databases available and provides excellent tools for developers, allowing them to define, debug, and profile their SQL.

Getting ready

Microsoft SQL Server is available in many different versions, ranging from the simple Local DB, through SQL Server Express up to SQL Server Enterprise. SQL Server is renowned for its power, yet the friendliness of the tools that are supplied with it.

SQL Server originally started out as Sybase, but the latest version is SQL Server 2014. In this recipe, we will be interfacing with SQL Server 2014 Express.

 For more information on SQL Server, visit `http://www.microsoft.com/en-us/server-cloud/products/sql-server/`.

Installing SQL Server is outside of the scope of this recipe; we will, however, concentrate on showing how to connect to SQL Server from within NetBeans.

To connect to SQL Server from within NetBeans, we need to use a JDBC driver. SQL Server JDBC drivers are not supplied with NetBeans—they need to be downloaded from Microsoft. You can download the JDBC drivers from `http://msdn.microsoft.com/en-US/sqlserver/aa937724/`.

The latest JDBC drivers provide support for SQL Server 2012. However, these are the latest drivers and depending upon your needs, will work with SQL Server 2014.

 Many other companies provide JDBC drivers for SQL Server; however, I recommend using the official Microsoft drivers as I find they work better in production environments. One of the downsides of the Microsoft JDBC drivers is that they cannot connect to the Local DB edition of SQL Server as Local DB requires clients to connect via **named pipes**. The Microsoft SQL Server drivers require client connections to be via TCP/IP and therefore any version of SQL Server from Express upwards is compatible with the official drivers.

Once you've installed SQL Server Express and downloaded and installed the Microsoft JDBC drivers for SQL Server, we can begin with our project.

How to do it...

Navigate to the **Services** explorer and perform the following steps:

1. Right-click on the **Databases** node and select **New Connection…**.
2. Since there are no SQL Server drivers supplied with NetBeans, we need to create a new driver. From the **Driver** drop-down menu, select **New Driver…**.

3. On the **New JDBC Driver** dialog, click on the **Add...** button and locate the `sqljdbc4.jar` file that you downloaded with the SQL Server JDBC driver download. The **Driver Class** and **Name** fields will be automatically populated by NetBeans querying the driver file, as shown in the following screenshot:

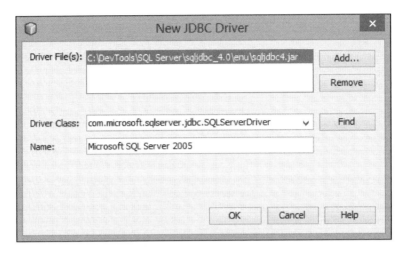

4. Click on the **OK** button to create the new driver.

5. You will now be returned to the **New Connection Wizard** dialog where the **Driver** field is set to **Microsoft SQL Server 2005**.

 Don't worry that the driver refers to Microsoft SQL Server 2005—it's just a name!

6. Click on the **Next** button.

The next step is to enter basic database connection information.

Note that the following information is not set in stone and you might have changed it when installing and configuring the database. However, if all the defaults were used, it is likely that the information is the same as presented here:

1. Enter the following connection information:

   ❑ **Driver Name: Microsoft SQL Server 2005**

   ❑ **Host**: localhost

   ❑ **Port**: 1433

   ❑ **Database**: Leave this blank

- ❑ **Instance Name**: `\SQLEXPRESS`
- ❑ **User Name**: `sa`
- ❑ **Password**: The password that was entered during installation

2. Now that everything looks more or less like the following screenshot, notice the pattern of **JDBC URL**. The **JDBC URL** field follows the standard naming scheme of commencing with `jdbc:` followed by the database type. The URL then contains details about the host, the instance name, and the port number to connect to the database on. The **New Connection Wizard** dialog is shown in the following screenshot:

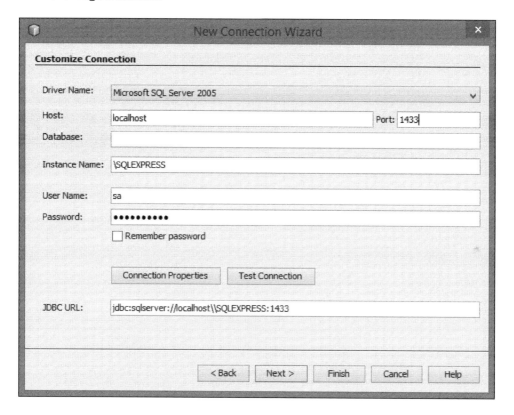

3. Click on the **Next** button.
4. In the **Select Schema** dropdown, select **dbo**.
5. Click on the **Finish** button to create the new connection to SQL Server.

How it works...

Unlike previous databases we have connected to, this is the first database connection that we have defined within this cookbook that requires an external `.jar` file to connect properly.

This is because NetBeans does not provide the SQL Server JDBC `.jar` (`sqljdbc4.jar`) file by default. You will not find this `.jar` file within NetBeans, or within a Maven repository, as it is proprietary to Microsoft Corporation.

As shown in the registration procedure, after entering the required information, the JDBC URL is of the format:

```
jdbc:sqlserver://localhost\\SQLEXPRESS:1433
```

This connection string shows that we are connecting to an SQL Server instance called `SQLEXPRESS` running on port `1433`. This is the default port for a SQL Server database.

When registering the database, NetBeans validates the entered information to ensure access to the database is available. This ensures that no misconfigured database is going to be used and prevents the user from using a misconfigured connection. The connection can also be tested while inputting connection details by pressing the **Test Connection** button.

When the **Finish** button is clicked, NetBeans connects to the SQL Server database and fetches existing schemas from the server. A new database connection is placed within the **Databases** node of the **Services** explorer.

There's more...

What if we wanted to connect to Oracle instead of MS SQL Server? Can we do that with NetBeans?

Connecting to an Oracle database

With NetBeans, it's straightforward to connect to an Oracle database. The procedure for connecting to Oracle is almost identical to that for connecting to Microsoft SQL Server. For Oracle, it's necessary to use the JDBC driver named `ojdbc7.jar`. This driver is provided with Oracle installations, but can also be downloaded from `http://www.oracle.com/technetwork/database/features/jdbc/index.html`.

When choosing an Oracle JDBC driver, it can be useful to know the naming scheme Oracle uses for its drivers. Oracle drivers are generally named `ojdbc<jdk_version>.jar`, so for example, `ojdbc7.jar` is the driver file to use with Java 7. Oracle also produces driver files that contain debug information. These all have the suffix, `_g`, so for example, `ojdbc6_g.jar` is the debug driver file to use with Java 6.

To configure Oracle, when selecting the driver on the **New Connection Wizard** dialog, select **Oracle Thin** as the driver and then add the `ojdbc7.jar` driver, as shown in the following screenshot:

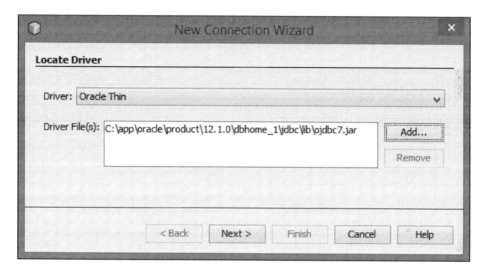

On the **Customize Connection** page of the **New Connection** dialog, the following information should be used to connect to Oracle:

- **Driver Name: Oracle Thin (Service Name)**
- **Host**: `localhost`
- **Port**: `1521`
- **Service**: `orcl`
- **User Name**: `system`
- **Password**: The password that was entered during installation

After entering all of this information, the JDBC URL for Oracle is of the following format:

`jdbc:oracle:thin:@//localhost:1521/orcl`

What if my Oracle database connection requires me to use TNS? Can I use this to connect from NetBeans? Certainly! When configuring a new connection, specify **Oracle Thin (TNS Name(v10.2.0.1.0 or later))** as **Driver Name**. The option is then presented to enter the **TNS Name** field for configuration rather than the **Service** field.

Connecting to PostgreSQL

PostgreSQL is a cross-platform object-relational database system that, like MySQL, is also open source and free. It is supported and used by a consortium of companies such as Red Hat, Skype, and HP. As with MySQL, PostgreSQL features a GUI for management activities—**pgAdmin**.

Setting up PostgreSQL with NetBeans is not as straightforward as with MySQL, but NetBeans still comes with the appropriate JDBC driver, so don't worry, it's still not rocket science.

Getting ready

For this recipe, we will be using PostgreSQL version 9.3.2 and pgAdmin III.

Installation and configuration of PostgreSQL and components onto the operating system is beyond the scope of this recipe. What will be learned here is how to configure PostgreSQL with NetBeans so that integration between the database and NetBeans can be achieved.

In this recipe, we will assume that the database is installed locally and that the password has been chosen by the user.

It is necessary to have an existing database in PostgreSQL for this recipe to work; we will assume that the name of the database is cookbook.

How to do it...

With NetBeans open and PostgreSQL running, perform the following steps:

1. Navigate to the **Services** explorer, right-click on the **Databases** node, and select **New Connection...**.

2. In the **New Connection Wizard** dialog, select **PostgreSQL** from the **Driver** dropdown and click on **Next**.

3. Enter the following information to define the PostgreSQL connection:

    - **Host**: 127.0.0.1
    - **Port**: 5432
    - **Database**: cookbook
    - **User Name**: postgres
    - **Password**: Enter the postgres user's password

The **New Connection Wizard** dialog for the PostgreSQL connection is displayed in the following screenshot:

4. Click on the **Next** button.

5. On the **Choose Database Schema** tab, click on the **Select Schema** dropdown and choose **public**.

6. Click on **Finish**.

7. A PostgreSQL JDBC connection node is added to the **Databases** node as shown in the following screenshot:

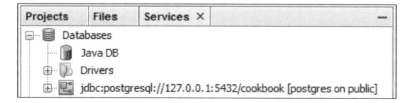

How it works...

NetBeans validates the entered information to access the database. This ensures that no misconfigured database is going to be used and prevents the user from using a misconfigured connection. The connection can also be tested while inputting connection details by clicking on the **Test Connection** button.

When the **Finish** button is clicked, NetBeans connects to the PostgreSQL database and fetches existing databases from the server. A new database connection is placed within the **Databases** node of the **Services** explorer.

There's more...

How can a user connect and disconnect from a PostgreSQL database from within NetBeans?

Connecting and disconnecting

It is possible to connect and disconnect from a database using the **Services** explorer.

Simply right-click on the desired connection and select **Connect...**, in the case of the database being disconnected; select **Disconnect** if it is connected, as shown in the following screenshot:

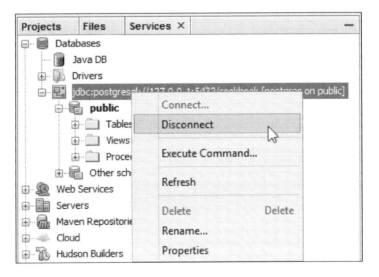

Managing a SQL database

In the previous recipes, we've seen how to connect to a variety of both open source and commercial relational databases. Connecting to a database is all well and good (after all, it's what we do in our applications), but we need to be able to easily create tables and views, and easily run SQL queries against our databases to see what data we have in them.

In this recipe, we'll see how we can perform these types of actions.

Getting ready

We'll be managing a Java DB instance in this recipe as Java DB is one of the easiest databases to configure and connect to from within NetBeans.

If you've not got a Java DB connected and configured within NetBeans, then please refer to the earlier recipe, *Connecting to Java DB*, to see how to connect. When creating a new Java DB database, name it `cookbook` and specify the username to connect to the database as `APP`.

How to do it...

Navigate to the **Databases** node within the **Services** explorer and perform the following steps:

1. Right-click on the `cookbook` database underneath the **Java DB** node and select **Connect...**. If the Java DB network server is not running, it will be started.

2. A connection will be made to the Java DB database called `cookbook`. This is accessed from within the **Databases** node, as shown in the following screenshot:

Note that when a database is not connected, the disconnected icon () is displayed next to the connection name instead of the connected icon ( ).

3. Before we can insert any data into the database, we must first make a table. Expand the Java DB connection node and the **APP** node within it to see sub nodes, **Tables**, **Views**, and **Procedures**, as shown in the following screenshot:

4. Right-click on the **Tables** node and select **Create Table...**.

5. The **Create Table** dialog will be displayed. Enter the **Table name** field as TASKS.

6. Click on the **Add column** button and create the following columns one by one:

Name	Type	Size	Default	Constraints
TASK_ID	INTEGER			Primary key, Unique, Index
TASK_NAME	VARCHAR	25		
TASK_COMPLETED	BOOLEAN		false	
TASK_DUE	DATE			Null

7. Once completed, the **Create Table** dialog should look like the following screenshot:

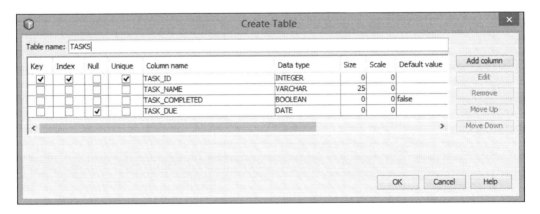

8. Click on the **OK** button to create the table.

9. The table will now be created and will be shown within the **Tables** node in the **Services** explorer.

10. Expand the TASKS node and notice how the columns and indexes for the table are available.

The primary key for this table has been declared as an autoincrementing identity field that can store integer values. At present, NetBeans does not allow columns to be created as identity columns within Java DB, so if this is required, then the table must be created via SQL and not via the **Create Table** dialog.

Now that we've created a table, let's insert some data into it with the following steps:

1. Right-click on the TASKS node and select **Execute Command...**.
2. A new SQL window will be opened into which we can type SQL commands.
3. Enter the following code into the SQL window:

```
insert into TASKS(TASK_ID, TASK_NAME) values (1, 'Read
Cookbook');
insert into TASKS(TASK_ID, TASK_NAME) values (2, 'Eat
sandwich');
insert into TASKS(TASK_ID, TASK_NAME, TASK_DUE) values (3,
'Do some programming', '2015-03-01');
```

It's a good point to note that SQL files can be saved within a project so that if you've got some SQL that you regularly need to run, you can quickly and easily access it at a later date.

4. Click to place the mouse cursor anywhere within the first insert statement as shown in the following screenshot:

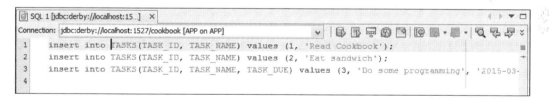

5. Click the **Run Statement** button (). This will execute the statement that is currently selected and not the entire contents of the SQL window.
6. Right-click on the TASKS table within the **Services** explorer and select **View Data...**.
7. A new SQL window will open where the SQL is already entered as select * from APP.TASKS;.
8. The SQL statement will be executed automatically showing the data beneath the query window.
9. Navigate back to the original **SQL** window.

10. Comment out the original SQL statement that we have already executed by appending – to the beginning of the line. The first SQL statement should now read:

```
--insert into TASKS(TASK_ID, TASK_NAME) values (1, 'Read
Cookbook');
```

11. Click on the **Run SQL** button (🌐). This will execute all of the SQL code that is currently within the **SQL** window. In this instance, this will be the final two SQL statements that we have defined.

12. Navigate back to the **SQL** window that contains the `select * from APP.TASKS;` SQL statement and click on the **Run SQL** button.

13. Note how there are now three rows stored in the database as shown in the following screenshot:

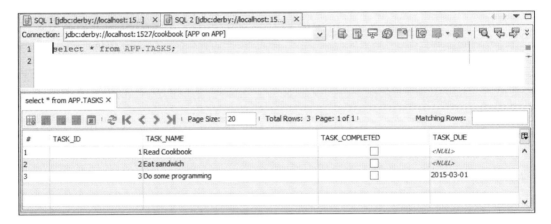

How it works...

In this recipe, we've seen how we can connect to a database within NetBeans via JDBC. In this instance, the database was Java DB; however, the procedure is the same for any database.

Once connected to the database, we use the **Create Table** dialog to allow us to graphically define the schema for a simple table. We noted that there are some restrictions within NetBeans with regards to creating tables in Java DB (namely that we can't create identity fields via the GUI).

Executing SQL statements is easily accomplished using either the **Run Statement** or **Run SQL** commands. When more than one SQL command is specified, each command needs to be separated by a semicolon, `;`, so that NetBeans knows where one command ends and another begins.

Finally, we saw that, not only can we execute SQL statements that don't return results, we can also execute SQL statements that return results. Not only that, but we can easily see the results in a nicely formatted paged table.

There's more...

NetBeans provides even more features than we've seen for manipulating data within a database.

Viewing data

What if we've got a table with a lot of columns in it and we only wish to view some of those columns? Right-clicking on a table and selecting **View Data...** returns all of the columns for the table. Is it possible to view only a few columns?

It certainly is! Instead of right-clicking on the table and selecting **View Data...**, simply select the columns to view (press *Ctrl* while clicking on a column name for multiselect) and then choose **View Data...**.

Creating indexes

Creating a table with no indexes is probably going to give us performance headaches when we start getting larger datasets. Fortunately, NetBeans allows us to easily create custom indexes on a table. Simply right-click on the **Indexes** node and select **Add Index....** The **Add Index** dialog allows an index name to be specified along with the columns to be part of the index and whether the index in unique or not. The following screenshot displays the **Add Index** dialog:

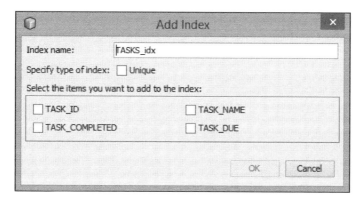

Inserting, deleting, and amending data graphically

We saw in this recipe how we can use SQL to insert data into tables. Sometimes, however, it can be useful to easily insert or delete data from a table, or even edit existing data. How can NetBeans help us here?

When viewing a dataset, some additional options are available for editing data. Clicking on the **Insert Record** button (▦) displays a form allowing all of the fields for one or more rows to be defined graphically. These new rows can then be inserted directly into the database or the SQL can be selected and manually executed against the database.

If we don't need some data in the database, then clicking on the **Delete Selected Records** button (▦) will do as the name says, and delete the rows that are selected in the dataset viewer.

We can also edit data within a dataset viewer by double-clicking on the cell we wish to edit and then simply specifying the new value of the data.

All of these operations are under transactional control, so to keep (commit) any changes we make graphically, we need to click on the **Commit Record(s)** button (▦). Conversely, to throw away (rollback) any edits we make, we need to click on the **Cancel Edits Selected Record(s)** button (▦).

Finally, if we simply wish to delete all of the rows within a table, we can click on the **Truncate Table** button (▦).

Exporting schemas

So, we've finally written an application, and we want to take a copy of the database schema, perhaps so that we can deploy it to another server, or pass it to a colleague for them to look at. How can we achieve that?

Right-clicking on a table within the **Tables** node in the **Services** explorer provides a **Grab Structure** option. This saves the structure of a table away into a binary file that can later be loaded into NetBeans using the **Recreate Table** option—again on the right-click menu from a table.

Connecting to MongoDB

MongoDB is a NoSQL database that allows JSON-style documents to be stored within it, rather than the traditional tables and rows that a relational database uses. The name MongoDB comes from the word humongous, giving an indication of the size of data that can be stored within MongoDB, as it is not uncommon to store billions of documents within MongoDB.

MongoDB is used by large corporations such as LinkedIn, SalesForce, and EA.

For further information about MongoDB, visit the project site at `http://www.mongodb.com`.

Getting ready

To complete this recipe, it is necessary to have an instance of MongoDB to connect to, however, installation of MongoDB is outside the scope of this recipe.

In this recipe, we will assume that MongoDB is installed locally, although by changing connection details, this recipe will work equally well for remote MongoDB servers.

How to do it...

MongoDB support is not included within NetBeans by default; so, first, we must add it with the following steps:

1. Click on **Tools** and then **Plugins** form the NetBeans main menu to open the NetBeans **Plugins** dialog.

2. Select the **Available Plugins** tab and check the **Install** checkbox for the **NBMongo** plugin, as shown in the following screenshot:

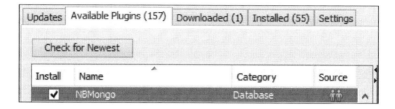

3. Click on the **Install** button to commence installation of the plugin.

4. NetBeans will confirm installation of the NBMongo plugin. Click on **Next**.

5. Read and accept the license agreement and then click on the **Install** button to complete installation of the plugin.

6. The plugin will now be installed. Click on **Finish** when installation is complete and then click on **Close** to exit the **Plugins** dialog.

7. A new option within the **Services** explorer is now available for connecting to MongoDB. Click on the **Services** explorer to see the **Mongo DB** option, as shown in the following screenshot:

Now that we've added MongoDB support into NetBeans, let's create a connection to a MongoDB server with the following steps:

1. Right-click on the **Mongo DB** node within the **Services** explorer and select the **New Connection** option.

2. The **New MongoDB Connection** dialog will be displayed.

3. Enter the **Name** field as `Mongo Cookbook` and the **Mongo URI** field as `mongodb://localhost/cookbook`.

4. Click on **OK** to add the new connection.

5. A new option is added into the **Services** explorer for the specified MongoDB; however, NetBeans is not yet connected to MongoDB. Right-click on the `Mongo Cookbook` node underneath MongoDB within the **Services** explorer and select **Connect**.

6. The connection to MongoDB is established and the `cookbook` database created is shown:

Let's now create a collection within MongoDB and add some data to it with the following steps:

1. Right-click on the `cookbook` node within the `Services` explorer and select **Add Collection**.

2. In the **Add Collection** dialog, enter the **Collection name** field as `Books` and click on **OK**, as shown in the following screenshot:

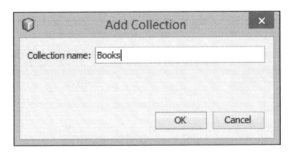

3. A `Books` collection is now displayed within the **Services** explorer underneath the `cookbook` database.

4. Right-click on the `Books` collection and select the **Open** menu option. The `Books` collection will now be opened within a new window titled `cookbook.Books`, as shown in the following screenshot:

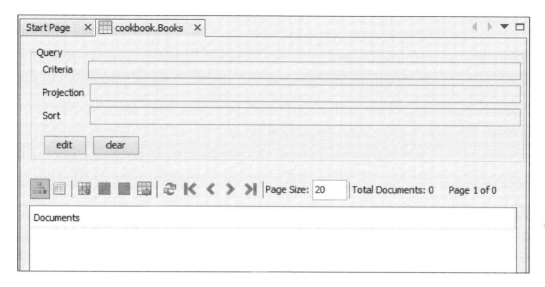

5. Click on the **Add Document** () button to invoke the **Add new document** dialog.

6. On the **Add new document** dialog, enter the document as:

```
{
    Name:"NetBeans Cookbook",
    Author: "David Salter"
}
```

We will have the **Add new document** dialog as shown in the following screenshot:

7. Click on the **OK** button to store the document.

8. The list of **Documents** stored within the collection is updated to reflect the newly added document, as shown in the following screenshot:

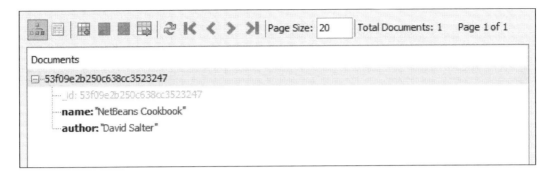

How it works...

In this recipe, we saw how to install MongoDB support into NetBeans via a third-party plugin called NBMongo. For more information about this plugin, visit `http://plugins.netbeans.org/plugin/52638/nbmongo`.

When connecting to the database, we specified a database name within the MongoDB connection URI. This database was then lazily created when we added a collection to it. If we need to customize the MongoDB connection URI, we can click on the **Browse** button on the **New MongoDB Connection** dialog. This allows us to specify items such as host name, port, credentials, and database options.

After connecting to MongoDB, we added a simple document to the database. The document was a simple JSON document containing two fields, `name` and `author`. Of course, adding only two fields like this does not show off the benefits of a NoSQL database, but shows how easy it is to store documents from within NetBeans.

Finally, we saw how NetBeans will easily list out the documents in a collection for us. NetBeans pages these documents for us instead of producing one long list of all the documents within a collection.

There's more...

In addition to adding and selecting documents, the MongoDB plugin allows us to edit and delete documents within a collection—just as we'd expect to do with a traditional relational database. We can import and even export collections as JSON files so that they can be used outside of MongoDB.

When viewing lists of documents, we can modify the criteria, projection, and sort ordering of the resultset directly from within the results window. If you're not familiar with MongoDB, please consult the MongoDB manual at `http://docs.mongodb.org/manual/` for more information on these operations.

The MongoDB shell

What if I want to perform some advanced operation that's only available from within the MongoDB shell? Can I do that from within NetBeans? You certainly can!

Right-clicking on a database within a MongoDB connection in the **Services** explorer provides the option to open **Mongo Shell**. To enable this option, the path to the MongoDB shell executable first needs to be specified. This path is specified within the **Miscellaneous** section of the NetBeans **Options** dialog, as shown in the following screenshot:

7

NetBeans JavaFX

In this chapter, we will cover the following recipes:

- ▶ Creating a JavaFX application
- ▶ Graphical editing of FXML files
- ▶ Styling a JavaFX application with CSS
- ▶ Creating and using a JavaFX custom control
- ▶ Deploying a self-contained application

Introduction

JavaFX is a software toolkit geared around developing rich GUI-based applications. It was first introduced at JavaOne in 2007 and has most recently been released as JavaFX Version 8 as part of the Java 8 release.

JavaFX used to be a separate installation from Java, but as of JDK 7u6, JavaFX has been bundled with both the Java JDK and JRE.

The long term strategy for JavaFX is surely to replace Swing as the dominant GUI development environment for Java developers as it provides a wealth of GUI components and provides developers the facility to easily create new components. JavaFX promotes the separation of user interface and application code by employing FXML files for developing the user interface. FXML files allow user interfaces to be developed with an XML format structure outside of Java code that can be styled by designers using standard CSS.

JavaFX applications can be executed as standalone native applications (for example, `.exe` files on Windows or `.app` files on Mac OS X), or can be launched via Java Web Start or by embedding within a web page.

These deployment strategies, along with the advanced design and layout tools for GUIs, make JavaFX an excellent choice for developing modern GUI-based applications.

For more information on JavaFX, check out Oracle's information page at `http://www.oracle.com/technetwork/java/javase/overview/javafx-overview-2158620.html`.

Creating a JavaFX application

In this recipe, we'll see how we can use NetBeans to create a JavaFX application. We'll create two windows; one of these will be developed in Java code and the second will be developed using FXML.

Getting ready

To complete this recipe, you can use either the Java SE or Java EE version of NetBeans.

You must have JDK 7u6 or higher installed to be able to develop and run JavaFX applications.

How to do it...

1. Click on **File** and then **New Project...**.

2. Select **JavaFX** from the **Categories** list and **JavaFX Application** from the list of **Projects**.

3. Click on **Next**.

4. Enter the **Project Name** field as `WelcomeToFX`. Ensure a valid project location is specified. Ensure **Create Application Class** is selected as `com.davidsalter.cookbook.welcometofx.WelcomeToFX`.

5. Click on **Finish**.

A blank JavaFX application will now be created for you. To check that everything is installed correctly, run the application. You should see a window with a **Say 'Hello World'** button within it, as shown in the following screenshot:

Now that we have validated that we can run JavaFX applications, let's change the application to ask for our name. We'll then display an FXML-designed window and see how we can develop JavaFX applications using both Java code and FXML. To do this, perform the following steps:

1. Double-click on the `WelcomeToFX.java` file from the **Projects** explorer to open it up for editing.

2. Change the `start(Stage primaryStage)` method to read:

```
@Override
public void start(Stage primaryStage) {
  primaryStage.setTitle("Hello World!");

  GridPane gridPane = new GridPane();
  gridPane.setAlignment(Pos.CENTER);
  gridPane.setHgap(15);
  gridPane.setVgap(15);
  gridPane.setPadding(new Insets(20));
  Label helloLabel = new Label("Hello");
  gridPane.add(helloLabel, 0, 0);

  Label nameLabel = new Label("What's your name?");
  gridPane.add(nameLabel, 0, 1);

  TextField nameTextField = new TextField();
  gridPane.add(nameTextField, 1, 1);

  Button helloButton = new Button("Say Hello");
  HBox horizontalBox = new HBox(10);
  horizontalBox.setAlignment(Pos.BOTTOM_RIGHT);
  horizontalBox.getChildren().add(helloButton);
  gridPane.add(horizontalBox, 1, 2);

  Scene scene = new Scene(gridPane, 350, 150);
  primaryStage.setScene(scene);
  primaryStage.show();
}
```

3. Right-click within the editor pane and select **Fix Imports** to add all of the import statements required for the class.

 Ensure that all the imports belong to the `javafx` packages and not `java.awt` packages. Some of the classes used by this code, for example, `Insets` exist both as `javafx.geometry.Insets` and `java.awt.Insets`. In this chapter, we always want to use the `javafx.*` versions.

This code generates a simple user interface that welcomes the user and asks them for their name. As of yet, there is no functionality behind the **Say Hello** button on the form. As we saw, the user interface was designed completely within Java code. The resultant window should look something like the following screenshot:

Let's now create another window that will echo the name that we will enter into this form welcoming us to JavaFX. We'll create this window as FXML with the following steps:

1. Right-click on the `WelcomeToFX` project within the **Projects** explorer and select **New** and then **Other....**

2. In the **New File** dialog, select **JavaFX** from the list of **Categories** and **Empty FXML** from the list of **File Types**.

3. Click on **Next**.

4. Enter the **FXML Name** field as `Greetings`.

> Remember, when creating a new file of a known type, we don't need to enter the file extension (`.fxml` in this case) as NetBeans will automatically add it for us.

5. Enter the **Package** field as `com.davidsalter.cookbook.welcometofx`.

6. Click on **Next**.

7. On the **New Empty FXML** page, check the **Use Java Controller** option.

8. Ensure the default option of the **Create New** controller is selected with the **Controller Name** field named `GreetingsController` and the **Package** field named `com.davidsalter.cookbook.welcometofx`, as shown in the following screenshot:

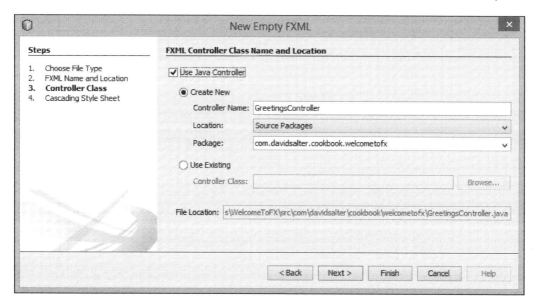

9. Click on **Next**.

10. On the **Cascading Style Sheet Name and Location** page, ensure that the **Use Cascading Style Sheets** option is not selected. We will see in a later recipe how to style JavaFX using CSS.

11. Click on the **Finish** button to create the FXML page.

12. Double-click on the `Greetings.fxml` file within the **Projects** explorer to open it up for editing.

13. Change the contents of the file to read:

```
<?xml version="1.0" encoding="UTF-8"?>

<?import javafx.scene.control.*?>
<?import javafx.scene.layout.*?>

<AnchorPane id="AnchorPane" prefHeight="150.0"
prefWidth="350.0"
    xmlns:fx="http://javafx.com/fxml/1"
    xmlns="http://javafx.com/javafx/2.2"
    fx:controller=
    "com.davidsalter.cookbook.welcometofx.
    GreetingsController">
  <children>
```

```
<GridPane layoutX="75.0" layoutY="35.0">
  <children>
    <Label text="Hi" GridPane.columnIndex="0"
    GridPane.rowIndex="0" />
    <Label fx:id="name" text="..your name here.."
    GridPane.columnIndex="0" GridPane.rowIndex="1" />
  </children>
  <columnConstraints>
    <ColumnConstraints hgrow="SOMETIMES"
    minWidth="10.0" prefWidth="100.0" />
    <ColumnConstraints hgrow="SOMETIMES"
    minWidth="10.0" prefWidth="100.0" />
  </columnConstraints>
  <rowConstraints>
    <RowConstraints minHeight="10.0" prefHeight="30.0"
    vgrow="SOMETIMES" />
    <RowConstraints minHeight="10.0" prefHeight="30.0"
    vgrow="SOMETIMES" />
    <RowConstraints minHeight="10.0" prefHeight="30.0"
    vgrow="SOMETIMES" />
  </rowConstraints>
</GridPane>
  </children>
</AnchorPane>
```

14. This FXML file simply creates a grid and then adds two labels into the grid. The first label says **Hi** and the second will show the name entered within the window we created earlier.

    Since we want to dynamically change what's shown in this window (we want to display the user's name in the `Label` tag identified as `fx:id="name"`), we need to add some code to the controller class to manage this.

15. Double-click on the `GreetingsController.java` file within the **Projects** explorer to open the file for editing.

16. Add a private member to store the inputted name as follows:

```
@FXML
private Label name;
```

17. Add a public method to store the name:

```
public void setName(String name) {
  this.name.setText(name);
}
```

18. Fix any imports using the **Fix Imports** tool.

When fixing imports, remember that some of the JavaFX classes have the same names as classes in the `java.awt` packages. Ensure you import the correct `javafx` packages rather than `java.awt` packages.

Now that we've created a screen to get some input from the user, and a screen to show the input back to the user, we need to wire the two screens together so that the greetings page is shown when the user clicks on the button on the first window with the following steps:

1. Double-click on the `WelcomeToFX.java` file within the **Projects** explorer to open up the file for editing.

2. Immediately before instantiating the `Scene` class (three lines from the bottom of the `start` method), insert the following code:

```
helloButton.setOnAction(new EventHandler<ActionEvent>() {

    @Override
    public void handle(ActionEvent event) {
      try {
        FXMLLoader loader = new
        FXMLLoader(getClass().getResource("Greetings.fxml"));
        Stage stage = new Stage(StageStyle.DECORATED);
        stage.setScene(new Scene((Pane) loader.load()));
        GreetingsController controller =
        loader.<GreetingsController>getController();
        controller.setName(nameTextField.getText());
        stage.show();
      } catch (IOException ex) {
        Logger.getLogger(WelcomeToFX.class.getName())
        .log(Level.SEVERE, null, ex);
      }
    }
});
```

This code adds an event handler onto `helloButton`, which when clicked, loads the window that is defined by `Greetings.fxml` and shows it.

3. Again, right-click within the code editing window and select the **Fix Imports** menu option to fix the file's `import` statements.

4. Press *F6* to run the application. Enter a name in response to the question **What is your name?** and click on the **Say Hello** button to be greeted.

How it works...

In this recipe, we saw how to create a JavaFX application and how to create user interfaces both using Java code and using FXML.

We coded a JavaFX window using pure Java and then we created a window using FXML. Neither of these windows had much styling on them. We'll see in a later recipe, *Styling a JavaFX application with CSS*, how we can style JavaFX applications using CSS.

 When dynamically loading FXML files using the `FXMLLoader` class, it's a good practice to catch `java.lang.IllegalStateExceptions` as these will be thrown with a `Location is not set` message if the FXML file cannot be found and loaded.

One of the main benefits of designing user interfaces in FXML is that it completely separates the user interface from the application code thus allowing designers more control over the UI and UX of an application. We saw, however, that the NetBeans editor for FXML files is just the plain old NetBeans text editor. Unless you can remember all of the syntax to FXML, you probably won't be too productive writing FXML this way. In the next recipe, *Graphical editing of FXML files*, we'll see how we can enhance the FXML editing abilities within NetBeans and bring them up to par, or even to better than those provided for Swing applications.

There's more...

What if I only want to create applications using FXML? Is it possible to create a JavaFX `Application` class without coding any user interface in Java?

Creating all user interfaces in FXML

It certainly is! When creating a project from the **New Project** wizard, select **JavaFX** from the list of **Categories** and **JavaFX FXML Application** from the list of **Projects**.

If you prefer to use Maven as your build tool, you'll be pleased to know you can also create JavaFX applications using Maven. Simply select **Maven** from the **Categories** list on the **New Project** wizard and then **JavaFX Application** from the list of **Projects**. This will create an application ready for developing user interfaces in FXML by default.

Manually creating controllers

When creating FXML files, we saw in this recipe how to create Java controller classes. What happens if I forgot to create a controller? Do I have to manually create a controller and then wire it up to the FXML file?

Fortunately, NetBeans helps in this regard. To create a controller and link it up to the FXML file, simply right-click on an FXML file within the **Projects** explorer and select the **Make Controller** option. NetBeans will then create a blank controller class and will also add the `fx:controller` attribute into the FXML file automatically wiring the two together.

Graphical editing of FXML files

In the previous recipe, *Creating a JavaFX application,* we saw how to create JavaFX applications using both Java code and the more designer friendly FXML.

We saw that the basic editing facility for FXML files within NetBeans is not much more than a text editor. In this recipe, we'll see how to use the JavaFX Scene Builder to provide a first-rate design tool for JavaFX applications.

Scene Builder is Oracle's JavaFX visual layout tool and is available as a separate download from Java for Windows, Mac OS X, and Linux.

Getting ready

To complete this recipe, you'll need to have either the Java SE, or the Java EE version of NetBeans 8 installed together with a minimum of JDK 7u6 installed.

You will also need the application we developed in the previous recipe, *Creating a JavaFX application*. If you have not completed this recipe, the complete application is available within the code download bundle for this chapter.

How to do it...

Before starting, ensure that NetBeans is closed down so that integration with Scene Builder can be completed with the following steps:

1. To enable graphical editing of FXML files, we need to install Oracle's Scene Builder application. Scene Builder integrates seamlessly with NetBeans by allowing FXML files to be edited automatically when they are opened within NetBeans.

    For more information about Scene Builder, including early access to the next release, check out `http://www.oracle.com/technetwork/java/javase/downloads/javafxscenebuilder-info-2157684.html`.

2. Download JavaFX Scene Builder Version 2.0 from `http://www.oracle.com/technetwork/java/javase/downloads/sb2download-2177776.html`.

3. Run the installer to install the product. The installer should run through very quickly and install the product without asking for any user input.

4. Launch NetBeans and open the `WelcomeToFX` project.

5. Expand the **Source Packages** node and double-click on the `Greetings.fxml` file.

6. The file will now be opened automatically within Scene Builder instead of within NetBeans' text editor, as shown in the following screenshot:

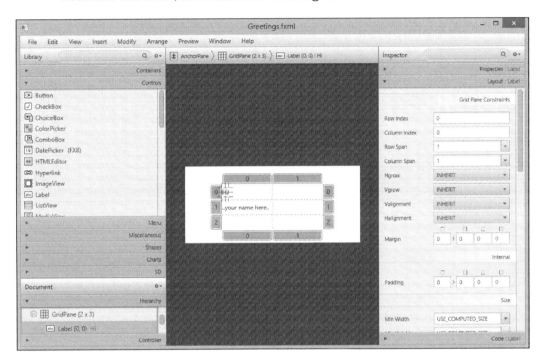

7. The FXML file can now be edited graphically in a similar fashion to editing Swing files within NetBeans. Since Scene Builder is working on the same file as NetBeans, when the file is saved in Scene Builder, it is automatically used when the application is executed in NetBeans.

How it works...

The standard installation of NetBeans allows FXML files to be edited within a text editor. When Oracle's Scene Builder product is installed, it sets up a reference to the installation location within NetBeans so that double-clicking on an FXML file opens the file within Scene Builder.

The location of Scene Builder is configured within NetBeans within the **Java** section of the **Options** window. Select **Tools** and then **Options** from the main menu to access the options window. From there, select the **Java** category and the **JavaFX** tab, as shown in the following screenshot:

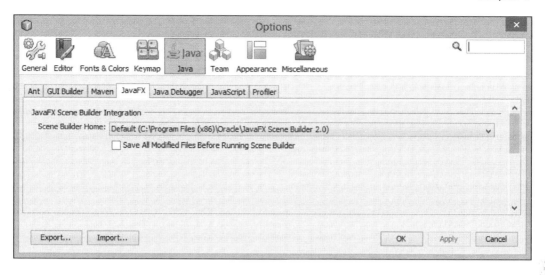

There's more...

When Scene Builder is installed and configured within NetBeans, it is still possible to edit FXML files directly within a text editor if required.

To edit a file directly within NetBeans, right-click on an FXML file and select the **Edit** option. Right-clicking on a file and selecting **Open** will perform the same action as double-clicking the file, that is, it will open the file within Scene Builder.

Styling a JavaFX application with CSS

One of the benefits of JavaFX applications is that their user interfaces can be designed rather than developed. This is typically a job done by a designer rather than a developer. As such, it's a good practice to place all of the application styling outside of Java code within a CSS file.

It's possible to style a JavaFX application within Java code by setting fonts and colors and layout padding (we saw an example of setting padding on elements within the *Creating a JavaFX application* recipe) within the Java code, but obviously, this makes it more difficult to make style changes to an application.

In this recipe, we'll see how we can apply CSS changes primarily to FXML files. We'll also show how CSS can be applied to Java files for those that are curious about how to do this.

Getting ready

To complete this recipe, you'll need to have either the Java SE, or the Java EE version of NetBeans 8 installed together with a minimum of JDK 7u6 installed.

You will also need the application we developed in the previous recipe, *Creating a JavaFX application*. If you have not completed this recipe, the complete application is available within the code download bundle for this chapter.

How to do it...

Ensure that NetBeans is open and that the `WelcomeToFX` project is loaded.

The first stage in styling an FXML file is to reference a style sheet that will contain all of the styling information with the following steps:

1. Right-click on the `Greetings.fxml` file and select **Edit** to open the file for editing within NetBeans rather than in Scene Builder (see the *Graphical editing of FXML files* recipe, for more details on installing Scene Builder).

2. To use CSS styling within an FXML file, we must reference the CSS file that we wish to use directly within the FXML file itself. Immediately before the `</AnchorPane>` tag, add the following code:

```
<stylesheets>
   <URL value="@style.css" />
</stylesheets>
```

3. This tells the runtime that the `style.css` file has got all the styling information for this FXML file. The @ prefix in front of the filename indicates that the `style.css` file is stored in the same location as the FXML file.

4. In order to use the URL tag, we need to add a reference to the appropriate Java library, namely `java.net.*`, as an `import` statement for the file.

5. Add the following `import` statement with the existing `import` statements at the top of the file:

```
<?import java.net.*?>
```

Now that we've referenced a style sheet, we need to define the style sheet and any associated styles within using the following steps:

1. Right-click on the `com.davidsalter.cookbook.welcometofx` package within the **Projects** explorer and select **New** and then **Other...**.

2. On the **New File** dialog, select **Other** from the list of **Categories** and **Cascading Style Sheet** from the list of **File Types**.

3. Click on **Next**.

4. Enter the **File Name** field as `style` and click on the **Finish** button to create the file.

5. The `style.css` file should be automatically opened within NetBeans for editing.

6. The first styling we are going to add is a background color to the window. Add the following into the CSS file:

```
.root {
    -fx-background-color:  linear-gradient(blue, gray);
}
```

7. This style sets the background color to be a linear gradient between the colors blue and gray. You can see that the selector is prefixed with . indicating that the style is for the root class rather than for an object with an ID of `root`.

 The `.root` style, as its name suggests, is applied to the root node of the Scene class's instance. As all the controls within a Scene class are stored in a hierarchy underneath the root node, any styles applied to the `.root` class are automatically applied to all controls within the form. The `.root` class is therefore a good place to add any styles that are consistent across all objects on a form.

8. Let's now add a style to all labels on the form. Add the following code to the end of the `style.css` file:

```
.label {
    -fx-font-size: 20px;
    -fx-text-fill: yellow;
}
```

9. As with the previous style, the style is prefixed with . indicating, in this case, that all elements of the `label` class are to have a font size of 20 pixels and are to be displayed in yellow.

10. Let's now override that rule for the `name` field that we have on the form. Add the following style to the end of the `style.css` file:

```
#name {
    -fx-font-size: 30px;
}
```

11. You can see that this selector is different from the previous selectors that we defined, as it begins with a # prefix instead of a . prefix. This indicates that the style should be applied only to objects that have `fx:id` of `name`. In our case, this is the label that displays the user's name.

At this point, you may be wondering how you can find out the names of all the CSS styles that can be applied to nodes within JavaFX. Well, you can get a full CSS reference guide from Oracle at `http://docs.oracle.com/javafx/2/api/javafx/scene/doc-files/cssref.html`.

12. Now that we've made some changes to CSS, let's run the application and see how it's been styled. Press *F6* to run the application. Enter a name and click on the **Say Hello** button. The resultant window should look something like the following screenshot:

So far we've seen how to style FXML files using CSS. Remember that we said we'd take a look at how to style Java-coded windows as well? We'll do it with the following steps:

1. Double-click on the `WelcomeToFX.java` file within the **Projects** explorer to open it for editing.

2. Within the `start()` method, add the following code immediately before the call to `primaryStage.show()`:

```
scene.getStylesheets().add(WelcomeToFX.class.
getResource("style.css").toExternalForm());
```

3. This line loads the style sheet file from the classpath and registers it for use against the `Scene` class.

 When using Java code instead of FXML to define user interfaces, you can still use all the same CSS selectors for style definition. A `Label` tag is a `Label` tag irrespective of whether it's defined in FXML or Java code.

When using Java code, however, we use the `.setId()` method to set a node's ID (in FXML, we use the `fx:id` attribute).

So, to set the ID of `nameLabel`, we would code this as:

```
nameLabel.setId("name");
```

4. Save the file and press *F6* to run the application. The first window should look something like the following screenshot:

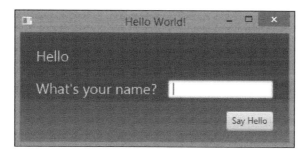

How it works...

Cascading style sheets are the standard way of defining web page and web application styling on the Internet. CSS is also the way to style JavaFX applications. Each scene can have one or more style sheets associated with it, which can then be referenced from FXML or from within the Java code.

Creating and using a JavaFX custom control

Like any good component-based framework, JavaFX allows developers to create custom components that can be used within the developer tools just like any of the built-in components.

In this recipe, we'll see how to create a custom JavaFX component and then see how it can be used from within Java code and also from within FXML. The custom component will be a text string and an input box that can be repeatedly used for asking for a single piece of information. The custom component will look like the following screenshot:

Getting ready

To complete this recipe, you'll need to have either the Java SE, or the Java EE version of NetBeans 8 installed together with a minimum of JDK 7u6 installed.

How to do it...

Before creating a custom component, let's create a basic JavaFX application so that we can host the component we are going to create with the following steps:

1. Create a new empty JavaFX Application with the following details:

    ❑ **Project Name**: FXCustomComponent

    ❑ **Create Application Class**: com.davidsalter.cookbook.fxcomponent. FXCustomComponent

 If you're having trouble creating a JavaFX application, see the *Creating a JavaFX application* recipe earlier in this chapter.

2. Custom components are typically written in FXML; so, let's now create an FXML page with a controller that can represent the custom control. Right-click on the **Source Packages** node of the FXCustomComponent project and select **New** and then **Other...**.

3. On the **New File** dialog, select **JavaFX** from the list of **Categories** and **Empty FXML** from the list of **File Types**.

4. Click on **Next**.

5. Enter the **FXML Name** field as CustomInput and the **Package** field as com. davidsalter.cookbook.fxcomponent.custom.

6. Click on **Next**.

7. Check the **Use Java Controller** checkbox and change the **Controller Name** field to be CustomInput.

 We've changed the name of the controller from the default naming scheme of <fxml>Controller to CustomInput (without the appended word Controller) as CustomInput will now be the name of our custom control. We don't have to do this, but CustomInput is a better name for a custom control than CustomInputController.

8. Click on **Finish** to create the FXML file and its controller.

9. We now want to edit the FXML file textually in NetBeans, so right-click on the CustomInput.fxml file and select **Edit**.

 If you don't have Scene Builder installed, you can simply double-click on the file to open it up in NetBeans. See the recipe, *Graphical editing of FXML files*, for further information about Scene Builder.

10. Change the contents of the `CustomInput.fxml` file to read:

```
<?xml version="1.0" encoding="UTF-8"?>

<?import javafx.geometry.*?>
<?import javafx.scene.control.*?>
<?import javafx.scene.layout.*?>

<fx:root type="javafx.scene.layout.HBox" alignment="CENTER"
xmlns:fx="http://javafx.com/fxml/1"
xmlns="http://javafx.com/javafx/2.2" >
  <children>
    <Label fx:id="label" text="Label" HBox.hgrow="ALWAYS">
      <HBox.margin>
        <Insets right="8.0" />
      </HBox.margin>
    </Label>
    <TextField fx:id="text" prefWidth="100.0" />
  </children>
  <padding>
    <Insets bottom="8.0" left="8.0" right="8.0"
    top="8.0" />
  </padding>
</fx:root>
```

11. This FXML file is very similar to those that we've seen before. We can see that there is a `Label` and `TextField` tags each of which have an `fx:id` attribute of `label` and `text` respectively. There is also a small amount of padding applied to the control to space the individual components out and make them more readable. What's new, however, is that the root node of the FXML file is now `<fx:root>` instead of a layout type. The `<fx:root>` tag is used when creating custom controls to set the root component of the control hierarchy directly via code. This allows us to explicitly set the controller of the component.

12. You'll also notice that we aren't setting the controller within the FXML file. This is because we're going to set the controller for the custom component within the Java code in the next step.

If we set the controller within the FXML file, bad things happen! Try it for yourself and see by adding an `fx:controller` attribute to the `fx:root` element.

When loading the FXML file, JavaFX would detect the presence of a controller class and try to instantiate it. This would then cause the FXML file to be loaded, at which point JavaFX would detect the presence of a controller class and try to instantiate it repeatedly.

13. Double-click on the `CustomInput.java` file to open it up for editing and change the body of the class to be:

```java
public class CustomInput extends HBox {

    @FXML private Label label;
    @FXML private TextField text;

    public CustomInput() {
        FXMLLoader loader = new FXMLLoader(
        getClass().getResource("CustomInput.fxml"));
        loader.setRoot(this);
        loader.setController(this);

        try {
            loader.load();
        } catch (IOException ex) {
            Logger.getLogger(CustomInput.class.getName()).
            log(Level.SEVERE, null, ex);
            throw new RuntimeException(ex);
        }
    }

    public String getLabel() {
        return labelProperty().get();
    }
    public void setLabel(String value) {
        labelProperty().set(value);
    }

    public StringProperty labelProperty() {
        return label.textProperty();
    }

    public String getText() {
        return textProperty().get();
    }
    public void setText(String value) {
        textProperty().set(value);
    }

    public StringProperty textProperty() {
        return text.textProperty();
    }
}
```

14. Looking at this code, we can again see a lot of similarities with the code that we've written before. We've created two private instance members of `Label` and `TextField` tags and annotated them with the `@FXML` annotation. This provides the link between the objects declared within the FXML file and the Java code that backs them. We've also created a constructor for the class that loads the FXML file and then sets the class as the controller and the root of the custom component. This is essential for creating custom components.

15. Each of the members that we've created on the form has an associated `StringProperty` property defined for it. These use the JavaBean technique for creating properties so that the custom component can be queried by reflection and a list of its properties obtained. This allows code completion and Javadoc tooltips to be displayed when using the custom control at a later date.

16. The final thing to note about this class is that it extends the `HBox` class as the default layout for the control. This ties in with the default layout that we defined within the root component of the `CustomInput.fxml` file:

```
<fx:root type="javafx.scene.layout.HBox"
```

Now that we've done everything necessary to create a custom control, let's see how we can access it from within the Java code.

 If you want to learn more about JavaFX programming, check out the Oracle JavaFX tutorials at `http://docs.oracle.com/javase/8/javase-clienttechnologies.htm`.

17. Double-click on the `FXCustomComponent.java` file from within the **Projects** explorer to open the file for editing.

18. At the top of the `start()` method, create an instance of the `CustomInput` control we have just defined:

```
CustomInput input = new CustomInput();
input.setLabel("What is your name?");
```

19. Change the root component to be `VBox` instead of `StackPanel` and add the new input component into it:

```
VBox root = new VBox();
root.setAlignment(Pos.CENTER);
root.getChildren().add(input);
root.getChildren().add(btn);
```

20. Finally, change the button event handler to print out the contents of the textbox in the custom control. Change the event handler to read:

```
@Override
public void handle(ActionEvent event) {
    System.out.println(input.getText());
}
```

21. Fix the imports on the `FXCustomComponent.java` class and then press *F6* to run the application. The application should look something like the following screenshot:

22. Enter a name and then click on the **Say 'Hello World'** button and note that the inputted name is displayed in the NetBeans output window.

There's more...

In the previous section, we saw how to instantiate a custom component within the Java code, but what if we want to instantiate it via FXML?

To instantiate a custom control within FXML, we just need to create a tag with the name of the custom control and then set properties on it just like any other control. For example, the code we wrote in step 19 of the preceding list would be like the following code within FXML:

```
<VBox>
  <children>
    <CustomInput label="What is your name"></CustomLabel>
    <Button …> </Button>
  </children>
</VBox>
```

What if we wanted to style a custom control? Can we do that? We certainly can! We can use exactly the same techniques that we used in the recipe, *Styling a JavaFX application with CSS*, to style custom components. This is where multiple style sheets would come in particularly useful as we could use one style sheet for the basic, stock custom component styling, and then have a separate one for each application or scene within our application.

Deploying a self-contained application

As we've seen in the previous recipes in this chapter, NetBeans, in conjunction with Scene Builder provides first-rate tools for developing JavaFX applications. Developing applications is only one stage in the development cycle, and we need to be able to deploy our applications to customers after they have been developed.

NetBeans provides tools to allow JavaFX applications to be packaged as self-contained applications that include any libraries used by the application as well as a complete copy of the JRE used for development. Self-contained applications can be packaged with native installers and easily distributed to customers.

In this recipe, we'll see how we can create a self-contained application and package it up for installation using **Inno Setup** from JR Software.

This recipe is primarily aimed at developers using Windows as their operating system; however, NetBeans provides tools for Mac OS X and Linux developers as discussed at the end of the recipe.

Getting ready

To complete this recipe, you'll need to have either the Java SE, or the Java EE version of NetBeans 8 installed together with a minimum of JDK 7u6 installed.

You will also need the application we developed in the previous recipe, *Styling a JavaFX application with CSS*. If you have not completed this recipe, the complete application is available within the code download bundle for this chapter.

How to do it...

Ensure that NetBeans is not loaded as we need to make changes to the system's path environment variable. If we make changes to this while NetBeans is running, the changes will not take effect within NetBeans.

1. Download the Inno Setup installer from `http://www.jrsoftware.org` and install it onto your development PC. Inno Setup is a free installer for Windows applications that can be used in both open source and commercial applications. We'll not go into details about how to use Inno Setup here as that could take a entire book on its own. Fortunately, NetBeans takes care of all of the interaction with Inno Setup for us.

2. Once Inno Setup has been installed, we need to add the path to the Inno Setup installation folder to our path. Access the environment variables for your system, as shown in the following screenshot:

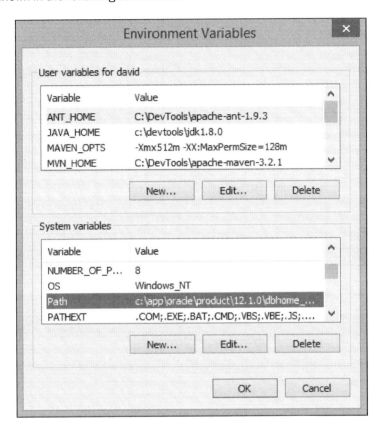

3. Once you have accessed the environment variables, amend the `Path` system variable and append the installation directory of Inno Setup to it. This is usually `C:\Program Files (x86)\Inno Setup 5`, as shown in the following screenshot:

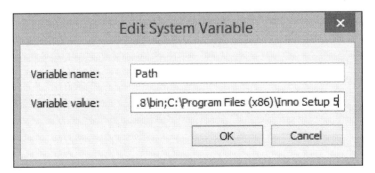

4. Once we've amended the `Path` environment variable, we can start NetBeans and open the `WelcomeToFX` project.

5. The first step to creating a self-contained application is to enable native packaging. Right-click on the `WelcomeToFX` project within the **Projects** explorer and select **Properties**.

6. On the **Project Properties** window, select **Deployment** from the list of **Categories** and check the **Enable Native Packaging** option, as shown in the following screenshot:

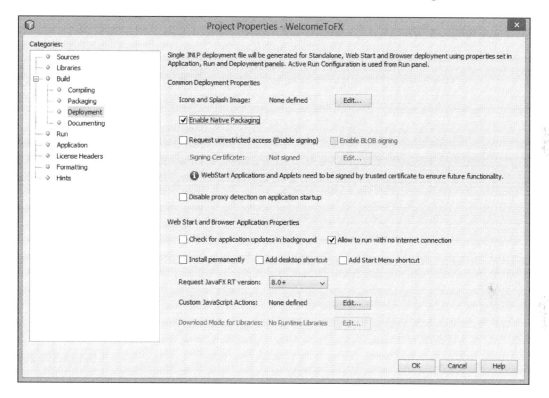

7. Before creating a self-contained application, let's first give the application a name and an author.

8. Within the **Project Properties** window, select **Application** from the list of **Categories**.

9. Change the **Title** field to be `Welcome To JavaFx` and the **Vendor** field to be `David Salter`. These fields will now be used as the application name and start screen group name within Windows.

10. Click on **OK** to enable NetBeans to create native packages for the application.

11. Right-click on the `WelcomeToFX` project within the **Projects** explorer and note that a new menu item **Package as** is now available, as shown in the following screenshot:

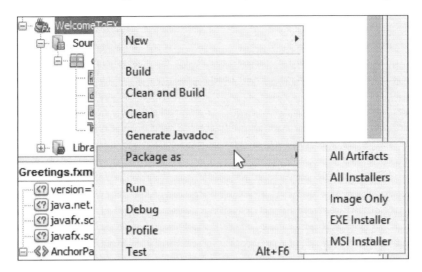

12. Within this menu, there are several different options:

- **All Artifacts**: Create all installation packages as well as the application distributable files
- **All Installers**: Create both an MSI installer package and a `.exe` installer package
- **Image Only**: Create the distributable files, but do not create any installers
- **EXE Installer**: Create a `.exe` installer only using Inno Setup
- **MSI Installer**: Create a `.msi` installer only using Wix

13. First, let's create an **Image Only** package. From the **Package as** menu, select the **Image Only** option.

14. NetBeans will now create an image only package, which is one without any installers. When the package is created, a **BUILD SUCCESSFUL** message will be shown within the **Output** window, as shown in the following screenshot:

```
jfx-build-native:
BUILD SUCCESSFUL (total time: 4 seconds)
```

15. Click on the **Files** explorer to show all the files within the project and expand the `bundles` node under the `dist` folder, as shown in the following screenshot:

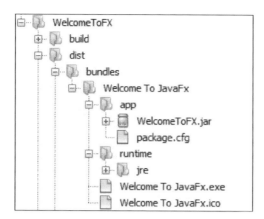

16. Within the `bundles` folder under the `dist` folder, you can see there is a folder for the application called `Welcome to JavaFx`. Inside that folder, there is a folder called `app` that contains the compiled version of our application as a `.jar` file. The runtime folder contains a complete JRE copied from our development machine—this is the same JRE that we used when running the application during development so it's guaranteed to be the correct version. You can also see that a native `.exe` file has been created along with an icon for the file.

17. Browse to this folder yourself in Windows Explorer and launch the `.exe` file to verify that the application will now run as a native `.exe` file.

    Now that we've seen that NetBeans is capable of creating a self-contained application from a JavaFX project, let's create an installer for the application.

18. Right-click on the `WelcomeToFX` project within the **Projects** explorer and select **Package as** and **EXE Installer**.

19. This time, the build process will take a little longer as it's building an installation package using Inno Setup.

20. When the build is completed, expand the `bundles` node under the `dist` folder for the `WelcomeToFX` project within the **Files** explorer, as shown in the following screenshot:

21. This time, we can see that there is only a single file within the `bundles` folder. This time, it's a `.exe` installer for the application. Locate the `Welcome To JavaFx-1.0.exe` file within Windows Explorer and double-click on it to install a copy of the application. Verify again that it's the application we developed earlier and that a link to the application has been added to the Windows Start screen, as shown in the following screenshot:

There's more...

What if I want to create a `.msi` installer instead of a `.exe` installer? Can I do that?

NetBeans allows `.msi` installers to be created via the Wix installer package. To create `.msi` packages, therefore, we need to follow a similar procedure to that above. We need to download and install Wix and then set the system's `Path` environment variable to have an entry for Wix in it. Typically, Wix is installed into the `C:\Program Files (x86)\Wix Toolset v3.8\bin` directory.

For more information about Wix, check out the `http://wixtoolset.org` site.

Once installed, the application uses the default Java logo as its icon. Can I apply my own branding to the installer? The application's icon can easily be changed via **Deployment** in the **Project Properties** window. Here, you can change the application's icon and splash screen image to those more suitable for your application. The following screenshot displays the **Icon and Splash Image** dialog:

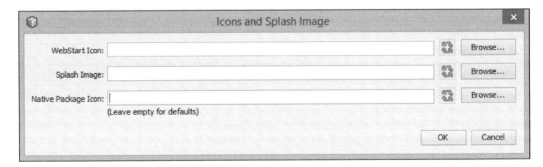

I don't use Windows for developing JavaFX applications. I use Mac OS X and/or Linux. Does NetBeans provide any tools for me?

On Mac OS X, NetBeans provides the facility to create `.dmg` packages instead of `.exe`/`.msi` packages. On Linux, the ability to create `.deb` packages is available.

8
NetBeans Mobile Development

In this chapter, we will cover the following recipes:

- ► Adding mobile support to NetBeans
- ► Creating an MIDP application
- ► Adding Android support to NetBeans
- ► Creating an Android application

Introduction

With the advent of smartphones and tablets, mobile development has had a renaissance. You just need to look at the number of mobile applications that are available for the major smartphones and feature phones to see how popular mobile development is.

It's not only on mobile phones and tablets that Java ME is used. It's also one of the major players in embedded technology (running on devices such as Raspberry Pi), in Blu-ray players, TVs, and smart cards.

In this chapter, we'll see how we can add mobile support to NetBeans so that we can develop applications for these types of devices. In particular, we'll look at creating applications for **Mobile Information Device Profile** (**MIDP**) and Android devices.

Adding mobile support to NetBeans

NetBeans 8 is not provided in a downloadable configuration that is explicitly available for the mobile application developer. The nearest preconfigured download is the **All** bundle, which includes all of the NetBeans tools ranging from those for the mobile developer to all of the tools required for an enterprise developer. Clearly, there's a need for the mobile developer to be able to install only the plugins they require without the need for additional unnecessary plugins.

Fortunately, it's a straightforward task to add mobile development support to the smallest NetBeans distribution—the Java SE download, as shown in this recipe.

Getting ready

To complete this recipe, you need to have downloaded and installed either the Java SE or Java EE download bundles of NetBeans.

How to do it...

The first step in adding mobile development support into NetBeans is to download a suitable Java ME SDK. Let's now download the Java ME 3.4 SDK and configure it within NetBeans using the following steps:

1. Browse to the Java ME download page and download the Java ME SDK 3.4.

    The Java ME download page can be found at `http://www.oracle.com/technetwork/java/javame/javamobile/download/sdk/index.html`.

2. Once the Java ME SDK has been downloaded, execute the setup application and install it in a location of your choice. The only option during installation is to choose the location in which you want to install the SDK. Take a note of this directory as we will need it later on.

3. After installing the Java ME SDK, launch NetBeans so that we can configure mobile development support.

4. Click on **Tools** and then **Plugins** from the main NetBeans menu.

5. Within the **Plugins** dialog, click on the **Available Plugins** tab.

6. Within this tab, locate the **Mobility** and **Visual Mobile Designer** plugins and select them for installation, as shown in the following screenshot:

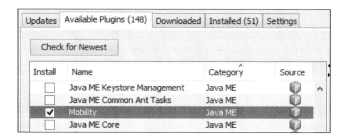

7. Click on the **Install** button to begin the installation process for the plugins. NetBeans will now identify the plugin dependencies and mark them also for installation.

8. Click on **Next** to display the license agreement for the new plugins.

9. Read and accept the license agreement, and then click on **Install** to add the Mobility plugins into NetBeans.

10. NetBeans will now need to restart to complete the installation. Click on **Finish** to restart NetBeans.

NetBeans will now restart with the Mobility plugins installed. We now need to add a reference to the Java ME SDK in NetBeans so that we can create Java ME applications, with the following steps:

1. Click on **Tools** and then **Java Platforms** from the main NetBeans menu.

2. The **Java Platform Manager** dialog will be displayed, showing that only the Java SE platform is installed.

3. Click on the **Add Platform...** button to allow a Java ME platform to be added.

4. In the **Add Java Platform** dialog, select the platform type as **Java ME CLDC Platform Emulator**, as shown in the following screenshot:

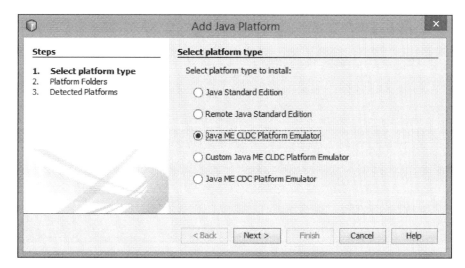

5. Click on **Next**.

6. NetBeans will now display the **Choose directory to search for platforms** dialog. Select the directory in which you installed the Java ME SDK in step 2 and click on the **Open** button.

7. NetBeans will confirm the folder selection. Click on **Next** to begin searching for Java ME platforms in the specified directory.

8. NetBeans will now take a few seconds to search within the specified folder for Java ME SDK installations. When a platform is detected, it will be displayed, providing details of the platform, as shown in the following screenshot:

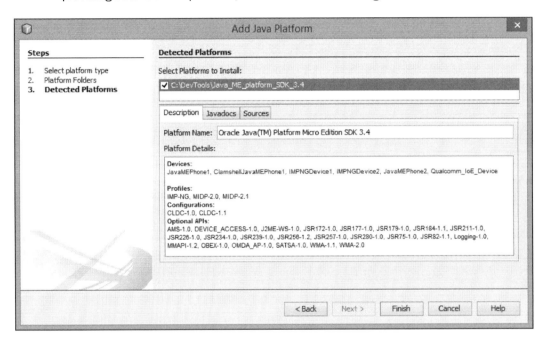

9. Click on **Finish** to add the Java ME platform.

10. The **Java Platform Manager** dialog will now show the newly added Java ME platform:

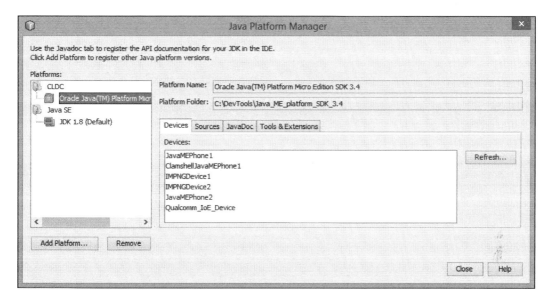

11. Click on the **Close** button to complete the procedure.

How it works...

Adding support for Java ME development in NetBeans was a three-stage process. First, we had to download an appropriate Java ME SDK. For this recipe, we downloaded the Java ME 3.4 SDK. We then added support for mobile development into NetBeans by adding the Mobility plugin. This plugin is hosted on the standard NetBeans update centers, so it could be easily installed without any additional configuration.

When the Mobility plugins were installed, they provided the ability within NetBeans to add a Java ME CLDC Platform Emulator. Without these plugins, we would only have been able to define Java SE 8 platforms within NetBeans. These plugins also provide us with all of the wizards necessary to create Java ME applications. We'll see more of those in the next recipe.

There's more...

What if we want to develop applications for a different mobile platform, for example, Nokia's Asha range of phones?

Developing for a different mobile SDK requires many of the same steps as shown in this recipe. Crucially though, we would need to download the appropriate mobile SDK (for the Asha, for example) and install that locally on our PC. After installing the SDK, we would need to add it as a platform within NetBeans, as shown in this recipe. After this, we could start developing mobile applications for the platform.

Creating an MIDP application

In this recipe, we will use the MIDP as the profile for a mobile application.

MIDP is the best-known Java ME profile, and provides core functionality that will run across many devices, giving applications more portability.

Getting ready

To complete this recipe, you will need to run NetBeans 8 with added mobile support. If you have not added mobile support in NetBeans, check out the previous recipe.

How to do it...

First, we must create a new Java ME project with the following steps:

1. Click on **File** and then **New Project...** from the main application menu.

2. In the **New Project** dialog, select **Java ME** from the list of **Categories** and **Mobile Application** from the list of **Projects**.

3. Enter in the **Project Name** field `MyMIDPApp`. Leave the other options with their default values and click on **Next**.

4. Select **Oracle Java(TM) Platform Micro Edition SDK 3.4** as **Emulator Platform**. The **Device**, **Device Configuration**, and **Device Profile** fields can be changed here, but the defaults are suitable in this instance, as shown in the following screenshot:

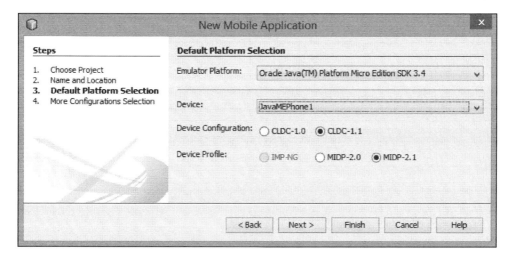

5. Click on **Finish** to create the application.

How it works...

The folder structure created by NetBeans for a Java ME project is rather extensive.
The project is created with an **Ant build file**, which already includes several targets.
On top of that, the `.properties` files are created for the convenience of the developer.

To have access to all of the files shown in the following screenshot, it is necessary to build the project. To do this, right-click on the project and select **Build**.

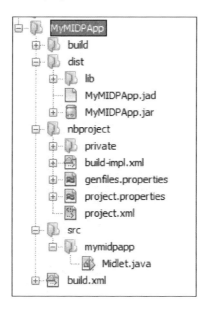

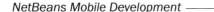

NetBeans then creates the `Midlet.java` file, which is our main class for developing with Java ME.

It is possible to edit the code in a MIDlet Java file in different ways.

If a MIDlet is created as a plain Java class, it can only be edited in the **Source** view. However, if a **Visual MIDlet** class is created, it can be edited in the **Source**, **Screen**, **Flow**, and **Analyzer** views. A Visual MIDlet is created by selecting **Visual MIDlet** from the **File Types** list when creating a file. A plain Java MIDlet is created by default when a Java ME project is created. Visual MIDlet editing is provided by the Visual MIDlet designer plugin. The different views for editing a Visual MIDlet are as follows:

- ▶ **Source**: This is where the developer can write the code. By clicking on it, the view changes to the Java code editor, where it is possible to see the code generated by NetBeans (the grayed-out and commented parts) and the user-editable code. This is very similar to editing Swing-generated code.

- ▶ **Screen**: This allows the developer to build the UI graphically by dragging-and-dropping components from the **Palette** window—much like creating a Swing or JavaFX user interface.

- ▶ **Flow**: This lets the developer create and build the flow between windows and add behaviors, in the form of commands, to the components from the **Palette** window. This is shown in a very user-friendly and graphical way to the developer, and is very similar to UML diagrams.

- ▶ **Analyzer**: Since every bit of memory counts in mobile applications, this view is responsible for analyzing the code for unused components, screens, or resources that might be left on our mobile device.

To run a mobile application, simply right-click on the project and select **Run**. The appropriate mobile emulator will launch with the application running within it.

There's more...

On project creation, we can select the device we are designing our application for and will be deploying it on.

The device can be selected at project creation time on the **Default Platform Selection** page within the **New Mobile Application** wizard.

On an existing project, the target device can be changed within the project's properties window with the following steps:

1. Right-click on the project within the **Projects** explorer and select **Properties**.

2. Click on **Platform** from within the **Category** list, and the list of available devices is shown under the **Device** dropdown, as shown in the following screenshot:

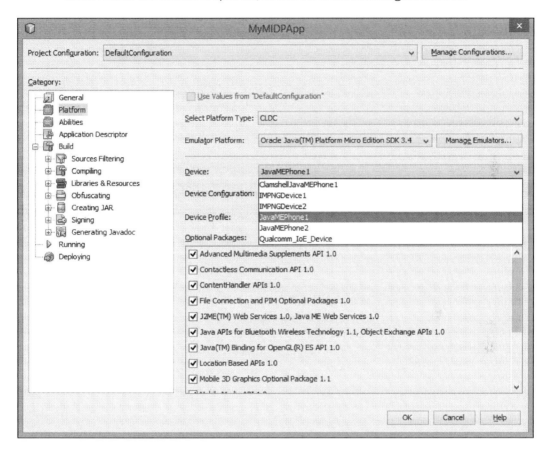

The function of **Optional Packages** selected in the preceding screenshot is to enable features in the Java ME application that would otherwise not be supported. For example, the `ContentHandler` API lets applications execute other registered applications by a URL.

To learn more about the available APIs within Java ME, please refer to `http://docs.oracle.com/javame`.

Alternatively, when testing, it is possible to select the device prior to running the application. Right-click on the project node and select **Run With...**, and you will be presented with the **Quick Project Run** dialog:

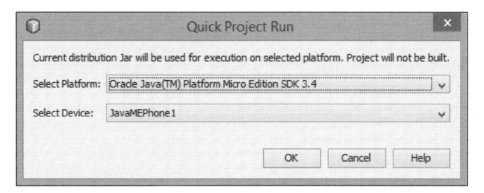

Adding Android support to NetBeans

The Android platform is one of the most popular smartphone and tablet platforms to develop for at the moment.

Developed by Google, the Android platform contains many different APIs, both inside and outside of the Google ecosphere. For example, Android provides location services and can also be integrated with Google Maps.

Fortunately (for the Java developer), Android applications are written in Java, which is then compiled into Android's proprietary bytecode to run on the Dalvik virtual machine (instead of the usual Java Virtual Machine that Java developers are used to).

For more information about Android and Android development, check out `http://www.android.com` and `http://developer.android.com`.

Since Android applications are essentially written in Java, we can install a plugin called **NBAndroid** to allow us to develop and test Android applications, all from within NetBeans. For more information about NBAndroid, check out the website at `http://www.nbandroid.org`.

Getting ready

To complete this recipe and enable Android support within NetBeans, we need to have either the Java SE, Java EE, or All bundle of NetBeans 8 installed. We also need to have downloaded and installed the Android SDK.

The Android SDK can be downloaded from `http://developer.android.com/sdk/index.html`.

How to do it...

1. The NBAndroid project is not distributed via the standard NetBeans Update Centers, so we need to add the NBAndroid Update Center into NetBeans. Click on **Tools** and then **Plugins** from the main NetBeans menu.

2. Click on the **Settings** tab, and then click on the **Add** button to add a new Update Center.

3. Enter the **Name** field as NBAndroid and the **URL** field as http://nbandroid. org/updates/updates.xml, as shown in the following screenshot:

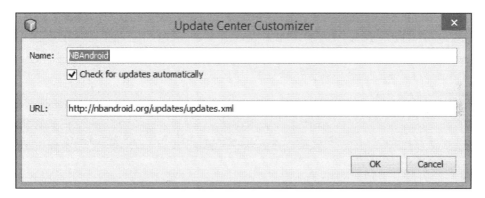

4. Click on **OK** to add the Update Center.

5. Click on the **Available Plugins** tab and select **Android** from the list of available plugins, as shown in the following screenshot:

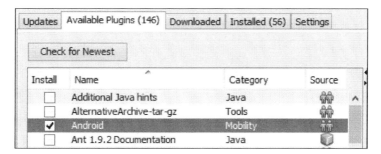

6. Click on **Install** to install the NBAndroid plugin.

7. The **NetBeans IDE Installer** dialog will now be shown, confirming that the Android plugin is being installed. Click on **Next**.

8. Read the license agreement, and if you agree to it, click on the **I accept the terms in all of the license agreements** checkbox and then click on **Install** to continue.

9. Click on **Close** on the **Plugins** dialog to complete the installation process for the NBAndroid plugin.

Now that we've installed the NBAndroid plugin into NetBeans, we need to configure it so that we can develop Android applications. We can achieve this with the following steps:

1. Click on **Tools** and then **Options** from the main NetBeans menu.

2. On the **Options** dialog, click on the **Miscellaneous** option and then on the **Android** tab.

3. Enter the location for your Android SDK under the **SDK Location** field, as shown in the following screenshot:

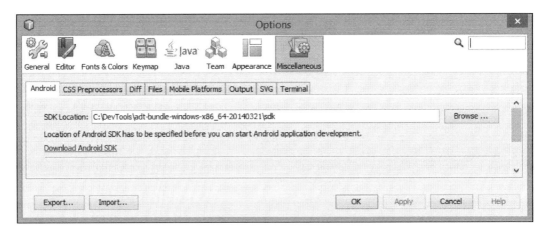

4. Click on **OK** to complete the configuration of the Android SDK.

How it works...

In this recipe, we added a custom Update Center in NetBeans, allowing us to install the NBAndroid plugin and, therefore, Android developer support in NetBeans.

The NBAndroid plugin allows us to specify an Android SDK to use when developing applications. The plugin provides wizards that can be used for creating Android applications (we'll see those in the next recipe) and enhances the XML text editors when editing Android XML files.

When developing for Android, different versions of the Android SDK can be configured using the Android SDK Manager (SDK Manager.exe) application. These can then be selected via the project's properties dialog in NetBeans as the target SDK for applications, as shown in the following screenshot:

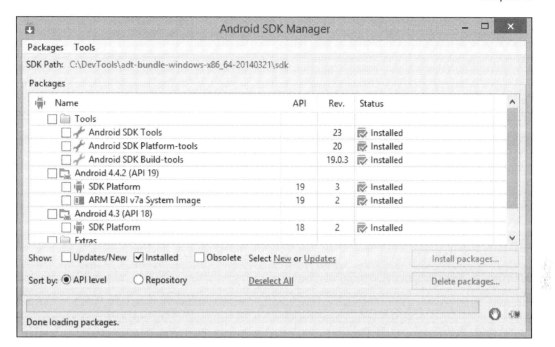

There's more...

The NBAndroid plugin that we've seen so far is provided free of charge and provides facilities for creating Android applications within NetBeans.

An additional plugin called **NBAndroid Extensions** is also available from the NBAndroid project. This plugin is available on a subscription basis, but provides additional facilities for NetBeans developers, the most important being the ability to provide a GUI layout preview.

For more information on this additional plugin, check out
`http://nbandroid.org/wiki/index.php/NBAndroid-ext`.

Creating an Android application

In this recipe, we'll see how we can use the NBAndroid plugin to create a basic Android application.

Getting ready

To complete this recipe, you'll need to use any version of NetBeans 8. You'll need to have downloaded and configured the Android SDK on your machine. Finally, you'll need to have installed the NBAndroid plugin as described in the previous recipe.

How to do it...

To create an Android application, perform the following steps:

1. Click on **File** and then on **New Project...** from the main NetBeans menu.

2. Select **Android** from the list of **Categories** and **Android Project** from the list of **Projects**.

3. Click on **Next**.

4. On the **New Android Application** dialog, enter the **Project Name** field as `HelloAndroid`, and the **Package Name** field as `com.davidsalter.cookbook. android`.

5. Select the latest Android platform within the list of platforms (**Android 4.2.2**, as shown in the following screenshot).

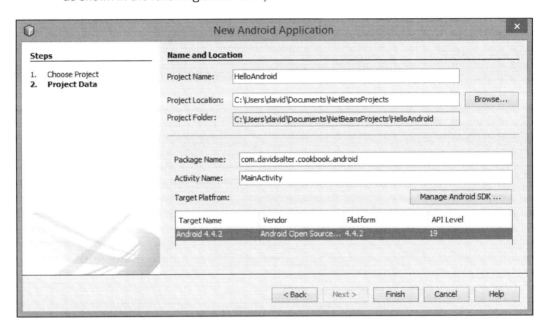

6. Click on **Finish** to create the application.

7. Double-click on the `main.xml` file located under `HelloAndroid\res\layout` to open it up for editing. This file contains the definition of the screen layout of the application.

8. Change the `TextView` node to the following code:

```
<TextView
    android:layout_width="fill_parent"
    android:layout_height="wrap_content"
    android:text="NetBeans Rocks !!"
/>
```

9. Right-click on the `HelloAndroid` project and select **Run** to start the Android emulator and launch the application within it. The resultant dialog will look like the following screenshot:

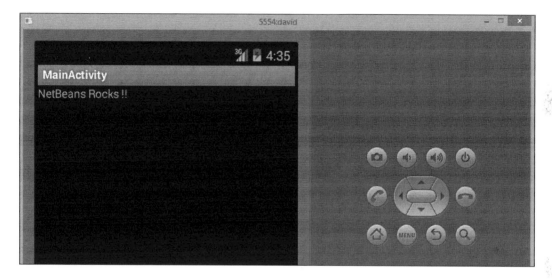

How it works...

In this recipe, we saw how the NBAndroid provides Android application support within NetBeans, allowing Android applications to be created.

For more information on how to develop for the Android platform, check out `http://developer.android.com`.

9
Version Control

In this chapter, we will cover the following recipes:

- ▶ Initializing a Git repository
- ▶ Cloning a Git repository
- ▶ Checking out from a Subversion repository
- ▶ Getting the history of a file
- ▶ Committing and pushing code changes
- ▶ Creating a Diff patch
- ▶ Branching a repository

Introduction

With all but the smallest projects, good source code management is essential. Source code management allows multiple developers to work together on projects whether they are working on the same piece of functionality or completely disparate parts of the system.

Probably, the most common source code control system at present is Git. Within this chapter, we'll see how we can manage Git repositories from within NetBeans allowing us to perform all of the common version control actions such as branching, committing, and merging.

Don't worry, though, if you don't use Git—this chapter includes recipes for Mercurial, Subversion, and CVS as well. To aid developers switch between different version control systems, NetBeans has been developed so that all the included version control functionality is very similar, if not the same across systems. So, for example, if you know how to check a file into Subversion within NetBeans, you know how to check it into Git.

Initializing a Git repository

Initializing a Git repository is often one of the first tasks that is performed when starting a new project. Initializing a repository creates the local repository and allows local source control actions to be performed such as checking in code and viewing a file's history.

In this recipe, we'll see how NetBeans allows us to initialize a Git repository for a specific project and how this gives us benefits over using the Git command-line tools.

Getting ready

You can use any of the Java download bundles of NetBeans (Java SE, Java EE, or the All bundle) to complete this recipe as they all have Git support built into NetBeans.

We will be initializing the `JarViewer` project that we created in *Chapter 4, Developing Desktop Applications with NetBeans*, so if you did not complete the recipes in that chapter, you will need to locate the `JarViewer` project from the code download bundle for this book.

How to do it...

To initialize a Git repository, perform the following steps:

1. Right-click on the `JarViewer` project within the **Projects** explorer and click on **Versioning** and **Initialize Git Repository...**.

2. The **Initialize a Git Repository** dialog will now be shown confirming the root path that the repository will be created in, as shown in the following screenshot:

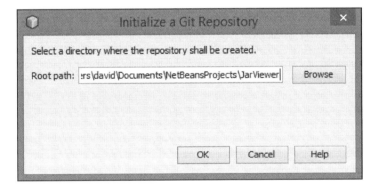

3. Click on the **OK** button to initialize the repository.

How it works...

Initializing a Git repository within NetBeans performs two tasks:

- ► Initializing the repository
- ► Adding the initial project files to the newly created repository

Initializing the repository is the same as executing the `git init` command from a command line within the root folder of the project. This command creates a local Git repository within the project files and creates a hidden folder called `.git` in which all of the repository files are stored. This folder is not visible from within NetBeans. If, however, we open up Windows Explorer (or Finder on the Mac), we can see that this folder has been created, as shown in the following screenshot:

Name	Date modified	Type
.git	03/06/2014 22:18	File folder
build	03/06/2014 22:18	File folder
dist	03/06/2014 22:18	File folder
nbproject	03/06/2014 22:18	File folder
src	03/06/2014 22:18	File folder
build.xml	03/06/2014 22:18	XML File
manifest.mf	03/06/2014 22:18	MF File

The second stage of initializing the repository within NetBeans is to add all of the project files into the repository. This is the equivalent of using the `git add` command.

When adding a project into a new Git repository through the **Initialize Git Repository** option, NetBeans only adds source files into the project. Any private files, or build-related files are not added for inclusion into the repository. This is one of the major benefits of initializing a repository this way over initializing and adding files manually using the `git` command.

After a project has been initialized within Git, different color codes and icons are displayed within the **Projects** explorer to show the status of files.

Newly added folders that have not been committed have a cylindrical icon (▣) next to them to indicate that they contain newly added files. Newly added files themselves are displayed in green. Files that have been excluded from the repository, for example, build files are displayed in gray, as shown in the following screenshot:

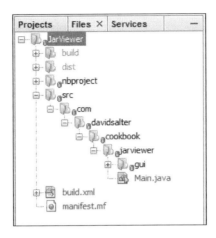

We'll make changes to the files within this project in the subsequent recipes in this chapter and see how the icons change when we delete or modify files.

There's more...

In many respects, Mercurial and Git are similar source code control systems, although in recent years, Git has become the more popular of the two. NetBeans, however, provides tools to allow Mercurial repositories to be initialized in a similar fashion to Git repositories.

Initializing a Mercurial repository

To initialize a Mercurial repository, however, the Mercurial tools need to be first installed onto your computer. If you've not got the Mercurial tools installed, you can download them from `http://mercurial.selenic.com`.

A quick way to check if you have the Mercurial tools installed correctly is to open a command prompt or terminal session and execute the `hg` command. If you have Mercurial installed correctly, you should see a list of commands that Mercurial supports. If it's not installed correctly, you'll see an error indicating that the `hg` command could not be found. In this case, you either need to install Mercurial or add it to your system path.

Once you've got Mercurial installed, you can initialize a Mercurial repository using the same steps mentioned in this recipe for Git repositories except that, in the initial step, you would right-click on the project and select **Versioning** and then **Initialize Mercurial Repository...** instead of **Initialize Git Repository...**.

Cloning a Git repository

In the previous recipe, *Initializing a Git repository*, we saw how to create a new local Git repository. This is a useful technique when starting new projects; however, most of the time we aren't starting new projects, but are instead working on existing projects.

In this recipe, we'll see how to clone a Git repository so that we can work on a project that is already stored in the source control.

Getting ready

You can use any of the Java download bundles of NetBeans (Java SE, Java EE, or the All bundle) to complete this recipe as they all have Git support built into NetBeans.

To complete this recipe, you will need to create a fork of the `JarViewer` repository on GitHub. A fork is essentially your own copy of a repository that you can make changes to without affecting the original product.

 With Git, it is possible to clone both remote repositories (such as on GitHub) and repositories that are stored on the local filesystem. A local Git repository functions exactly the same as a remote Git repository.

The process of forking repositories is integral to how many open source projects work. To make a fix to a project, a fork is first made, which creates your own copy of the Git repository. The code can then be fixed and committed on the forked repository before issuing a pull request. A pull request indicates to the owner of the original repository that some new changes have been made in a forked repository that we'd like committing to the main repository. Using Git and GitHub, this process is very straightforward.

In this recipe, we will be cloning your personal fork of the `cookbook-jarviewer` project created in *Chapter 4, Developing Desktop Applications with NetBeans*. We'll see how to create the fork on GitHub and then how to clone it into NetBeans.

To complete this recipe, you will need an account with GitHub. For more information about GitHub and to create an account there, visit `http://www.github.com`.

How to do it...

The first step in completing this recipe is to create a fork of the `cookbook-jarviewer` project on GitHub. We can achieve this with the following steps:

1. Navigate to `http://github.com` and log in to your account.
2. Navigate to the `cookbook-jarviewer` project by browsing to `http://github.com/doobrie/cookbook-jarviewer`.
3. At the top right of the page, you will see the **Fork** button (shown in the following screenshot). Click on this button to create your own copy of the repository on your account.

4. It will now take GitHub a few moments to fork the repository. The forked repository will have a URL of `https://github.com/<your-username>/cookbook-jarviewer.jar`.

Now that we've forked the `cookbook-jarviewer` project, let's see how we can clone it into NetBeans with the following steps:

1. Click on the main NetBeans **Team** menu, then click on **Git**, and finally on **Clone....**.
2. The **Clone Repository** dialog will be shown. Enter the **Repository URL** field as `https://github.com/<your-username>/cookbook-jarviewer.jar` remembering to change `<your-username>` to your GitHub username.
3. Enter your GitHub username and password into the **User** and **Password** fields, as shown in the following screenshot:

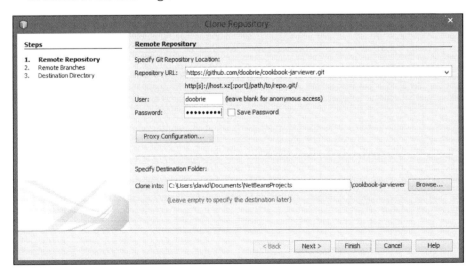

If you are using a proxy server to connect to the Internet, you may need to configure that within NetBeans before continuing. Clicking on the **Proxy Configuration...** button on the **Clone Repository** page allows a proxy server to be configured.

4. Click on the **Next** button.

5. A list of remote branches to clone will be displayed. This repository only has one branch, called `master`. Ensure the branch is checked and click on **Next**.

6. The **Destination Directory** page will now be shown confirming the information we have entered so far in the wizard, as shown in the following screenshot:

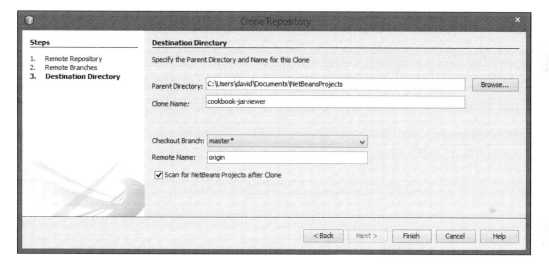

7. Ensure the **Scan for NetBeans Projects after Clone** checkbox is selected. When this checkbox is selected, NetBeans will look for NetBeans projects in a cloned repository and will provide the user with an easy option to open any that are found. Click on **Finish** to clone the repository.

8. A confirmation dialog will be shown when the cloning process has completed showing that NetBeans has found a NetBeans project within the repository. Click on the **Open Project** button to open the project, as shown in the following screenshot:

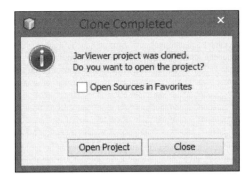

How it works...

Cloning a Git repository is a very useful technique for taking a copy of a remote repository onto your local development machine.

Cloning a repository from within NetBeans is similar to performing the `git clone` command from a command line; however, NetBeans has the facility to scan the cloned repository for NetBeans projects, which can then be easily opened.

In this recipe, we cloned a GitHub repository; however, we don't have to clone repositories on GitHub. The same procedure works for cloning repositories on BitBucket or any other Git-hosted repository.

There's more...

In the previous recipe, *Initializing a Git repository*, we saw that when a project is integrated with a **Source Code Control System** (**SCCS**) such as Git, different colors and icons are used to visually show the status of files.

Since we've just cloned a repository and not made any changes to it, we shouldn't expect to see the icon on the project (◉) indicating that files have been changed.

If we look at the project, however, we can see that the icon is present next to the project name indicating that something has changed. Expanding all of the project nodes, we can see that no files have been changed though, as shown in the following screenshot. So why then do we see this icon?

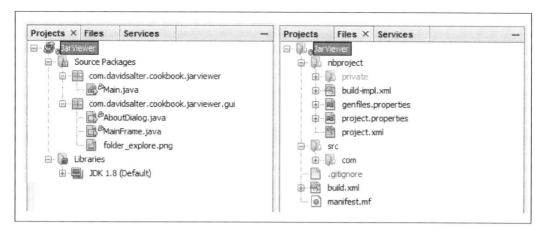

If we open up the **Files** explorer, we can see that NetBeans has added a file called
`.gitigore`. Opening up this file, we can see that it contains a single line:

```
/nbproject/private/
```

This file tells Git to ignore the contents of the `private` folder located in the `nbproject`
folder within the project and not to commit anything within this folder into source control.
This is a very useful feature to stop private files from being committed and therefore visible
to other users.

This file is displayed in green within the **Files** explorer as it's a new file that hasn't yet been
added into the repository.

Cloning a Mercurial repository

In this recipe, we looked at cloning a Git repository. What happens if we want to clone a
Mercurial repository instead? Both Git and Mercurial support distributed (offline) repositories,
so can NetBeans help us here?

NetBeans can certainly help us when using Mercurial instead of Git. To use Mercurial,
however, requires an extra step that is not required for using Git. Before we can use Mercurial
from within NetBeans, we need to ensure that we have installed the Mercurial tools from
`http://mercurial.selenic.com` and added them to the systems path, as NetBeans
executes these commands to provide Mercurial functionality.

Once we've installed Mercurial support, we can click on the **Team** menu item from within the main NetBeans menu. We then choose **Mercurial** and then **Clone Other...** to access the **Clone External Repository** dialog. From there on, we can specify connection details to a remote Mercurial repository and check projects out and then open them within NetBeans.

Updating to a specific revision

Sometimes when working with a repository, we don't want to get the latest files (the last commit performed on the repository). NetBeans allows us to get a specific revision from a repository once we have cloned it.

To check out a specific revision, right-click on the project within the **Projects** explorer and click on **Git**, then on **Checkout**, and finally on **Checkout Revision...**. NetBeans will then display the **Checkout Selected Revision** dialog from which we can choose a specific revision to check out.

Checking out from a Subversion repository

In the previous recipe, *Cloning a Git repository*, we saw how to clone a remote Git repository so that we could make changes to it. In this recipe, we'll show how to check out a Subversion repository. Subversion works differently from Git, in that when files are checked out from Subversion, they are stored locally with the repository being stored somewhere on a server. In Subversion, there is no local repository like there is in Git. This means that with Git, you can perform SCCS operations offline. With Subversion, these operations must be performed online. These differences therefore explain why we don't clone a Subversion repository, instead, we **check out** files from a Subversion repository.

Getting ready

You can use any of the Java download bundles of NetBeans (Java SE, Java EE, or the All bundle) to complete this recipe as they all have Subversion support built into NetBeans.

To complete this recipe, we will be checking out a copy of the `JarViewer` application from *Chapter 4, Developing Desktop Applications with NetBeans*, from a Subversion repository hosted on Google Code. For more information about Google Code and how to create hosted projects there, check out `https://code.google.com/hosting`.

How to do it...

1. Click on **Team**, then on **Subversion**, and finally on **Checkout...** from the main NetBeans menu.

2. The **Checkout** dialog will be displayed. Enter the **Repository URL** field as `https://cookbook-jarviewer-svn.googlecode.com/svn/trunk`.

3. Since public commit access has not been granted to this repository, leave the **User** and **Password** fields blank. If you were to check out a repository to which you had commit access (or one that simply requires authentication to check out code), you would enter the username and password here. The **Checkout** dialog is shown in the following screenshot:

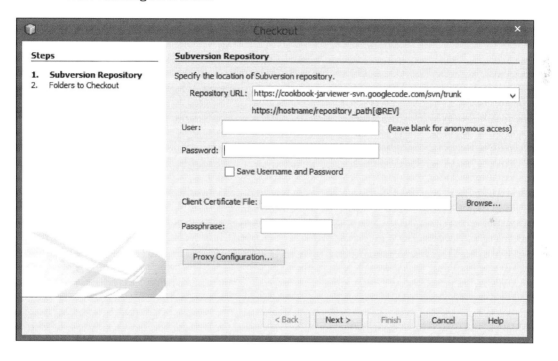

4. Click on **Next**.

5. On the **Folders to Checkout** page, NetBeans provides confirmation about the repository that is being checked out. The **Repository Folder(s)** field defaults to `trunk` indicating that the main trunk branch from the repository is to be checked out. The **Repository Revision** field is set to `HEAD` meaning that the latest version of trunk will be checked out. Ensure the **Scan for NetBeans Projects after Checkout** checkbox is checked, as shown in the following screenshot:

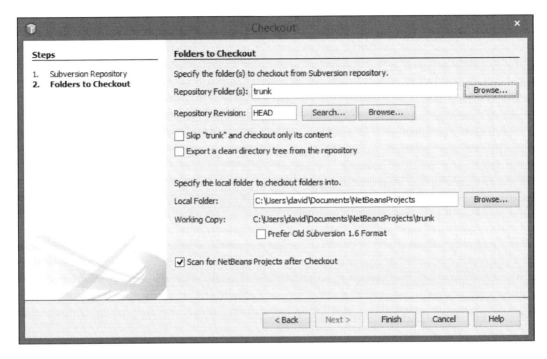

6. Click on the **Finish** button to check out the project.
7. After a few moments, NetBeans will indicate that the checkout was completed successfully. Click on the **Open Project** button to open the checked out project.

How it works...

Checking out a project from within NetBeans is a similar process to performing the `svn co` command from the command line. NetBeans connects to the remote Subversion repository and checks out the required folder and revision using the supplied credentials.

If we now right-click on the project or any files within the project from the **Projects** explorer, we can see that a **Subversion** menu item has been added. We can access all of the Subversion functionality from this menu.

There's more...

When interacting with Subversion, it can sometimes matter what version of the Subversion client is used for communicating with the server. By default, NetBeans uses the JavaHL bindings. This is a Java API built on top of the native Subversion client files and generally provides the best experience for communicating with Subversion.

If a different version of the Subversion client is required, however, this can be configured within the **Team** section of the NetBeans **Options** menu. Within this page, **Preferred Client** for Subversion can be configured as `CLI`. Selecting this option allows a specific version of the Subversion client to be specified and used for all communication between NetBeans and the Subversion server.

The final option is to use `SvnKit`. This is a pure Java implementation of the Subversion client libraries and will give better performance than the CLI option, but not as good as the JavaHL option.

If you do not have to specify a certain version of the Subversion client to communicate with your Subversion server, it is best to leave the **Preferred Client** option at its default setting of **JavaHL**, as shown in the following screenshot:

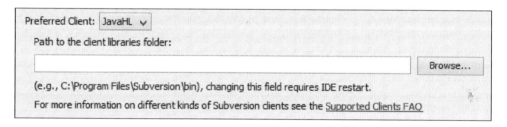

Importing files into a Subversion repository

In this recipe, we saw how to check out files from a Subversion repository, but is there any way that NetBeans can help us to store the initial files within a Subversion repository? Fortunately, there is.

From an open project (that is not stored in Subversion), simply right-click on the project in the **Projects** explorer and select the **Versioning** and then select the **Import into Subversion Repository...** menu options.

On the **Import** dialog, enter values in the **Repository URL**, **User**, and **Password** fields. Complete the wizard by entering the initial commit message and the NetBeans project will be stored within a Subversion repository. We can see the **Import** dialog in the following screenshot:

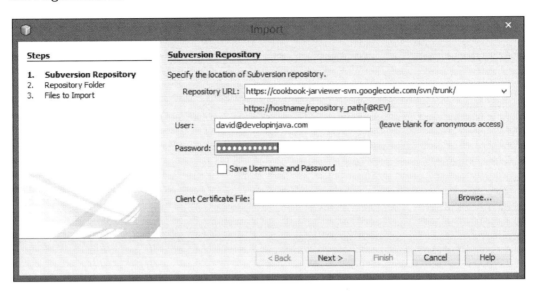

In many respects, Subversion is a natural replacement for the CVS source code control system. Both Subversion and CVS require online access to repositories as neither of them has the concept of local distributed repositories like Git and Mercurial. Subversion provides benefits over CVS though, mainly in terms of atomic commits, which CVS does not support. One of the major downsides of CVS is that commits are not atomic, so if something goes wrong in the middle of a commit, the repository can be left in an unstable state. Subversion overcomes this problem by ensuring that all commits are atomic, that is either everything is committed in one step, or nothing is committed at all.

Using CVS from within NetBeans

CVS is a relatively old source code control system, and as such, support from it has been removed from the base NetBeans product. CVS support can, however, be easily added via a NetBeans plugins. Click on **Tools** and then **Plugins** to open the **Plugins** dialog. On the list of **Available Plugins**, the **CVS** plugin provides support for CVS. Select the plugin and click on the **Install** button to add CVS support to NetBeans.

Once CVS support has been added into NetBeans, it can be accessed in a similar fashion to how we used Subversion earlier in this recipe.

We can import a project into CVS by right-clicking on the project and selecting **Versioning** and then the **Import into CVS Repository...** menu option. The procedure is almost identical to that of importing into a Subversion repository.

Similarly, we can check out from a CVS repository by selecting the **Team** option and then **CVS** and finally the **Checkout...** menu option from the main NetBeans menu. Again, the procedure is almost identical to that of checking out from a Subversion repository.

Getting the history of a file

So far we've seen how to initialize source code repositories and how we can get a working copy for us to develop against.

In this recipe, we'll use NetBeans to query a Git repository so that we can view the history of files within it. We'll concentrate on Git within this recipe as it is probably one of the most widely used source code control systems at the moment. You can apply the principles for other types of repository as the general procedures are the same.

Getting ready

To complete this recipe, we'll need to have cloned the `cookbook-jarviewer` repository from GitHub as described in the earlier recipe, *Cloning a Git repository*.

Ensure that this project is open within NetBeans before starting this recipe.

How to do it...

We can view the history of files with the following steps:

1. Expand the `JarViewer` project within the **Projects** explorer so that the **Source Packages** node of `com.davidsalter.cookbook.jarviewer` is opened.

2. Right-click on the `Main.java` file and select **Git** and then **Show History**.

3. The history for the file is now displayed. Looking at the history view, you can see that two commits have been made to the file. Each commit is listed along with its identifier (**430c537** and **3098371**), a description for the commit, the author, and the date the commit was performed, as shown in the following screenshot:

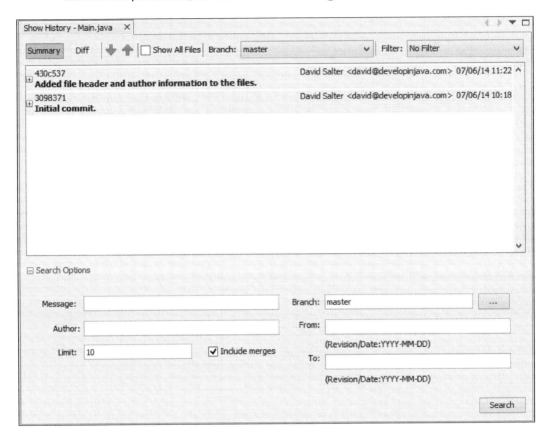

If there are a lot of commits, and we wish to search for a specific one, we can use the fields at the bottom of the history window to narrow the search down by commit description, author, branch, and date span.

4. Enter the text `file header` into the **Message** edit box and click on the **Search** button.

5. Note how the history has been filtered to only display entries matching the input criteria.

Once we've viewed the history of a file, we can also see what changes were made to the file during a specific commit. We can also perform several actions on a previous commit such as tagging or reverting the commit with the following steps:

1. Click on the plus button (⊞) at the left of the file history with an ID of **430c537**.

2. The history line will expand showing several options: **Diff to Previous**, **Checkout 430c537**, **Tag Commit**, **Export Commit...**, and **Revert Commit....** They are described as follows:

   ❑ **Diff to Previous**: This option compares the specified version of the file with the previous version

   ❑ **Checkout**: This option checks out the specified version of the repository into the local working copy

   ❑ **Tag Commit**: This option adds a source control tag to the specified version

   ❑ **Export Commit**: This option creates a Diff file of the commit and saves it to the disk

   ❑ **Revert Commit**: This option reverts the changes made in the specified commit to that state which the file was in before the commit was made

   All these options are displayed in the following screenshot:

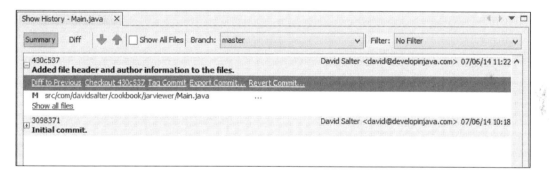

3. Click on the **Diff to Previous** link to view the differences of the file to the previous version of the file. The resultant dialog is displayed in the following screenshot:

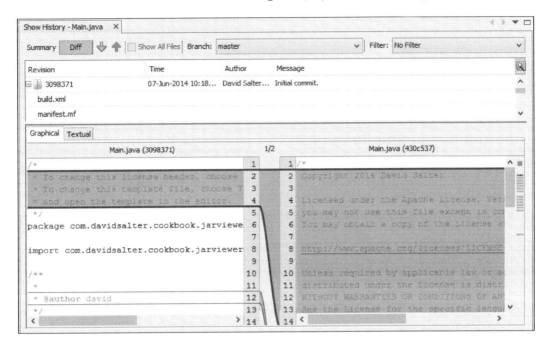

4. Any additions to a file are displayed with a blue background, while any modifications to a file are shown with a green background.

So far we've seen how we can view the differences between files that have been committed to the repository. NetBeans also allows us to see the changes that have been made to a project since it was last committed with the following steps:

1. Double-click on the `Main.java` file to open it for editing.

2. Use the **Insert Code...** refactoring to insert a logger into the file and then log a start message immediately after the definition of the `main()` method:

```
LOG.info("Starting application: "+args.length+"
arguments.");
```

3. Note that wherever we've changed the file, NetBeans has added a green band in the left margin to indicate the lines that have changed, as shown in the following screenshot:

```
31   public static void main(String[] args) {
32       LOG.info("Starting application: "+args.length+" arguments.");
33       java.awt.EventQueue.invokeLater(new Runnable() {
```

4. Right-click on the `JarViewer` node within the **Project** explorer and click on **Git** and then on **Show Changes**.

5. The output window is opened showing that the `Main.java` file has been modified.

6. Click on the **Open Diff** button (▓) to show what changes have been made to the file. A file differences window similar to the one shown previously is displayed showing what changes have been made to the file.

There's more...

In this recipe, we showed you how to view the history for a file by right-clicking on it within the **Projects** explorer and selecting the **History** option. A shortcut to this operation is to click on the **History** button at the top of a file when it is open within the editor. Upon selecting the **History** tab, we are presented with the option of filtering the history to show either local changes, or changes that have been committed to Git. Using both of these options provides a powerful tool for managing the history of files. We can see the **History** tab in the following screenshot:

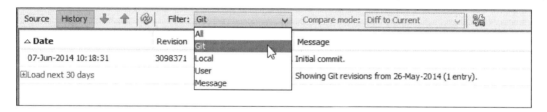

In this recipe, we saw how to view the history for a file and how to show what changes were made to the file over the previous version. What if we wanted to show all the changes in a commit though, and not just the changes made to a single file?

NetBeans allows the history for the entire project to be shown by right-clicking on the root node of the project in the **Projects** explorer and selecting **Git** and then **Show History**. NetBeans then shows the history search screen as shown previously, but does not perform the search until some criteria have been entered and the **Search** button has been clicked.

Committing and pushing code changes

In the previous recipe, *Getting the history of a file*, we made a change to a file under source control so that we could see how NetBeans could show us the differences that we'd made to our local code.

In this recipe, we'll see how we can commit these changes back to source control on our local Git repository and then how we can push the changes back to the remote repository.

Getting ready

To complete this recipe, you will need to have completed the previous recipe, *Getting the history of a file*, so that there are local changes to the repository. It's possible to complete this recipe by making your own changes to the local code; however, the descriptions in this recipe may not then match exactly with your code base.

How to do it...

1. Right-click on the root node of the `JarViewer` project within the **Projects** explorer and click on **Git** and then on **Commit...**.

2. The **Commit** dialog will now be displayed. Enter `Added startup logging` in the **Commit Message** field. Ensure your GitHub e-mail address is specified in the **Author** and **Committer** fields, as shown in the following screenshot:

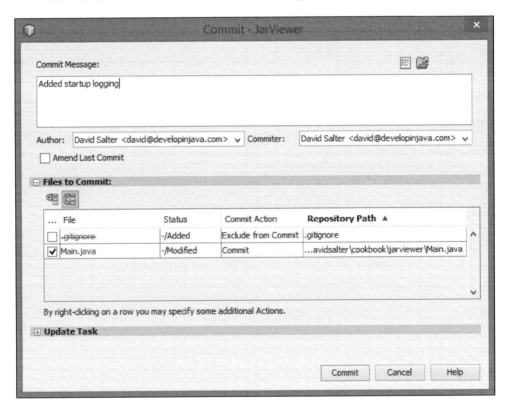

3. Click on the **Commit** button to commit the changes to the repository.

NetBeans will now commit any changed files to the local Git repository. If you wish to verify this, check out the history for the project. If you need help with this, check out the preceding recipe, *Getting the history of a file*. Note how any of the files that were changed locally are no longer displayed in blue within the **Projects** explorer, and any blue or green marking in the gutter when editing a file have also been removed as the local file is now the same as the file in the local Git repository.

With Git, when we've made changes to a local repository, we can push the changes to the remote repository so that they are available for everyone to clone with the following steps:

1. Right-click on the `JarViewer` root node within the **Projects** explorer and select **Git**, then **Remote**, and then **Push...**.

2. The **Push to Remote Repository** dialog will be displayed:

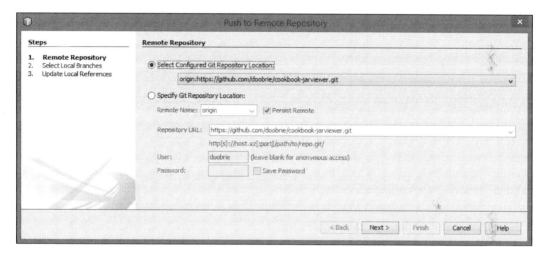

3. Since we originally cloned a remote repository, NetBeans knows where to push the local repository to. The **Select Configured Git Repository Location** option should be automatically selected. If you wish to push to a different remote repository, or you have initialized a local repository without cloning a remote repository, then enter the details under the **Specify Git Repository Location** option.

4. Click on **Next**.

5. NetBeans will show a list of **Local Branches** that are to be pushed. On this page, NetBeans will indicate that we are updating the `master` branch (as we have not created any other branches). Click on **Next**.

6. NetBeans will now show a list of **Remote Branches** that will be updated. Again, as there is only one branch on the remote repository, this is all that will be displayed.

7. Click on **Finish** to push the local repository to the remote repository.

There's more...

When we are about to commit files to a repository, it's good practice to first perform an update procedure, so that we know that we are working on the very latest code and we will minimize chances of code conflicts when committing code. Performing an update gets the latest code base from the repository and merges it into our code base flagging up any conflicts that we will need to resolve. When we're in a situation where we are happy with our code, it's also good practice to run any tests that we may have before committing to the repository (we'll discuss testing in *Chapter 10, NetBeans Testing and Profiling*). When we've updated to the latest code and run our tests, we should be confident that committing our code will not break any other code within the project.

Managing new files

When we commit files to a repository, how does NetBeans handle new files that we've added to the project? Do we need to manually add them to Git?

When we add new files into a project via the NetBeans **New File** wizard, the files are automatically flagged within Git to be added to the local repository next time a commit is performed. If we have added files outside of NetBeans into the project structure, however, we need to manually flag them to be added to Git. This is achieved by right-clicking on the file in question and choosing **Git** and then the **Add** option.

Creating a Diff patch

When working on projects that are hosted in Subversion or CVS, it's often necessary to create a Diff patch and submit this to project owners. A Diff patch details all of the changes made between two code bases, with all of the information being held within a single file.

Creating a Diff patch is particularly common in open source projects where a user does not have commit rights, but wishes to submit a patch or a piece of new functionality to a project.

In this recipe, we'll show how to use NetBeans to create a Diff patch for changes made to a locally checked out Subversion repository.

Getting ready

To complete this recipe, you will need to have completed the previous recipe, *Checking out from a Subversion repository,* so that we have a local repository to make changes to and so that we can create a Diff file for these changes.

Ensure that the `JarViewer` project checked out from Subversion is open within NetBeans before proceeding with this recipe.

How to do it...

In order to create a Diff patch, we first need to make some changes to the project so that it is different to the remote repository with the following steps:

1. Double-click on the `Main.java` file to open it for editing.
2. Use the **Insert Code...** refactoring to insert a logger into the file and then log a start message immediately after the definition of the `main()` method:

   ```
   LOG.info("Starting application: "+args.length+"
   arguments.");
   ```
3. Now that we've made some changes so that our local copy of the repository is different from the remote repository, we can create a Diff file.
4. Right-click on the `JarViewer` root node within the **Projects** explorer and select **Subversion**, then **Patches**, and then **Export**.
5. On the **Export Diff Patch** dialog, select a filename to save the Diff patch and then click on the **OK** button to create the Diff patch.

 Although you can use any file extension when creating Diff patches, the standard file extension is either `.diff` or `.patch`.

6. The Diff patch will be created and opened within NetBeans showing all the changes made to the project.

There's more...

If you only want to create a Diff patch for a single file within NetBeans, you can select the **Team** menu and then **Diff** and the **Diff Files** menu option. This **Diff Files** option will cause a list of files that have changed from the remote repository to be displayed. Clicking on any of the files shows a graphical representation of what has changed in that file. This is very easy to follow and makes viewing the changes to a particular file very easy. Clicking on the **Textual** tab will show the changes for the specified file in the Diff format, as shown in the following screenshot:

```
Graphical  Textual
# This patch file was generated by NetBeans IDE
# It uses platform neutral UTF-8 encoding and \n newlines.
--- Remotely Modified (Based On HEAD)
+++ Locally Modified (Based On LOCAL)
@@ -16,17 +16,20 @@
 package com.davidsalter.cookbook.jarviewer;
```

Right-clicking on any changed file and selecting **Export Diff Patch** will create a Diff patch for the specified file only and not for all the files that have changed.

Applying a Diff patch

The opposite of creating a Diff patch is applying a Diff patch to a project. If you receive a Diff patch, and wish to apply it to a project, this can easily be performed with NetBeans.

Right-click on the root node of the project from within the **Projects** explorer and click on **Subversion**, then **Patches**, and then **Apply Diff Patch...**. NetBeans will then ask for a Diff patch file to be selected. Upon selecting the file, NetBeans will attempt to apply it to the current project. The **Output** window will show the status of applying the patch and whether it has succeeded or failed (most likely because NetBeans cannot correctly perform a complex merge). NetBeans will also show both a **Graphical** and **Textual** result of a merge so that you can see exactly what parts of the Diff patch have been applied and to what files.

Branching a repository

When multiple people are working on a project, there is usually more than one piece of development being performed at a single time. It's a good practice to only commit production-ready code to the trunk or master branches of a repository, so we need somewhere else to commit code that we've not finished with. This is where branching and branches comes in.

A branch is a separate development stream that has been taken from the master/trunk branch at a certain point of time, usually with the intention of completing a specific piece of functionality, whether it's a bug fix or a new feature.

Within this recipe, we'll show how to create a branch within a Git repository, although the procedure is the same for other types of repositories.

Getting ready

To complete this recipe, we'll need to have cloned the `cookbook-jarviewer` repository from GitHub as described in the earlier recipe, *Cloning a Git repository*.

Ensure that this project is open within NetBeans before starting this recipe.

How to do it...

1. Right-click on the `JarViewer` node within the **Projects** explorer and select **Git**, then **Branch/Tag**, and then **Create Branch...**.

2. The **Create Branch** dialog will be displayed. Enter `Bug911` in the **Branch Name** field.

3. Click on the **Checkout Created Branch** checkbox so that it is checked, as shown in the following screenshot:

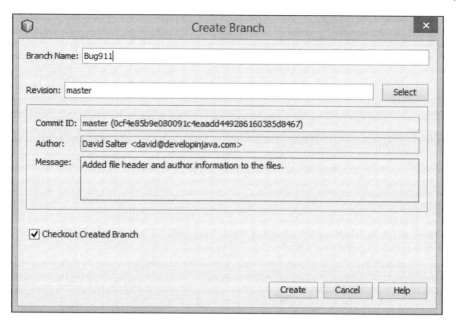

4. Click on the **Create** button.

The new branch will be created and checked out. Any commits to code will now be applied to this new branch and not committed to the master/trunk branch.

Once we've made changes to a branch, and completed a piece of development, we usually want to merge the branch back into the master/trunk so that it is available for others. Let's make a change to the project now and then merge this back into the master with the following steps:

1. Change the `Main.java` file so that the `LOG` statement uses a message template rather than concatenating strings:

   ```
   LOG.log(Level.INFO, "Starting application: {0} arguments.",
   args.length);
   ```

2. Commit this change to the branch using the **Commit** option within NetBeans (remember, we're still on a bug branch at the moment and not on the master branch).

3. Right-click on the `JarViewer` node within the **Projects** explorer and select **Git**, then **Branch/Tag**, and then switch to the master branch. Note how the changes we've just made to the file have now disappeared because we've switched to the master branch and haven't merged the changes into it yet.

4. Right-click on the `JarViewer` node within the **Projects** explorer and select **Git**, then **Branch/Tag**, and then **Merge Revision…**.

5. The **Merge Revision** dialog will now be displayed. Click on the **Select** button to select a revision to merge into master.

6. From the list of branches, select the **Local** branch `Bug911`. Click on the **Select** button to select the branch for merging, as shown in the following screenshot:

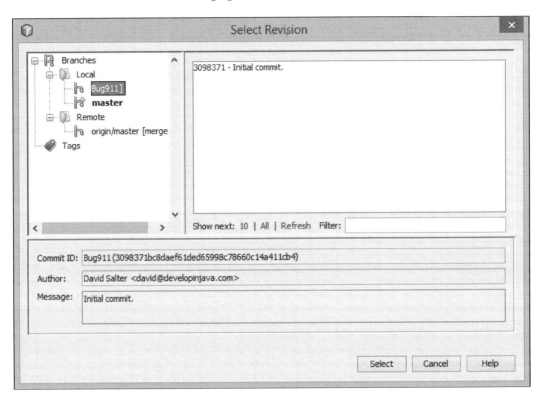

7. Click on the **Merge** button to merge the changes into master.

There's more...

Instead of creating branches, we can also make **tags** within a repository. A tag is essentially a label whose purpose is to identify a specific location within a repository, for example, a specific release. Common names for tags could be names such as `Release_1_0_0` or `Beta_1`. Creating a tag within a repository is a similar process to creating a branch (a tag is essentially an uneditable branch so tags and branches share a lot in common). To create a tag, select the **Branch/Tag** menu option and then **Create Tag...**. Tags can be managed (deleted) from the **Manage Tags** dialog that is accessible by selecting the **Branch/Tag** menu option and then by selecting **Manage Tags...**.

10
NetBeans Testing and Profiling

In this chapter, we will cover the following recipes:

- ▶ Installing JUnit support into NetBeans
- ▶ Creating a JUnit test for an existing class
- ▶ Creating a JUnit test
- ▶ Creating a JUnit test suite
- ▶ Running tests
- ▶ Creating a TestNG test and test suite
- ▶ Profiling an application

Introduction

In recent years, writing tests for applications has become a much more widely used practice. In many ways, this is due to the rise of open source software and the need to prove that software will function as expected.

In software development, there are now many different unit testing frameworks, many of which are based upon the xUnit architecture. This architecture, originally defined by Kent Beck in the late 1990s, defines a basic set of components to run tests.

xUnit specifies that tests are executed by a **test runner**, which is responsible for running all of the necessary tests and generating results indicating either the success or failure of each test. Each test is defined as a separate **test case**. For each test case, we define a number of **assertions** that must equate to true for the test to be successful.

To run a test, any number of preconditions need to be defined. In xUnit, these are called **test fixtures**. When there are multiple test cases that require the same test fixtures, these are grouped together into a **test suite**.

In the world of Java software development, JUnit and TestNG are the two most common testing frameworks, both of which follow the xUnit architecture. In this chapter, we'll discuss how to use both JUnit and TestNG within NetBeans.

In addition to looking at unit testing, we'll take a look at profiling and performance testing. We'll see how NetBeans' internal profiler can be used to monitor application performance.

Installing JUnit support into NetBeans

Since Version 7 of NetBeans, JUnit has not been included with the standard installation of NetBeans. JUnit uses the Common Public License, and as such, cannot be installed by default with fresh installs of NetBeans.

You may have noticed when installing NetBeans that you are asked partway through the installation if you wish to install JUnit support. To install JUnit support during installation, you must agree to the JUnit license agreement.

If you did not install JUnit during NetBeans installation, this recipe will show you how to install JUnit support. The **JUnit License Agreement** page of **NetBeans IDE Installer** is shown in the following screenshot:

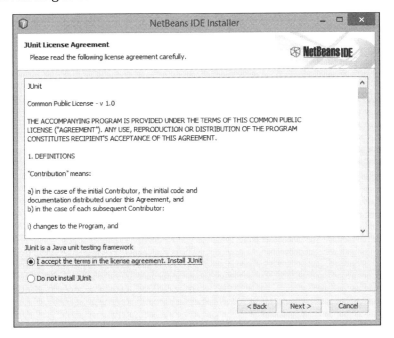

Getting ready

To complete this recipe, you must use either the Java SE, Java EE, or All NetBeans download bundle. Additionally, this recipe assumes that JUnit was not installed with NetBeans.

How to do it...

To install JUnit support, perform the following steps:

1. Click on **Tools** and then **Plugins** from the main NetBeans menu bar.
2. On the **Plugins** dialog, select the **Available Plugins** tab.
3. Locate the **JUnit** plugin and check the **Install** checkbox, as shown in the following screenshot:

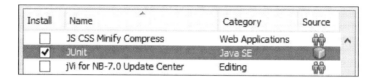

4. Click on the **Install** button.
5. The **NetBeans IDE Installer** dialog will be displayed confirming that the JUnit plugin is to be installed. Click on the **Next** button.
6. Read and accept the license agreement, then click on the **Install** button to continue the installation.
7. Click on the **Finish** button to complete installation.

How it works...

With NetBeans 8, JUnit support is available as a NetBeans plugin that can be downloaded and installed via the NetBeans **Plugins** option. Installing the plugin does not require a restart of NetBeans, but does install and activate all of the functionality required to write and run JUnit tests. In the next recipe, *Creating a JUnit test for an existing class*, we'll see how to write JUnit tests within NetBeans.

Creating a JUnit test for an existing class

NetBeans provides facilities to easily create JUnit tests. In this recipe, we'll see how we can create tests for an existing class. We'll initially create a new library project within NetBeans and create a very simple class to do some basic math. We'll then see how to use NetBeans to create tests for the library.

Getting ready

To complete this recipe, you need to ensure that you have installed the JUnit support into NetBeans as described in the previous recipe, *Installing JUnit support into NetBeans*.

How to do it...

To create a JUnit test for an existing class, perform the following steps:

1. Click on **File** and then **New Project...**. Create a new **Java Class Library** project called `Calculator`. If you are unsure of the steps necessary to create this project, check out the *Creating a library* recipe in *Chapter 1, Using NetBeans Projects*, of this book.

2. Create a new class called `Calculator` in the `com.davidsalter.cookbook.testing` package. Change the body of the class to read:

```
public class Calculator {

    public int add(int x, int y) {
        return x + y;
    }

    public double divide(double x, double y) {
        return x / y;
    }
}
```

3. Now that we've created a very simple class, we can create a test for it. Note that we have no `main` method in our class library, so we can't simply run the class to see how it behaves.

4. Right-click on the `Calculator` node within the **Projects** explorer and click on **New** and then **Other...**.

5. In the **New File** dialog, select **Unit Tests** from the list of **Categories** and **Test For Existing Class** from the list of **File Types**.

6. Click on **Next**.

7. On the **New Test for Existing Class** dialog, click on the **Browse...** button and select the **Class To Test** field as `Calculator.java`, as shown in the following screenshot:

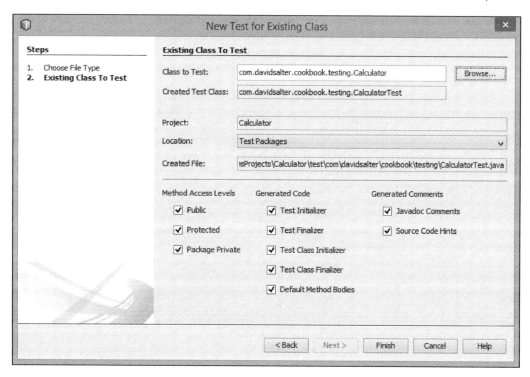

8. Leave all the default settings as they are and click on **Finish** to create the test class.

How it works...

Creating a new test for an existing class is a simple way to automatically create stub test methods for an existing class. This is useful for writing tests after the class has been written.

If you're a fan of **test-driven development** (**TDD**), you may be wondering if it's possible to create tests before classes are created as that is the working practice for TDD. Don't worry, NetBeans provides a way for creating "blank" tests. We'll see this in the next recipe, *Creating a JUnit test*. For more information on TDD, check out `http://en.wikipedia.org/wiki/Test-driven_development`.

When creating a test for an existing class, NetBeans asked us which class we'd like to write tests for. A list of all the classes within the project was displayed for us to choose from.

After choosing a class, we can see that NetBeans generated a test class with the same name as the class under test, but with the suffix `Test`. In our example, we created a test class called `CalculatorTest` from the application `Calculator` class.

> It's useful to maintain this naming scheme when creating additional classes as NetBeans uses this pattern for test class discovery and execution.

NetBeans automatically specified the location of the test class as within the **Test Packages** node of the project. This node is clearly shown within the **Projects** explorer, as shown in the following screenshot:

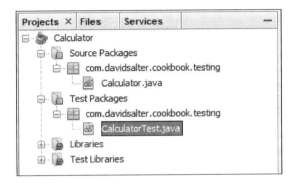

The idea behind storing test classes separately within a project is twofold:

- Test classes can be kept entirely separate from application classes making it easier to find and distinguish test and application code
- Test classes can be compiled separately from application classes and do not need to be distributed with release code

The next information required for creating a class was to specify **Method Access Levels**. We left these at the default values (all checked). These levels dictate whether tests are created for the different access level methods in the source class. For example, we can decide to generate tests only for `public` methods within a class and not generate tests for `protected` or package or `private` methods. The default option is to create test methods for all methods found in the source class.

Next to this, we can specify what code is to be generated (again, we chose the default option of having all options selected). We can choose to generate code for the following options:

- **Test Initializer**: This creates a method that is called before each instance of the test class is created. In JUnit terms, this method is annotated with `@BeforeClass`.
- **Test Finalizer**: This creates a method that is called after each instance of the test class has been executed. In JUnit terms, this method is annotated with `@AfterClass`.

▸ **Test Class Initializer**: This creates a setup method that is invoked before each test within the test class. In JUnit terms, this method is annotated with `@Before`.

▸ **Test Class Finalizer**: This creates a teardown method that is invoked after each test within the test class. In JUnit terms, this method is annotated with `@After`.

▸ **Default Method Bodies**: This tells NetBeans to create a test method for each method defined within the source class (taking into account the method access level). In our `CalculatorTest.java` class that we created in this recipe, we can see that two methods, `testAdd()` and `testDivide()`, were created corresponding to the `add()` and `divide()` methods in the `Calculator` class.

The final options provided by NetBeans were to generate **Javadoc Comments** and **Source Code Hints**. Generating Javadoc adds standard comments before each method in the test class, whereas, the source code hints option adds to-do comments into the code indicating where the test needs filling out.

If we look at the test that was generated for the `add()` method, we can see how NetBeans has tried to write a test for the `add` functionality with the following code:

```
@Test
public void testAdd() {
    System.out.println("add");
    int x = 0;
    int y = 0;
    Calculator instance = new Calculator();
    int expResult = 0;
    int result = instance.add(x, y);
    assertEquals(expResult, result);
    // TODO review the generated test code and remove the default
    call to fail.
    fail("The test case is a prototype.");
}
```

Within the code, we can see that the test creates a new instance of the `Calculator` class (sometimes, referred to as the **System Under Test** (**SUT**)). The `add()` method is invoked and the assertion, `assertEquals`, is called to check that the result from invoking the `add()` method is the same as the expected result. Clearly, NetBeans doesn't know what the `add()` method is supposed to do; so, a comment is added indicating that we need to review the assertion. The test is then configured to `fail` irrespective of the results.

To make this into a useful test requires very few changes as can be seen in the working of the following code:

```
@Test
public void testAdd() {
    int x = 4;
    int y = 5;
```

```
        Calculator instance = new Calculator();
        int expResult = 9;
        int result = instance.add(x, y);
        assertEquals(expResult, result);
    }
```

All that's needed in this instance to make the test useful is to set up some inputs to the SUT and define the expected results. In this case, validating that adding 4 and 5 gives 9.

There's more...

In addition to creating tests for classes using the **New File** wizard, it is also possible to create tests for a class directly from within the **Projects** explorer. To create or update a set of tests for a class in this way, locate the class to be tested within the **Projects** explorer and right-click on it. On the pop-up menu, select **Tools** and then the **Create/Update Tests** option. And then select the **Code Generation** options as required, as shown in the following screenshot:

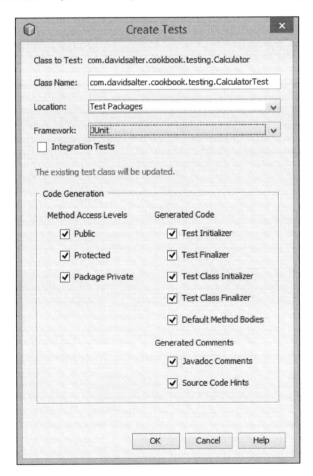

Creating a JUnit test

For some types of development, for example, TDD, the best practice for testing is to write the test before writing the functionality for the application. This allows the developer to think carefully about the architecture of the application, and helps to ensure better test coverage.

NetBeans helps in this area by allowing developers to create test classes that are not based upon existing application code (this is the opposite of what we saw in the previous recipe, *Creating a JUnit test for an existing class*, where the application code already existed).

In this recipe, we'll see how to create a basic JUnit test class.

Getting ready

To complete this recipe, you need to ensure that you have installed the JUnit support into NetBeans as described in the earlier recipe, *Installing JUnit support into NetBeans*.

You'll also need the sample project we created in the previous recipe, *Creating a JUnit test for an existing class*. If you have not completed that recipe, the project is available as part of the code download bundle for the book.

How to do it...

Perform the following steps to create a JUnit test:

1. Right-click on the **Test Packages** node of the `Calculator` project within the **Projects** explorer and click on **New** and then **Other...**.

2. In the **New File** dialog, select **Unit Tests** from the list of **Categories** and **JUnit Test** from the list of **File Types**.

3. Click on **Next**.

4. In the **Class Name** field, enter `CalculatorUnitTest`.

5. Ensure the **Location** dropdown is set to **Test Packages** and enter the **Package** field as `com.davidsalter.cookbook.testing`.

6. Uncheck all options under **Generated Code** and **Generated Comments** so that a blank JUnit test class is created, as shown in the following screenshot:

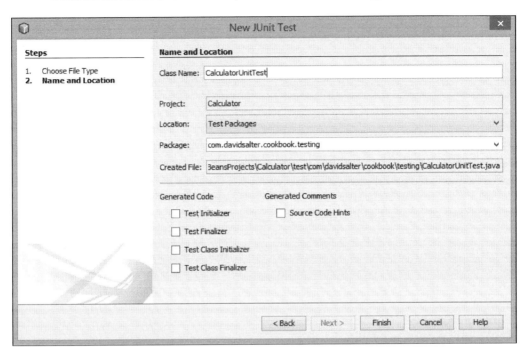

7. Click on **Finish** to create the test class.

Now that we've created the skeleton for a test case, let's add a test method into it to test the Calculator class we defined earlier.

8. Ensure the CalculatorUnitTest.java class is open for editing and add the following method to the class:

```
@Test
public void testAddNumbers() {
    Calculator calc = new Calculator();
    assertEquals("Invalid addition", 10, calc.add(2, 8));
}
```

This code uses the `@Test` annotation to declare that the `testAddNumbers()` method is a JUnit test method. The method creates an instance of the SUT and then uses JUnit's `assertEquals` method to check that the `calc.add(2,8)` method returns the value `10`. If this value is not returned, the error message `Invalid addition` will be logged to the test output.

> JUnit supports many different assertions, including `assertArrayEquals`, `assertEquals`, `assertFalse`, `assertNotNull`, `assertNotSame`, `assertNull`, `assertSame`, `assertThat`, and `assertTrue`. The general format of each of these methods is `assert(String message, Object expected, Object results);` however, the message parameter is optional. Although this parameter can be missed out, it's recommended to add it so that test failures can be more easily recognized.

How it works...

In this recipe, we created a JUnit test case without any foreknowledge of the SUT. This is a useful pattern when performing TDD.

We used the NetBeans wizard to create a blank test case for us. A blank test case is essentially a `public` class with no methods in it; however, it's located within the **Test Packages** section of the project rather than within the **Source Packages** section.

To create a test, we created a method and annotated it with the `@Test` annotation. We then used a JUnit `assert*` method to check that our SUT was generating the correct results.

Looking at the `CalculatorUnitTest.java` class, you'll notice that the JUnit assertions are all static imports. This allows unqualified access to the assert methods so we can call:

```
assert(…);
```

Instead of:

```
org.junit.assert.assert(…);
```

There's more...

In this recipe, we identified a test method with the `@Test` annotation. JUnit allows a couple of parameters to be specified with this annotation to change the expected behavior of the test.

If we are expecting that a test method must complete within a certain amount of time, we can add the timeout parameter to the annotation. For example:

```
@Test(timeout=5000)
```

This would declare that the test must complete within 5000 milliseconds; otherwise, it will have deemed to have failed.

Similarly, if we expect that a test method will throw an exception, we can add the expected parameter to the annotation. For example:

```
@Test(expected=java.io.IOException.class)
```

Creating a JUnit test suite

A JUnit test suite is a convenient way of specifying a set of test cases and the order in which they should run.

Within JUnit, the `@Suite` annotation is used to specify which test cases are within the suite. JUnit uses the `Suite` test runner to run the classes.

Getting ready

To complete this recipe, you need to ensure that you have installed the JUnit support into NetBeans as described in the earlier recipe, *Installing JUnit support into NetBeans*.

You'll also need the sample project we created in the previous recipe, *Creating a JUnit test*. If you have not completed that recipe, the project is available as part of the code download bundle for the book.

How to do it...

Perform the following steps to create a JUnit test suite:

1. Right-click on the **Test Packages** node within the `Calculator` project in the **Projects** explorer and click on **New** and then **Other....**

2. In the **New File** dialog, select **Unit Tests** from the list of **Categories** and **Test Suite** from the list of **File Types**.

3. Click on **Next**.

4. Enter the **Class Name** field as `CalculatorTestSuite`. Ensure the **Location** field is set to **Test Packages** and enter the **Package** field as `com.davidsalter. cookbook.testing`.

5. Uncheck the options under **Generated Code** and **Generated Comments**, as shown in the following screenshot:

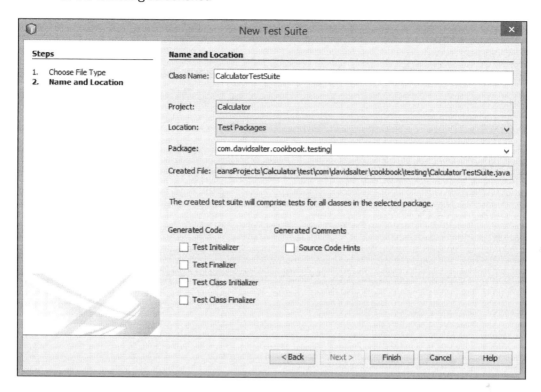

6. Click on **Finish** to create the test suite.

How it works...

In this recipe, we created a test suite called `CalculatorTestSuite` and added it to the `com.davidsalter.cookbook.testing` package. The body of the generated test suite class is as shown in the following code:

```
@RunWith(Suite.class)
@Suite.SuiteClasses(
  {com.davidsalter.cookbook.testing.CalculatorUnitTest.class,
    com.davidsalter.cookbook.testing.CalculatorTest.class
})
public class CalculatorTestSuite {
}
```

Looking at the code, we can see that NetBeans has created a public class called `CalculatorTestSuite` and annotated it with the `@RunWith(Suite.class)` annotation. This is the JUnit way of declaring a test suite.

The class is also annotated with the `@Suite.SuiteClasses({..., ...})` annotation. This annotation defines which classes are part of the test suite. In this case, NetBeans took a list of all the test classes within the package we created the suite in and added them to the suite. As we had two test classes, both these were added to the suite.

When running the suite, JUnit will run the classes in the order that they are specified within the `@Suite.SuiteClasses` annotation.

You will note that the `CalculatorTestSuite` class has no body as it is essentially a placeholder telling JUnit how to construct the test suite. Within the **New Test Suite** wizard, however, there is the option to add test initializers and finalizers into the test suite defining code that can be run outside of the individual test fixtures themselves.

There's more...

If, at a later date, we create more test classes, we can add these manually to the `@Suite.SuiteClasses` annotation to add the classes to the test suite. This is, however, a manual process.

Running tests

In the previous few recipes, we've seen how to create JUnit tests from scratch and based upon existing classes. We've also seen how to create a test suite that defines a set of tests and the order in which they can be executed.

In this recipe, we'll see how we can run all of those tests within NetBeans and see the reporting of the tests we've run.

NetBeans provides several ways to run tests and test suites. We'll look at all of these techniques within this recipe.

Getting ready

To complete this recipe, you need to ensure that you have installed the JUnit support into NetBeans as described in the earlier recipe, *Installing JUnit support into NetBeans*.

You'll also need the sample project we created in the previous recipe, *Creating a JUnit test suite*. If you have not completed that recipe, the project is available as part of the code download bundle for the book.

How to do it...

Ensure that the `Calculator` project is open within NetBeans. To run tests and test suites, perform the following steps:

1. Right-click on the `CalculatorUnitTest.java` class within the **Test Packages** node and click on **Test File**.

2. NetBeans will find all of the tests located within the `CalculatorUnitTest.java` class and run them. The results of the tests (in this case, there is only one test) will be shown in the **Test Results** window, as shown in the following screenshot:

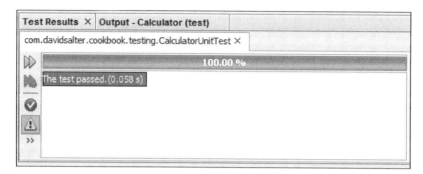

3. NetBeans shows a **100.00%** green bar indicating that 100 percent of the tests have passed. Great going so far!

4. Right-click on the `CalculatorTest.java` class within the **Test Packages** node and click on **Test File**.

5. As before, NetBeans will find all of the tests located within the specified class and run them. In this case, there are two tests, one of which passes and the other of which fails, as shown in the following screenshot:

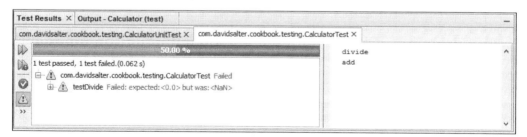

6. NetBeans now shows a **50.00%** green bar and a **50.00%** red bar indicating that half of the tests in the test run have failed. We can also see any test output (such as that generated by calls to `System.out.println`) displayed within the right-hand side window of the test results.

7. Expand the `com.davidsalter.cookbook.testing.CalculatorTest` node within the **Test Results** window, as shown in the following screenshot:

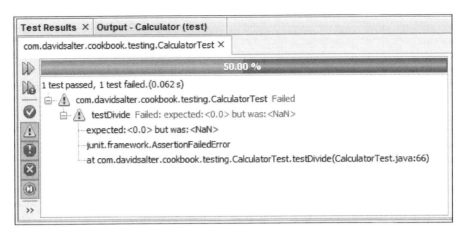

8. In the **Test Results** window, we can see that the `testDivide` method has failed. It was expecting a result of `0.0`, but found a result of `NaN` (Not a Number).

9. Double-click on the line beginning **testDivide Failed** within the **Test Results** explorer and NetBeans will open the appropriate test class for us and take us to the assertion that failed.

10. We can see that the `testDivide` method has failed because it was just a stub method generated for us by the **New Test for Existing Class** wizard. Let's fix the `testDivide()` method by changing it to read:

```
@Test
public void testDivide() {
    System.out.println("divide");
    double x = 10.0;
    double y = 2.0;
    double delta = 0.0001;
    Calculator instance = new Calculator();
    double expResult = 5.0;
    double result = instance.divide(x, y);
    assertEquals("Division not correct",
                expResult,
                result,
                delta);
}
```

Note that the `assertEquals` method that we are using in this example has an additional `delta` parameter at the end. This is required due to the inaccuracies that may occur when performing floating point arithmetic. This parameter says that if the expected result and the actual result are different by an amount smaller than `delta`, then they are considered to be the same.

11. Since we've only fixed one test within the class, we don't necessarily need to run all of the tests within it. Let's just run the `testDivide()` method test again. Right-click within the body of the `testDivide()` method and select **Run Focussed Test Method**.

12. NetBeans will run only the `testDivide()` method and a **100.00%** green bar will be displayed within the **Test Results** window indicating that we wrote the test correctly!

How it works...

Running JUnit tests within NetBeans is a straightforward process. We can run all of the tests within a class by right-clicking on the class within the **Test Packages** node and selecting the **Test File** option.

 Pressing *Ctrl + F6* or selecting the **Run File** option will also run tests on the selected file.

Running a test suite follows the same procedure—right-click on the test suite class and select the **Test File** option.

Within the **Test Results** window, several options are available to help us to navigate and manage test runs. They are explained in the following table:

Option	Description
▷▷	Rerun all the tests from the last test run
▷▷	Rerun all the failed tests from the last test run
✓	Show all passed tests in the **Test Results** window
⚠	Show all failed tests in the **Test Results** window
!	Show errors in the **Test Results** window

Option	Description
⊗	Show aborted tests in the **Test Results** window
⊚	Show skipped tests in the **Test Results** window
⬆	Move to the previous failure
⬇	Move to the next failure
⬕	Always open the **Test Results** window
⬔	Always open a new tab in the **Test Results** window

There's more...

NetBeans also provides the option to run all tests within a package. To perform this operation, right-click on a package within the **Test Packages** node and select **Test Package**.

To run all the tests for a project, simply select **Run** from the main menu and then the **Test Project** menu item.

If your tests/code aren't running as expected, NetBeans provides the option to debug tests. Instead of selecting **Test File** or **Run Focused Test Method**, select the debug variant, **Debug File** or **Debug Focused Test Method**. You can then use all of the NetBeans debugging functionality to help fix your code/tests.

Creating a TestNG unit test

TestNG is another popular Java testing framework that was inspired by early versions of JUnit that did not use annotations. TestNG is described as more powerful and easier to use than JUnit. For more details about this, check out the project's home page at `http://testng.org`.

Getting ready

To complete this recipe, you'll need the sample project we created in the earlier recipe, *Creating a JUnit test suite*. If you have not completed that recipe, the project is available as part of the code download bundle for the book.

How to do it...

Ensure the `Calculator` project is open within NetBeans. Perform the following steps to complete this recipe:

1. Right-click on the **Test Packages** node within the **Projects** explorer and select **New** and then **Other...**.

2. In the **New File** dialog, select **Unit Tests** from the list of **Categories** and **TestNG Test Case** from the list of **File Types**.

3. Click on **Next**.

4. Enter the **Class Name** field as `CalculatorTestNGTest`. Ensure the **Location** field is set to **Test Packages** and enter the **Package** field as `com.davidsalter.cookbook.testing`.

5. Check all of the **Generated Code** options and the **Generated Comments** option.

6. Click on **Finish** to create the test case.

7. Add the following test to the `CalculatorTestNGTest.java` class:

```
@Test
public void testAdd() {
    int x = 4;
    int y = 5;
    Calculator instance = new Calculator();
    int expResult = 9;
    int result = instance.add(x, y);
    assertEquals(expResult, result);
}
```

8. Fix the imports on the class using the **Fix Imports** refactoring (note, use the `org.testng` packages instead of the `org.junit` packages).

9. Right-click on the `CalculatorTestNGTest.java` class and select **Test File**. Note how the test is executed and shows results in a similar fashion to when running the JUnit tests.

How it works...

Creating and running a TestNG test and test suite works exactly the same way as creating and running a JUnit test suite.

When testing a package or running all the tests for a project, NetBeans will run all tests irrespective of whether they are JUnit or TestNG tests. You can try this out by running all of the tests in the `com.davidsalter.cookbook.testing` package or by selecting **Run** and then the **Test Project** menu item.

Profiling an application

NetBeans provides the facilities to profile both local and remote applications. Profiling allows you to get a view of the threads, CPU, and memory usage of your application. This can be very useful when tracking down memory leaks or application bottlenecks that are causing applications to run slowly.

In this recipe, we'll add an extra method to the `Calculator` class we defined earlier in this chapter and see how it fares when profiled.

Getting ready

To complete this recipe, you'll need the sample project we created in the earlier recipe, *Creating a JUnit test suite*. If you have not completed that recipe, the project is available as part of the download bundle for the book.

How to do it...

To profile our application, perform the following steps:

1. Double-click on the `Calculator.java` file and add the following method to it; this will calculate the factorial of a number recursively:

```
public long factorial(int x) {
    if (x <= 1) {
        return 1;
    } else {
        Calculator calc = new Calculator();
        return (x * calc.factorial(x-1));
    }
}
```

2. Since we're profiling an application, we need to add a main method to our project so that we have something to profile. Use the **New File** wizard to create a new **Java Main Class** (this is located within the **Java** category). Create the main class `Main` and place it in the `com.davidsalter.cookbook.testing` package.

3. Change the contents of the `main` method in `Main.java` to read:

```
public static void main(String[] args) {
    Calculator calculator = new Calculator();

    long x = calculator.factorial(20);
```

```
        System.out.println("x! = "+ x);
}
```

Now that we've created a simple application that performs some math, let's profile the memory of the application.

4. Click on **Profile** on the main NetBeans menu and then click on **Profile Project**. The **Profile Calculator** dialog will be displayed:

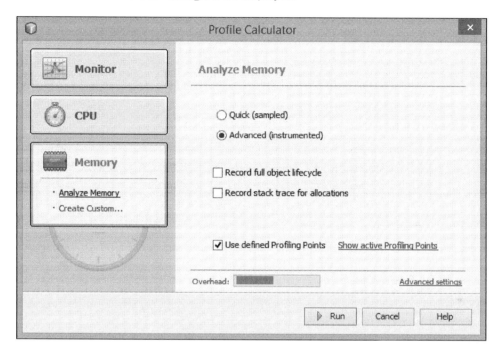

5. Click on the **Memory** profiler button at the left of the dialog and check the **Advanced (instrumented)** radio button. This will allow us to see memory usage for all code that is called by our application.

6. Click on the **Run** button.

7. The application will now run while NetBeans profiles execution of the code.

8. When the application has completed, a dialog will be displayed stating the application has finished execution and asking **Do you want to take a snapshot of the collected results?**. Click on **Yes**.

9. A memory snapshot window will now be displayed showing what classes are allocated to objects during the application's execution. The percentage of bytes allocated along with the number of bytes allocated and the objects allocated is shown in the following screenshot:

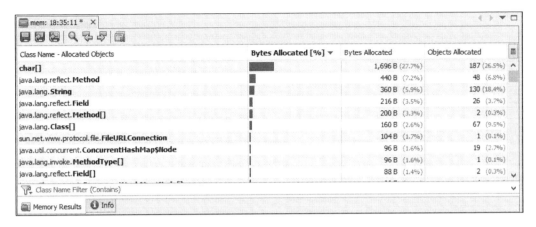

10. At the bottom of the memory snapshot window, there is a filter that allows the memory snapshot list to be filtered down. Enter the name `Calculator` into the filter box and press *Enter*.

11. The memory snapshot window will be contain only one entry—for our calculator class, as shown in the following screenshot:

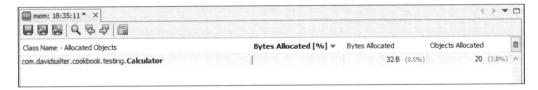

12. Click on the close button to close the memory snapshot window, and when prompted, save the results snapshot. This is now shown within the **Profiler** explorer. We can double-click on the snapshot at any time to view it again. The **Saved Snapshots** section is shown in the following screenshot:

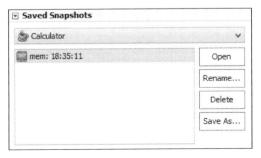

13. Looking at this entry, we can see that we allocated 20 objects during the execution of our code. This seems a bit excessive, so double-click on the line within the memory snapshot to open up the `Calculator` class. Looking at the class, we can see that we instantiate a `Calculator` object every time we call the `factorial()` method. This isn't necessary. Change the `else` clause within the `factorial()` method to read:

```
return (x * factorial(x-1));
```

14. Profile the application again, and filter to show only the `Calculator` class again. Note this time, how only one object is allocated—a potentially significant saving over the previous execution.

15. Click on the last button on the snapshot window (icon). This button allows us to compare the current memory with a saved memory snapshot.

16. The **Select Snapshot to Compare** dialog will be displayed. Select the previous snapshot and click on the **OK** button to compare the memory snapshots.

17. As before, filter the view to contain only the `Calculator` class. Note this time that the report tells us that initially we allocated 19 more objects than in our subsequent run.

There's more...

In addition to profiling memory, we can also profile the CPU usage and monitor the application's performance.

Monitoring the application is useful when we have multiple threads running as it shows us how many threads were allocated and how long they ran for, as shown in the following screenshot:

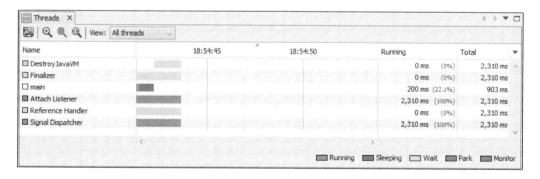

Monitoring CPU usage shows us how much CPU time is spent within each method of our application. When starting up monitoring CPU usage we can specify which classes we are interested in looking at, so for example, when running within an application server, we only look at the CPU overhead of our own classes and not that of the application server. The following screenshot shows an example of profiling the CPU usage time in the example application we created earlier:

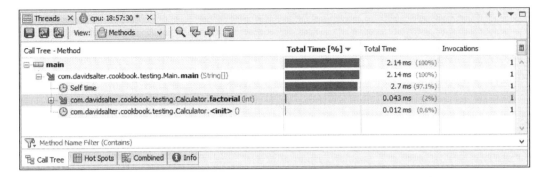

Profiling the CPU usage also gives us an indication of the hot spots, that is, the CPU intensive areas of our application. This can be invaluable when tracking down performance bottlenecks in an application.

11

Using External Web Services

In this chapter, we will cover the following recipes:

- ▶ Getting a list of Delicious bookmarks
- ▶ Adding a Delicious bookmark
- ▶ Getting a list of recent photos on Flickr
- ▶ Geocoding with Google Maps
- ▶ Verifying an e-mail address with StrikeIron
- ▶ Adding an additional web service into NetBeans

Introduction

With the ubiquitous nature of the Internet in the modern world, software developers are having to build connected applications more and more frequently. It's not enough to have standalone applications nowadays. Customers are demanding applications that can talk to other systems and that can mine data from multiple sources, bringing data together as valuable information.

Not long ago, XML was considered the answer to any integration problem with SOAP web services being hailed as the preferred integration mechanism. Despite SOAP's claims to be "simple", REST-based APIs have become increasingly common, with them generally offering an easier integration solution than SOAP-based web services. One of the major advantages of REST-based web services is their ability to return JSON data that can be consumed directly by JavaScript-based APIs.

Fortunately, NetBeans provides developers with an abstraction above all of these technologies and a Java-centric approach to invoking web services. Whether it's something comparatively simple such as validating an e-mail address or searching for online purchases on Amazon, NetBeans provides rapid access to many different web services.

Getting a list of Delicious bookmarks

Delicious (`http://delicious.com`) is a free online service allowing users to maintain collections of bookmarks that can be tagged and shared with other members of the community. Not only can bookmarks be tagged and shared, but Delicious provides facilities to discover new bookmarks based upon an individual user's interests.

NetBeans integrates with the Delicious web services, providing rapid access to manage both Delicious posts and their associated tags.

In this recipe, we'll see how we can get a list of all the bookmarks that we've stored in Delicious based on querying for a specific tag.

Getting ready

To complete this recipe, you'll need a Delicious account. Creating a Delicious account is free and easy. Head on over to `http://www.delicious.com` and create an account if you haven't got one already.

Once you've created a Delicious account, let's continue and create a standalone console application to display our bookmarks.

You can use either the Java EE or All download bundle of NetBeans to complete this recipe.

How to do it...

Perform the following steps to get a list of Delicious bookmarks:

1. Click on **File** and then on **New Project...** to create a new NetBeans project. Create a Java application called `DeliciousBookMarks` ensuring that a main class called `com.davidsalter.cookbook.delicious.BookMarks` is created.

    If you are having trouble creating a new project, check out the *Creating a Java application* recipe in *Chapter 1, Using NetBeans Projects*, of this book.

2. Ensure that the `BookMarks.java` file is open for editing.

3. Click on the **Services** explorer and expand the **Web Services** node. Locate the **Delicious** node and expand this to show the **Bookmarking Service** node. Expand this node and then the **[posts]** node within it:

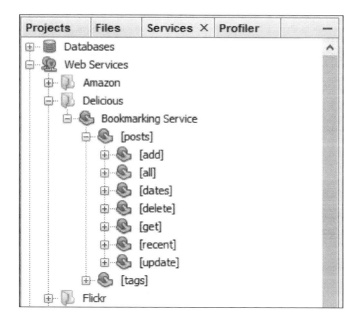

4. Expand the **[get]** node and note the **getPosts** web service inside it:

5. Drag the **getPosts** method from the **Services** explorer into the body of the `main()` method within the `BookMarks.java` class that is open within the editor window.

6. A dialog will briefly appear entitled **Generating Code for GET Saas Service** and then the **Customize GET Saas Service** dialog will be displayed.

7. Enter `Java` as the **Default Value** field for the **tag** parameter:

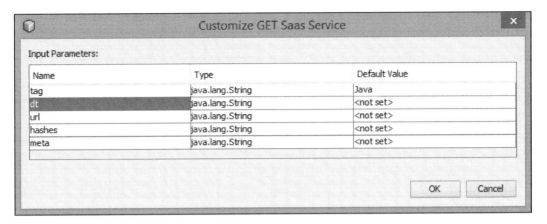

8. Click on **OK**.

9. NetBeans will now add the relevant files to the project allowing the Delicious web service to be invoked.

10. Edit the `BookMarks.java` class and add the following code as the last statement within the `if {}` statement:

```java
for (Post post : resultObj.getPost()) {
    System.out.println(post.getDescription());
    System.out.println(post.getHref());
}
```

11. Press *F6* to run the application.

12. NetBeans will display a **User Authentication** dialog for the Delicious web services. Enter your Delicious username and password and click on **Submit**.

13. Any bookmarks that you have tagged with Java will now be listed within the **Output** window of NetBeans:

How it works...

When using NetBeans to create connections to the Delicious web services, several helper classes are created within the project that allow the web services to be called:

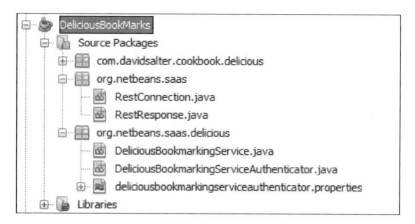

General purpose REST connection and response handler classes are created within the `org.netbeans.saas` packages. Classes designed specifically to invoke the Delicious bookmarking service are created within the `org.netbeans.saas.delicious` package.

To query for a list of bookmarks, the `DeliciousBookmarkingService.getPosts` method is invoked taking parameters that define the types of bookmarks returned. In our example, we queried for all posts that were tagged with the word `Java`.

To access the documentation for the Delicious web services, right-click on the **Bookmarking Service** node within the **Delicious** group in the **Services** explorer and select **View API Documentation**. This will open the default system browser and display the Delicious API help pages.

There's more...

When querying the Delicious web services, an authentication dialog is shown every time asking for username and password credentials. Instead of entering these credentials each time the application is executed, they can be stored within the `deliciousbookmarkingserviceauthenticator.properties` file that is stored within the `org.netbeans.saas.delicious` package. This is a simple properties file that uses the `username` and `password` keys to store login credentials.

You must remember to exclude this file from source control if you enter Delicious credentials into it. This file is not encrypted and allows anyone with access to the file to see your Delicious username and password.

Adding a Delicious bookmark

In this recipe, we'll see how we can store a bookmark within the Delicious social bookmark sharing system. If you are not familiar with Delicious, you should read the previous recipe, *Getting a list of Delicious bookmarks*.

Getting ready

To complete this recipe, you'll need a Delicious account. Creating a Delicious account is free and easy. Head on over to `http://www.delicious.com` and create an account if you haven't got one already.

Once you've created a Delicious account, let's continue and use NetBeans to store links within the service.

This recipe builds upon the application created in the previous recipe, *Getting a list of Delicious bookmarks*. If you have not completed this recipe, you can get the source code from the code download bundle for this chapter.

You can use either the Java EE or All download bundle of NetBeans to complete this recipe.

How to do it...

Perform the following steps to add a Delicious bookmark:

1. Create a new **Java Main Class** called `StoreBookMark.java` within the `com.davidsalter.cookbook.delicious` package.

2. Open the **Services** explorer and navigate to **Web Services | Delicious | Bookmarking Service | [posts] | [add]**.

3. Locate the **addPosts** web service and drag it into the body of the `StoreBookMark.main` method within the Java text editing window. The **addPosts** web service is shown in the following screenshot:

4. The **Customize GET Saas Service** dialog will be displayed.

5. Specify the following default values for **Input Parameters**:

   ❏ **url**: `http://www.packtpub.com/netbeans-ide-8-cookbook/book`

   ❏ **description**: `NetBeans 8 CookBook`

   ❏ **tags**: `Java, NetBeans`

We can see the **Customize GET Saas Service** dialog in the following screenshot:

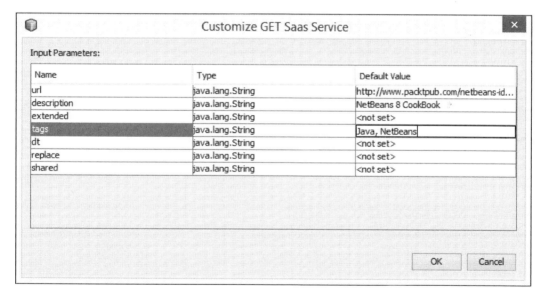

6. Click on the **OK** button.

7. NetBeans will now add the code to add a bookmark into the `StoreBookMark.java` class.

8. Right-click on the `StoreBookMark.java` class within the **Projects** explorer and select **Run File**.

9. Enter your Delicious credentials when requested.

10. The new bookmark will now be added to Delicious.

11. Open your browser and log in to your Delicious account to see the new bookmark you have stored, as shown in the following screenshot:

How it works...

When we dragged-and-dropped the **addPosts** web service onto our class, NetBeans correctly established that the helper classes required to invoke the Delicious web services were already added to our project. You'll remember that these helper classes were added to the project automatically in the previous recipe, *Getting a list of Delicious bookmarks*, when we initially dragged the **getPosts** web service into our code.

To store a bookmark within Delicious, NetBeans invoked the `DeliciousBookmarkingService.addPosts()` method passing in the information specified on the **Customize GET Saas Service** dialog.

To access the documentation for the Delicious web services, right-click on the **Bookmarking Service** node within the **Delicious** group in the **Services** explorer and select **View API Documentation**. This will open the default system browser and display the Delicious API help pages.

There's more...

If we want to check the response code of a call to any of the Delicious web services (and why wouldn't we!), we can query the returned object from the call.

In this example, the `addPosts()` method returns a `RestResponse` object, which has a `getResponseCode()` method. This method should return an HTTP 200 status code if everything is successful. Any other code would be an indication that something has not gone as expected.

For a discussion on the available HTTP status codes, check out the URL `http://www.w3.org/Protocols/rfc2616/rfc2616-sec10.html`.

In addition to storing bookmarks on Delicious, and querying them (as shown in the previous recipe, *Getting a list of Delicious bookmarks*), we can also delete and update bookmarks by dragging the appropriate web service into our code and customizing the input parameters. We can also manage the tags that we use to classify bookmarks by dragging the equivalent tag management web service into our code.

Getting a list of recent photos on Flickr

Flickr (`http://flickr.com`) is an online photo sharing site that allows members to store and share photos online.

With Flickr, you can search or browse photo collections. You can tag photos based upon location, title, camera type (and more) allowing easy retrieval at a later date.

NetBeans integrates with the Flickr web services, providing rapid access to manage both photos and their associated tagged data.

In this recipe, we'll see how we can get a list of the most recent photos uploaded to Flickr.

Getting ready

To complete this recipe, you'll need a Flickr account. Creating a Flickr account is free and easy. Head on over to `http://www.flickr.com` and create an account if you haven't got one already. You'll need a Flickr account to access the Flickr web services.

Once you've created a Flickr account, let's continue and create a standalone console application to query the latest photos uploaded to Flickr.

You can use either the Java EE or All download bundle of NetBeans to complete this recipe.

How to do it...

To get a list of recent photos on Flickr, perform the following steps:

1. Click on **File** and then on **New Project...** to create a new NetBeans project. Create a **Java Application** called `FlickrRecentPhotos` ensuring that a main class called `com.davidsalter.cookbook.flickr.FlickrRecentPhotos` is created.

If you are having trouble creating a new project, check out the
Creating a Java application recipe in *Chapter 1, Using NetBeans
Projects*, of this book.

2. Ensure that the `FlickrRecentPhotos.java` file is open for editing.

3. Click on the **Services** explorer and expand the **Web Services** node. Locate the **Flickr** node and expand this to show the **Photo Service** node. Expand this node and then the **[services]** and **[rest]** nodes within it, as shown in the following screenshot:

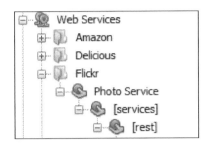

4. Locate the **photos_recentlyUpdated** web service underneath the **Flickr** web services and drag it into the `main` method of the `FlickrRecentPhotos.java` class.

5. The **Customize GET Saas Service** dialog will be displayed. Enter the following information into the dialog:

    ☐ **min_date**: `1388534400`

    ☐ **extras**: `Rain`

    ☐ **per_page**: `10`

    ☐ **page**: `1`

6. Click on the **OK** button.

7. NetBeans will now add the code to the `FlickrRecentPhotos.java` class to obtain a list of photos updated since January 1, 2014 (that is the equivalent to the UNIX timestamp 1388534400) that are tagged with the keyword `Rain`. A single page of results will be returned with a maximum of 10 photos.

8. Now, let's change the `FlickrRecentPhotos.java` class so that it prints out the titles of all the photos returned from the web service. Modify the body of the `if {}` statement to read:

```
flickr.photoservice.flickrresponse.Rsp resultObj =
        result.getDataAsObject(
            flickr.photoservice.flickrresponse.Rsp.class);

for (Rsp.Photos.Photo photo :
```

```
resultObj.getPhotos().getPhoto()) {
    System.out.println(photo.getTitle());
}
```

9. This code loops through the returned photos from the Flickr web service call and prints out the title of each post.

10. To invoke the Flickr web services, we need to specify our application key and secret key. Log in to your Flickr account and browse to `https://www.flickr.com/services/apps/create/`. From there, you can request an API key. Follow the onscreen instructions to request a key. You will then be provided with a `Key` and the corresponding `Secret`.

11. Back in NetBeans, edit the `org.netbeans.saas.flickr.flickrphotoserviceauthenticator.properties` file, entering the API `Key` and `Secret` values you have just got from Flickr, as shown in the following screenshot:

```
1  # To change this template, choose Tools | Templates
2  # and open the template in the editor.
3  api_key=<my api key>
4  secret=<my api secret>
```

12. That should be enough to run our application and query Flickr for our recently added photos. Unfortunately (or is it fortunately), the Flickr API requires SSL access to any of its services. This obviously helps prevent security issues when passing keys across the Internet. The NetBeans code to access Flickr, however, uses HTTP instead of HTTPS, so we need to make a small modification to the NetBeans generated files to allow them to use HTTPS instead of HTTP.

13. Edit the `FlickrPhotoServiceAuthenticator.java` class. Search and replace all instances of `http` with `https`. There should be three instances to change.

14. Now, edit the `FlickrPhotoService.java` class. Search and replace all instances of `http` with `https`. There should be only one instance to replace.

15. We've now made all the changes necessary to run the application. Press *F6* to run the application.

16. A **Flickr Authorization Dialog** will be displayed showing a URL that must be accessed to allow your application to access Flickr. Copy this URL and paste it into your browser to authorize. When you've authorized in the browser, click on the **OK** button, as shown in the following screenshot:

17. The titles of the 10 most recent images you have uploaded to Flickr matching our search criteria will now be displayed within the NetBeans console.

How it works...

When we added the Flickr web services to our NetBeans project, NetBeans automatically created the necessary classes to interact with the web services, doing much of the hard work for us.

The `org.netbeans.saas.RestConnection` and `org.netbeans.saas.RestResponse` classes are the standard classes that NetBeans creates for consuming any REST-based web service.

Specifically, the `org.netbeans.saas.flickr.FlickrPhotoService` and `org.netbeans.saas.flickr.FlickrPhotoServiceAuthenticator` classes were generated for interacting with Flickr. Within the `FlickrPhotoService` class, we can see that there is a single `photosRecentlyUpdated` method that queries a user's Flickr account and returns a list of recently updated photos. If we were to invoke more Flickr web services, then additional methods would be added into this class. As the name suggests, the `FlickrPhotoServiceAuthenticator` class deals with user authentication against Flickr.

One final point of note is that, when querying Flickr, we had to use a UNIX timestamp instead of a more traditional date format. This is simply due to the requirements of the Flickr API.

For more information about UNIX timestamps, check out this article on Wikipedia at `http://en.wikipedia.org/wiki/Unix_time`.

There's more...

You must have noticed that when authorizing your application at Flickr, the default method of operation is to grant full access to your Flickr account. This includes the ability to edit and delete photos from your account. The following screenshot shows these Flickr authorization options:

By authorizing this link, you'll allow **FlickrPhotos** to:

- ✓ **Access** your Flickr account (including private content)

- ✓ **Upload**, **Edit**, and **Replace** photos and videos in your account

- ✓ **Interact** with other members' photos and videos (comment, add notes, favorite)

- ✓ **Delete** photos and videos from your account

OK, I'LL AUTHORIZE IT   NO THANKS

If you're writing an application that requires read-only access to your account, you can edit the `FlickrPhotoServiceAuthenticator.java` class and change the `readOnly` member to be equal to `true`, as shown in the following screenshot:

```
private static boolean readOnly = true;
```

Now, whenever your application requires authentication with Flickr, it will only be able to read information and will not be able to perform any actions that may result in editing or deletion of data.

Geocoding with Google Maps

Geocoding is the process of converting place names or addresses into positional coordinates, returning any other salient information along the way. Once coordinates for a place or landmark are known, the location can be easily represented on a map providing easy-to-use information to consumers.

Google, as one of the premiere mapping service providers, supplies a Geocoding API that can be invoked directly from within NetBeans by simply dragging-and-dropping the web service into an appropriate Java class.

More information on Google Geocoding, including license terms, data formats, and general information about the API can be found at `https://developers.google.com/maps/documentation/geocoding/`.

In this recipe, we'll see how we can convert a location name into more useful information including positional latitude and longitude.

Getting ready

To complete this recipe, you'll need a Google account and a Google API key that allows geocoding. All these are free to obtain, but check out the Google licensing conditions before creating an account and API key.

To obtain an API key, navigate to `https://code.google.com/apis/console` and create a new project (this is simply so that an API key can be created—your application is not stored on Google's servers anywhere). For the application, ensure you activate the Geocoding API so that a key is generated, as shown in the following screenshot:

Clicking on the **Credentials** tab for your application will then give you access to your public API key. The resultant window will look like the following screenshot:

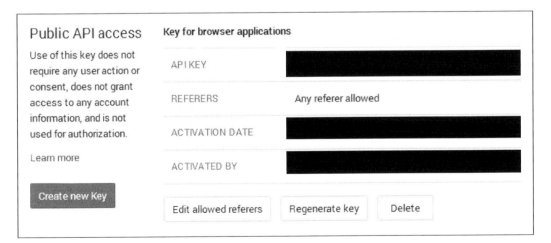

Once you've created a Google account and a project that has access to the Geocoding API, let's continue and create a standalone console application that can geocode a place name and provide useful information (including location) about the place.

You can use either the Java EE or All download bundle of NetBeans to complete this recipe.

How to do it...

To convert a location name into more useful information, perform the following steps:

1. Click on **File** and then on **New Project...** to create a new NetBeans project. Create a Java application called `Geocoding` ensuring that a main class called `com.davidsalter.cookbook.geocoding.Geocoding` is created.

> If you are having trouble creating a new project, check out the *Creating a Java application* recipe in *Chapter 1, Using NetBeans Projects*, of this book.

2. Ensure that the `Geocoding.java` file is open for editing.

3. Click on the **Services** explorer and expand the **Web Services** node. Locate the **Google** node and expand this to show the **Geocoding Service** node. Expand this node and then the **[geo]** node within it, as shown in the following screenshot:

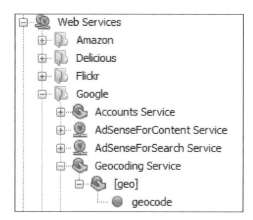

4. Locate the **geocode** web service underneath the **Geocoding Service** web services and drag it into the `main` method of the `Geocoding.java` class.

5. The **Customize GET Saas Service** dialog will be displayed. Enter the following information into the dialog:

   ☐ **q**: `trafalgar square, london`

   ☐ **output**: `json`

   We can see the **Customize GET Saas Service** dialog in the following screenshot:

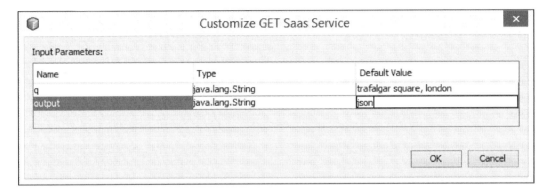

6. Click on the **OK** button.

7. NetBeans will now add the code to the `Geocoding.java` class to query the Google Geocoding service and to retrieve information about Trafalgar Square in London in a JSON format.

8. We need to change the generated code within the `main()` method within the `Geocoding.java` class in order to see the results of the API call. Since we're not retrieving XML, we can simply check the `return` response code and print out the response as a string if `Success` is returned. Modify the `Geocoding.main()` method to read as follows:

```
public static void main(String[] args) {
    try {
        String q = "trafalgar square, london";
        String output = "json";

        RestResponse result =
            GoogleGeocodingService.geocode(
                q,
                output);
        if (result.getResponseCode()==200) {
            System.out.println(
                "The SaasService returned: "
                +result.getDataAsString());
        }
    } catch (Exception ex) {
        ex.printStackTrace();
    }
}
```

9. As when calling most API methods, we need to specify the API key that we obtained from Google allowing access to the Geocoding API. Edit the `org.netbeans.saas.google.googlegeocodingauthenticator.properties` file and enter your Google API key, as shown in the following screenshot:

```
1  # To change this template, choose Tools | Templates
2  # and open the template in the editor.
3  api_key=<my api key>
```

If we were to run the application now, we'd expect to see lots of information, including latitude and longitude, about Trafalgar Square in London. Unfortunately, if we run the application, we get an HTML error result stating that Google can't process the request, as shown in the following screenshot:

```
Output - Geocoding (run)  X

 run:
 java.io.IOException: <html><head><meta http-equiv="content-type" content="text/html; charset=utf-8"/><title>Sorry...</title>
 <style> body { font-family: verdana, arial, sans-serif; background-color: #fff; color: #000; }</style></head><body><div><tab
 le><tr><td><b><font face=times color=#0039b6 size=10>G</font><font face=times color=#c41200 size=10>o</font><font face=times
  color=#f3c518 size=10>o</font><font face=times color=#0039b6 size=10>g</font><font face=times color=#30a72f size=10>l</font
 ><font face=times color=#c41200 size=10>e</font></b></td><td style="text-align: left; vertical-align: bottom; padding-bottom
 : 15px; width: 50%"><div style="border-bottom: 1px solid #dfdfdf;">Sorry...</div></td></tr></table></div><div style="margin-
 left: 4em;"><h1>We're sorry...</h1><p>... but your computer or network may be sending automated queries. To protect our user
 s, we can't process your request right now.</p></div><div style="margin-left: 4em;">See <a href="https://support.google.com/
 websearch/answer/86640">Google Help</a> for more information.<br/><br/></div><div style="text-align: center; border-top: 1px
  solid #dfdfdf;">&copy; 2013 Google - <a href="https://www.google.com">Google Home</a></div></body></html>

         at org.netbeans.saas.RestConnection.connect(RestConnection.java:207)
         at org.netbeans.saas.RestConnection.get(RestConnection.java:92)
         at org.netbeans.saas.google.GoogleGeocodingService.geocode(GoogleGeocodingService.java:44)
         at com.davidsalter.cookbook.geocoding.Geocoding.main(Geocoding.java:26)
 BUILD SUCCESSFUL (total time: 1 second)
```

This error occurs because Google has slightly changed the API endpoint for its geocoding web services. As a result, we need to modify the `org.netbeans.saas.google.GoogleGeocodingService.java` class that was automatically generated for us by NetBeans with the following steps:

1. Open the `org.netbeans.saas.google.GoogleGeocodingService.java` class for editing by double-clicking on it within the **Projects** explorer.

2. Change the `geocode` method to read as follows:

```
public static RestResponse geocode(String q, String output)
throws IOException {
    String apiKey = GoogleGeocodingServiceAuthenticator.
        getApiKey();
    String[][] pathParams = new String[][]{};
    String[][] queryParams = new String[][]
        {{"address", q},
        {"key", "" + apiKey + ""},
```

```
                    {"output", output}};
          RestConnection conn = new RestConnection(
              "https://maps.googleapis.com/maps/api/geocode/json",
              pathParams,
              queryParams);
          sleep(1000);
          return conn.get(null);
    }
```

3. Now that we've written some code to query the Google geocoding web service and output the results to the **Output** window, we can run the application and check out the results. Press *F6* to run the application. We will get the output as shown in the following screenshot:

```
Output - Geocoding (run)  X
                    "short_name" : "WC2N 5DN",
                    "types" : [ "postal_code" ]
              }
          ],
          "formatted_address" : "Trafalgar Square, London WC2N 5DN, UK",
          "geometry" : {
             "location" : {
                 "lat" : 51.508039,
                 "lng" : -0.128069
             },
             "location_type" : "APPROXIMATE",
             "viewport" : {
                 "northeast" : {
                     "lat" : 51.50938798029149,
                     "lng" : -0.126720019708498
                 },
                 "southwest" : {
                     "lat" : 51.5066900197085,
                     "lng" : -0.129417980291502
                 }
             }
          },
          "types" : [ "point_of_interest", "establishment" ]
       }
    ],
    "status" : "OK"
 }

 BUILD SUCCESSFUL (total time: 2 seconds)
```

4. If we scroll towards the bottom of the **Output** window, we can see that the information for latitude and longitude is retrieved for our chosen location.

How it works...

When we added the Google Geocoding web services to our NetBeans project, NetBeans automatically created the necessary classes to interact with the web services doing much of the hard work for us.

The `org.netbeans.saas.RestConnection` and `org.netbeans.saas.RestResponse` classes are the standard classes that NetBeans creates for consuming any REST-based web service.

Specifically, the `org.netbeans.saas.google.GoogleGeocodingService` and `org.netbeans.saas.google.GoogleGeocodingServiceAuthenticator` classes were generated for interacting with Google's Geocoding API.

Within the `org.netbeans.saas.google.GoogleGeocodingService` class, there is a single `geocode()` method. Since Google has slightly modified the REST endpoint for its geocoding web service, we had to modify the NetBeans autogenerated code to take this into account. The underlying REST endpoint for Google Geocoding is `https://maps.googleapis.com/maps/api/geocode/json`.

The `org.netbeans.saas.google.googlegeocodingserviceauthenticator.properties` file is where we stored our private API key that provides access to the Google Geocoding API.

> For more information about Geocoding and its uses and issues, check out the article on Wikipedia at `http://en.wikipedia.org/wiki/Geocoding`.

Verifying an e-mail address with StrikeIron

StrikeIron is a **Data-as-a-Service** (**DaaS**) provider that offers many solutions for data validation. For example, it offers services to validate e-mail addresses, postal addresses, and telephone numbers.

StrikeIron is a paid-for service; however, it offers free trials of all of its APIs so you can evaluate them before deciding whether to proceed.

More information on StrikeIron and on its DaaS offering can be found at `http://www.strikeiron.com`. Information about the *StrikeIron Email Verification* service can be found at `http://www.strikeiron.com/product-list/email/email-verification`.

In this recipe, we'll see how we can validate an e-mail address using StrikeIron.

Getting ready

To complete this recipe, you'll need a StrikeIron account. Creating a StrikeIron account is free of charge and provides you free trial access to all of StrikeIron's services. You can create a StrikeIron account to access a free trial of its e-mail validation web services at `http://offers.strikeiron.com/email-verification-hygiene-1`.

Once you've created a StrikeIron account and have a username and password, let's continue and create a standalone console application that can validate an e-mail address.

You can use either the Java EE or All download bundle of NetBeans to complete this recipe.

How to do it...

To validate an e-mail address using StrikeIron, perform the following steps:

1. Click on **File** and then on **New Project...** to create a new NetBeans project. Create a Java application called `EmailValidator` ensuring that a main class called `com.davidsalter.cookbook.email.EmailValidator` is created.

> If you are having trouble creating a new project, check out the *Creating a Java application* recipe in *Chapter 1, Using NetBeans Projects*, of this book.

2. Ensure that the `EmailValidator.java` file is open for editing.

3. Click on the **Services** explorer and expand the **Web Services** node. Locate the **StrikeIron** node and expand this to show the **Email Verification v5** service. Expand this node and the **EmailVerificationSoap** node within it, as shown in the following screenshot:

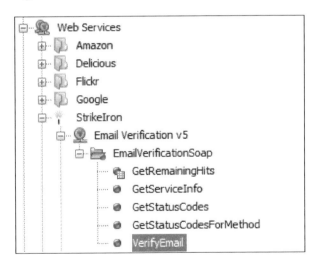

4. Locate the **Verify Email** web service underneath the **Email Verification v5** web services and drag it into the `main` method of the `EmailValidator.java` class.

5. The **Customize VerifyEmail Saas Service** dialog will be displayed. Enter the following information into the dialog:

   ❑ **userID**: Your StrikeIron user ID

   ❑ **password**: Your StrikeIron password

   ❑ **email**: `iaminvalid@nowhere`

   ❑ **timeout**: `15`

   We can see the **Customize VerifyEmail Saas Service** dialog in the following screenshot:

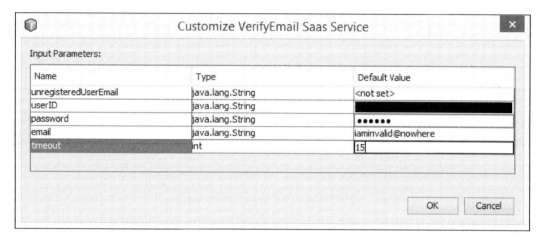

6. Click on the **OK** button.

7. NetBeans will now add the code to the `EmailValidator.java` class to query the e-mail address we entered (`iaminvalid@nowhere`).

8. We need to change the generated code within the `main()` method within the `EmailValidator.java` class in order to see the results of the API call. Immediately after the call to `port.verifyEmail(...)`, add the following code:

```
System.out.println(verifyEmailResult.value.
getServiceStatus().getStatusDescription());
```

9. We've now entered all of the information we need, so press *F6* to run the application and validate the e-mail address.

10. The application will launch, and a message will be displayed in the **Output** window indicating that the e-mail address has an invalid domain name (shown in the following screenshot)—StrikeIron is telling us that the e-mail address is invalid:

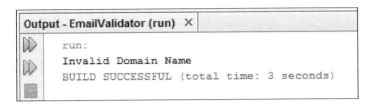

Now, let's change the code so we can see what happens when we try to validate a valid e-mail address with the following steps:

1. Edit the `EmailValidator.java` class and change the email variable to contain your e-mail address. So, for example, if your e-mail address is `cookbookreader@gmail.com`, change the email variable to read:

```
java.lang.String email = "cookbookreader@gmail.com";
```

2. Press *F6* to run the application again, and note that this time StrikeIron has successfully validated the e-mail address:

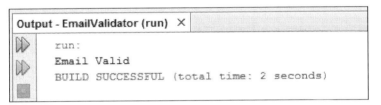

How it works...

When validating e-mail addresses with the StrikeIron tools, NetBeans creates five variables to hold the input parameters to StrikeIron:

▸ `unregisteredUserEmail`: This variable is a hangover from when StrikeIron used to allow unregistered users access to its API by specifying an e-mail address. This field is best left empty.

▸ userID: This is your user ID provided by StrikeIron. Most probably, this will be the e-mail address that you registered with at StrikeIron.

▸ password: This is your API password that was generated for you by StrikeIron when you created an account.

▸ email: This is the e-mail address that you wish to validate.

▸ timeout: This is the timeout period in seconds for querying the StrikeIron web services. This has to be within the range of 15 to 120 for the API call to succeed.

Unlike the previous recipes where NetBeans created specific classes for interacting with REST endpoints, NetBeans has used JAX-WS in this recipe to query the SOAP web services we have called. Classes representing the entities used by the web services are defined within the EmailVerification.jar library that NetBeans has automatically created and added to our project.

 For more information on JAX-WS, check out the documentation at https://jax-ws.java.net/.

NetBeans automatically generated code to instantiate the web service (com.strikeiron.EmailVerification service) and the port (com.strikeiron.EmailVerificationSoap port) for us to invoke web service operations.

We then invoked the web service operation to verify the provided e-mail address (port.verifyEmail(..)).

Finally, we checked the result of the web service call to establish whether the e-mail address was valid or not. We did this by checking the statusDescription field of the web service result.

There's more...

So far, we've written code to query the StrikeIron services to validate e-mail addresses. What if we just want to quickly test a web service without writing any code? Can this be done?

It certainly can. If we expand the node under the **Email Verification v5** web service in the **Services** explorer and then right-click on the **Verify Email** web service (rather than dragging it into a class), we get the **Test Method** option. Selecting this option causes the **Test Web Service Method** dialog to be displayed where we can enter different data for the different web service parameters and get rapid feedback on how the web service works. The **Test Web Service Method** dialog is shown in the following screenshot:

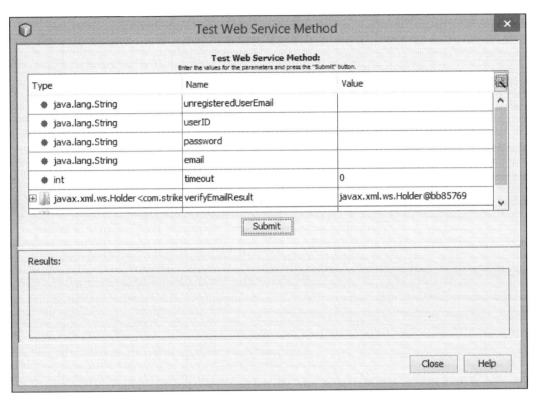

In addition to verifying e-mails, StrikeIron provides many other data and validation services, all of which can be invoked and tested in a similar fashion to the **Email Validation v5** web service described earlier. This is shown in the following screenshot:

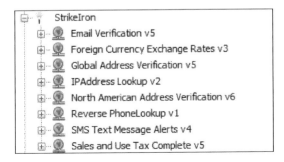

Adding an additional web service into NetBeans

In this chapter, we've looked at recipes that show how to consume different web services easily, all from within NetBeans by simply dragging-and-dropping the web service into an appropriate Java class. NetBeans is supplied with easy access to a wide variety of different web services from Amazon, Delicious, Flickr, Google, StrikeIron, WeatherBug, Zillow, and Zvents.

Although this is a huge number of web services, there are numerous others that aren't included by default within the **Services** explorer within NetBeans.

In this recipe, we'll see how we can add new web services into the **Services** explorer so that we can then drag-and-drop these into NetBeans classes, thereby easily consuming the web services from the client code.

Getting ready

To complete this recipe, we'll be accessing the web services defined at `http://webservicex.net`. Specifically, we'll be adding the Stock Quote web service into NetBeans and then testing that it works correctly.

WebserviceX.NET is a free collection of web services covering a wide range of topics such as stock quotes, global weather, and address verification. A full list of services can be found at `http://www.webservicex.net/WS/wscatlist.aspx`.

You don't need to create an account to use the WebserviceX.NET.

You can use either the Java EE or All download bundle of NetBeans to complete this recipe.

How to do it...

Perform the following steps to add a new web service:

1. Ensure the **Services** explorer is selected and then right-click on the **Web Services** node. A pop-up menu will be displayed with the **Add Web Service...** and **Create Group** options, as shown in the following screenshot:

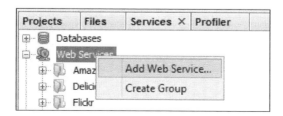

2. Click on **Add Web Service....** The **Add Web Service** dialog will be displayed. On this dialog, we must enter the WSDL for the web service that we are adding to NetBeans.

3. In the **URL** field, enter the value `http://www.webservicex.net/stockquote.asmx?WSDL`, as shown in the following screenshot:

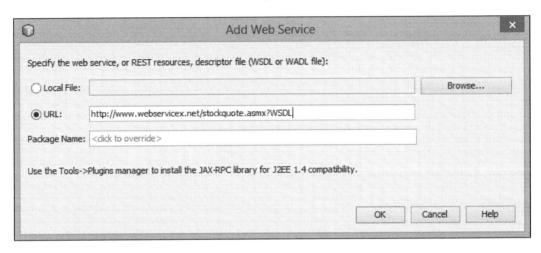

4. Click on **OK**.

5. After a few seconds, the new web service will be displayed as the last entry underneath the **Web Services** node within the **Services** explorer:

Now that we've added the web service into NetBeans, let's quickly test that it's working correctly with the following steps:

1. Expand the **stockquote-asmx** node underneath **Web Services** in the **Services** explorer.

If you have the **Output** window open while expanding the **stockquote.asmx** node, you will see a lot of output generated from NetBeans as it loads the WSDL for the web service and generates the necessary artifacts to invoke the web service. Reading this output gives a good indication of what NetBeans has to do to enable us to easily invoke the web service.

2. Expand the **StockQuoteSoap** web service and right-click on the **GetQuote** operation within. From the pop-up menu, select the **Test Method** option.

3. The **Test Web Service Method** dialog will be displayed, so let's find out the value of Oracle stock.

4. Enter the **Value** field as ORCL. This is the stock market symbol for Oracle Corporation.

5. Click on the **Submit** button.

6. After a few seconds, the **Results** field will be populated with the results of the web service call, as shown in the following screenshot:

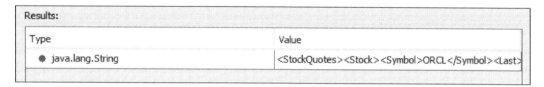

7. Click on the XML code displayed within the **Value** field to display a dialog box that shows all of the XML code. Reading the XML code, we can see that at the time of this writing the Oracle stock was worth $40.33 a share, as shown in the following screenshot:

How it works...

When we add a web service reference into NetBeans, we must specify either the REST resource for the service, or the service's description file (WSDL or WADL). In this recipe, we specified a WSDL for a SOAP-based web service.

NetBeans gave us the option of specifying a **Package Name** field when defining the WSDL; however, we deliberately left this blank so that the default package name would be used. The package name is that of the Java classes that NetBeans automatically creates (using JAX-WS in this example) for invoking the web service. If no package name is specified, then NetBeans calculates one based on the URL of the WSDL file. So, the package name for WebserviceX. NET's Stock Quote web service is `net.webservicex`.

 If we are planning on using more than one web service from the same provider, it would be useful to specify the package; thus, for example, we could have `net.webservice.stock` for the stock service and perhaps `net.webservicex.weather` for the weather service.

There's more...

If at any time, the WSDL for the web service changes, we can right-click on the web service (**stockquote-asmx** in this recipe) and select the **Refresh** option. This will cause NetBeans to re-read the WSDL and regenerate the client classes for invoking the web service.

We can also view the WSDL for a web service by right-clicking on the web service and selecting the **View WSDL** option.

Finally, if we no longer wish to use the web service, we can delete it from the **Services** explorer by right-clicking on the web service and selecting the **Delete** option.

If we have added a lot of web services into the **Services** explorer, it can be useful to group them so that they can easily be found when required. This can be achieved by right-clicking on the **Web Services** node and selecting the **Create Group** menu option. After selecting this option, NetBeans allows us to specify a new name for a group (basically, an empty node underneath the **Web Services** node). Upon creating the group, we can drag any existing web services into the group, allowing us to categorize them further. For further classification, NetBeans allows us to create groups within groups so that a hierarchy of web services can be specified.

12
Extending NetBeans

In this chapter, we will cover the following recipes:

- ▶ Creating a NetBeans module
- ▶ Packaging a NetBeans module for deployment

Introduction

NetBeans is a fully fledged IDE that provides many features to aid in a developer's day-to-day activities when developing applications.

We take some of the features available within NetBeans for granted, such as the ability to load and save Java source files. The majority of these features are provided, by default, with a standard installation of NetBeans. We don't need to install any extra plugins or components to get the desired functionality. This all adds up to NetBeans being an excellent feature-rich IDE.

Some features that we, as developers, use daily are not provided as standard with NetBeans and have to be installed separately via the NetBeans plugin center. Some of these plugins are developed by the NetBeans team, whereas others are contributed via third-party developers. For example, the WildFly plugin that allows Java EE developers to manage and deploy to the WildFly application server was not developed by NetBeans, but was contributed to the NetBeans plugin center and helps to advance the functionality provided by the IDE.

 The WildFly plugin was not provided as standard with NetBeans 8, but due to its popularity, has been included with NetBeans 8.0.1 and higher.

In addition to being a comprehensive IDE for multiple language development, NetBeans is also a platform that can act as a basis for developing complex Swing-based applications. When using NetBeans as a platform, many basic plumbing tasks are taken care of automatically, such as window management and connecting application logic to menu options and toolbar buttons.

In this final chapter, we'll take a look at how we can develop additional plugins for NetBeans and how we can package them up for deployment by other users. Extending NetBeans is a massive topic that warrants an entire book, so we'll just be scratching the surface of it, showing the sort of things that can be done to extend NetBeans.

 For more information on the NetBeans platform, and the types of modules that can be developed, check out the platform documentation at `https://netbeans.org/features/platform/all-docs.html`.

Creating a NetBeans module

The NetBeans IDE has been developed in a fashion that allows third-party developers to write additional plugins (sometimes called **modules**), which can provide additional functionality for the NetBeans IDE. Once written, these plugins are usually published at the NetBeans Plugin Center, where they can be discovered by other NetBeans users.

In this recipe, we'll show how to write a NetBeans Code Generator plugin that will allow us to easily add the basics of a JUnit test into a Java class. The plugin will be invoked by pressing *Alt + Insert* for the code generation option within NetBeans.

Getting ready

No special steps are required before completing this recipe.

Any version of NetBeans (Java SE, Java EE, or the All bundle) can be used to perform this recipe.

How to do it...

To create a NetBeans module, perform the following steps:

1. Click on **File** and then **New Project...** to open the **New Project** dialog.
2. Select **NetBeans Modules** from the list of **Categories** and **Module** from the list of **Projects**. Click on **Next**.

3. Enter the **Project Name** field as `AddUnitTest`. Ensure that the **Standalone Module** option is selected with **Development IDE** as the NetBeans Platform, as shown in the following screenshot:

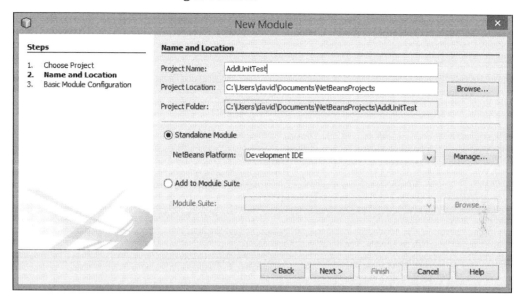

4. Click on **Next**.

5. On the **Basic Module Configuration** page of the **New Module** dialog, enter the **Code Name Base** field as `com.davidsalter.cookbook.codegenerator`. Change the **Module Display Name** field to `Add Unit Test` (we are just adding spaces here to make it more readable). Ensure that the **Localizing Bundle** field is automatically updated to `com/davidsalter/cookbook/codegenerator/Bundle.properties` after we have made these changes, as shown in the following screenshot:

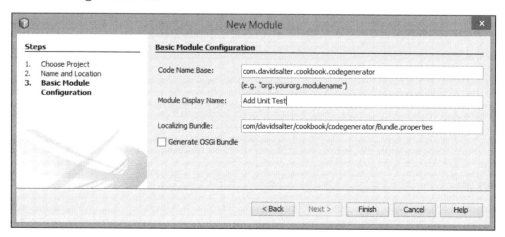

6. Click on **Finish**.

7. A new module project will now be created by NetBeans. Note how this project has a different icon from other projects we have created so far within this book. This new icon represents a NetBeans module project rather than a Java project or a Java web project, as shown in the following screenshot:

Now that we've created an empty module project, we need to add some functionality into it so that we can quickly add a test into our Java code. Let's do that now with the following steps:

1. Right-click on the `Add Unit Test` project within the **Projects** explorer and select **New** and then **Other...**.

2. Select **Module Development** from the list of **Categories** and **Code Generator** from the list of **File Types**, as shown in the following screenshot:

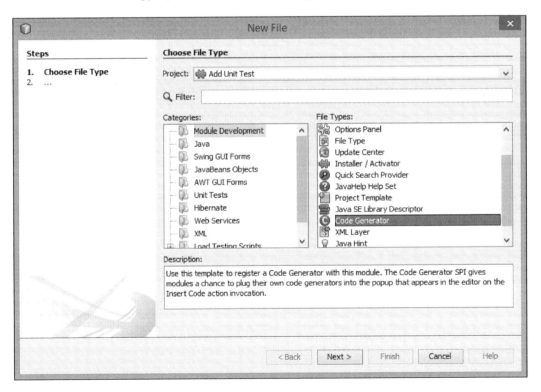

3. Click on **Next**.

4. The **New Code Generator** dialog will be displayed. Enter the following information into this dialog:

   - **Class Name**: AddUnitTest
   - **Package**: com.davidsalter.cookbook.codegenerator
   - **MimeType**: text/x-java

5. Click on **Finish**.

6. The **New Code Generator** dialog will now close.

In order to modify a class via our plugin (so that we can insert a new test method), we need to specify that we will be referencing the NetBeans **Java Source**, **Javac API Wrapper**, and **Utilities API** modules. Let's do that now with the following steps:

1. Right-click on the Add Unit Test project within the **Projects** explorer and select **Properties**. The **Project Properties** dialog will be displayed.

2. Select **Libraries** from the list of **Categories**, as shown in the following screenshot:

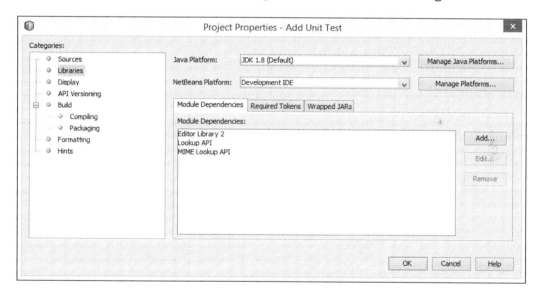

3. Click on the **Add** button within the **Module Dependencies** section to open the **Add Module Dependency** dialog.

4. Select the **Java Source**, **Javac API Wrapper**, and **Utilities API** modules and click on the **OK** button, as shown in the following screenshot:

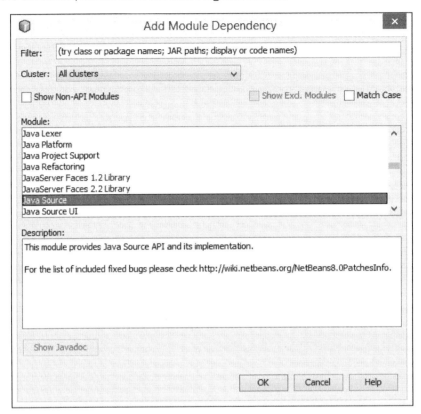

5. The list of **Module Dependencies** used by the project will now be updated to include the **Java Source**, **Javac API Wrapper**, and **Utilities API** modules, Javac API Wrapper, and Utilities API modules, as shown in the following screenshot:

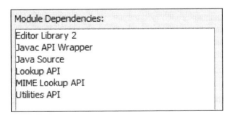

6. Click on the **OK** button to close the properties dialog.

We've now created an empty code generation module within our NetBeans module. Let's now define the name that is displayed for our module in the *Alt + Insert* **Generate** pop-up menu and then write the code that will add an empty JUnit test into our code with the following steps:

1. Ensure that the `AddUnitTest.java` file is open for editing within NetBeans.

2. Locate the method name `getDisplayName()` (at or around line 39). Modify the returned string to read `JUnit Test...`, as shown in the following screenshot:

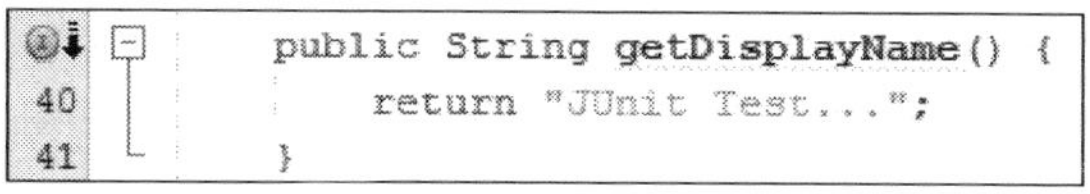

3. Locate the `invoke()` method (at or around line 47). Change the contents of this method to read:

```
public void invoke() {
  try {
    CancellableTask task = new
    CancellableTask<WorkingCopy>() {

      @Override
      public void cancel() {
      }

      @Override
      public void run(WorkingCopy workingCopy) throws
      Exception {
        workingCopy.toPhase(Phase.RESOLVED);
        CompilationUnitTree compilationUnitTree =
        workingCopy.getCompilationUnit();
        TreeMaker treeMaker = workingCopy.getTreeMaker();
        for (Tree typeDecl :
        compilationUnitTree.getTypeDecls()) {
          if (Tree.Kind.CLASS == typeDecl.getKind()) {
            ClassTree clazz = (ClassTree) typeDecl;
            ModifiersTree methodModifiers = treeMaker.
            Modifiers(Collections.<Modifier>
            singleton(Modifier.PUBLIC),
            Arrays.asList(treeMaker.Annotation
            (treeMaker.Identifier("Test"),
            Collections.EMPTY_LIST)));
            String methodName = "testAbc";
```

```
                    String methodBody = "{ fail(\"Test not written
                    yet\"); }";

                    TypeElement typeElement = workingCopy.
                    getElements().getTypeElement
                    ("java.lang.Exception");
                    ExpressionTree throwsClause = treeMaker.
                    QualIdent(typeElement);
                    MethodTree newMethod = treeMaker.
                    Method(methodModifiers, methodName,
                    treeMaker.PrimitiveType(TypeKind.VOID),
                    Collections.<TypeParameterTree>emptyList(),
                    Collections.EMPTY_LIST,
                    Collections.<ExpressionTree>
                    singletonList(throwsClause),
                    methodBody,null);
                    ClassTree modifiedClazz =
                    treeMaker.addClassMember(clazz, newMethod);
                    workingCopy.rewrite(clazz, modifiedClazz);
                }
            }
        }
    };
    Document doc = textComp.getDocument();
    JavaSource javaSource = JavaSource.forDocument(doc);
    ModificationResult result =
    javaSource.runModificationTask(task);
    result.commit();
    } catch (Exception e) {
    Exceptions.printStackTrace(e);
    }
}
```

We've now added all the code necessary to modify any open Java source file and insert a test method into it. Let's run the code and see how it works with the following steps:

1. Right-click on the `Add Unit Test` project within the **Projects** explorer and select **Run**.

2. NetBeans will build the module and a new instance of NetBeans will be started up.

3. Within this new instance of NetBeans, create a simple Java project with a `main` method class in it. The name of the project and class are unimportant as this is just a test project to see how our plugin works.

4. Right-click within the source for a Java file and select **Insert Code...**. The **Generate** pop up is displayed with our new **JUnit Test...** option within it, as shown in the following screenshot:

```
Generate
JUnit Test...
Constructor...
Logger...
toString()...
Override Method...
Add Property...
Call Web Service Operation...
Generate REST Client...
```

5. Select the **JUnit Test...** option and note how a blank JUnit test is added into the class methods, as shown in the following screenshot:

```
@Test
public void testAbc() throws IOException {
    fail("Test not written yet");
}
```

<h2>How it works...</h2>

In this recipe, we created a NetBeans module that plugs in to the **Insert Code...** menu option allowing us to quickly add the basics of a JUnit test into a Java class.

We started off by creating a NetBeans module and targeting it at the development IDE. This means that the module is compiled against the artefacts provided by the IDE that the plugin is currently being developed in. In my case, this is the All distribution of NetBeans 8.0. For the module, we defined a display name and a base package. A localization bundle was created for us automatically, although we didn't use this specifically in this recipe in order to keep a complex example more understandable.

We then used the **New File** wizard to add a Code Generator class into the module. A Code Generator class is a standard Java class that implements the `org.netbeans.spi.editor.codegen.CodeGenerator` interface. It's the fact that we implement this interface and define the methods within it that allows NetBeans to dynamically locate our plugin at runtime and add it's functionality into NetBeans as though it's part of the default product.

The `CodeGenerator` interface is defined as shown in the following code:

```
public interface CodeGenerator {
    @MimeLocation(subFolderName="CodeGenerators")
    public static interface Factory {
```

```
        public List<? Extends CodeGenerator> create(Lookup lkp);
    }

    public String getDisplayName();

    public void invoke();
}
```

Let's take a look at how we implemented these methods.

When creating the Code Generator, we were asked to specify a MIME type. A **MIME (Multipurpose Internet Email Extension)** type simply represents the type of a file just as it does with e-mail attachments. There are many different MIME types such as text/plain for a textual file or image/png for a .png graphics file. We chose text/x-java as this is the MIME type for a Java source code file. NetBeans took this information and added it into the Factory class it created for us.

 For more information on MIME types, check out http://en.wikipedia.org/wiki/MIME.

The following is a screenshot of the Factory class:

```
@MimeRegistration(mimeType = "text/x-java", service = CodeGenerator.Factory.class)
public static class Factory implements CodeGenerator.Factory {
  public List<? extends CodeGenerator> create(Lookup context) {
    return Collections.singletonList(new AddUnitTest(context));
  }
}
```

This MIME type specifies that the Code Generator that we are creating works on all Java source files. We could have used different MIME types, for example, text/html had we wanted to make our Code Generator work on HTML files.

The next method in the CodeGenerator interface is getDisplayName(). This method determines the text that will be displayed within the pop-up menu when the **Insert Code...** option is selected. The following is a screenshot of the getDisplayName() method:

```
public String getDisplayName() {
  return "JUnit Test...";
}
```

Finally, we implemented the `invoke()` method of the `CodeGenerator` interface. It is this method that gets called whenever the code generation options is invoked. The following is a screenshot of the `invoke()` method:

```
public void invoke() {
  try {
    CancellableTask task = new CancellableTask<WorkingCopy>() {

      @Override
      public void cancel() {...2 lines }

      @Override
      public void run(WorkingCopy workingCopy) throws Exception {...29 lines }

    };
    Document doc = textComp.getDocument();
    JavaSource javaSource = JavaSource.forDocument(doc);
    ModificationResult result = javaSource.runModificationTask(task);
    result.commit();
  } catch (Exception e) {
    Exceptions.printStackTrace(e);
  }
}
```

Within this method, we instantiated a `CancellableTask` class to perform the modification of the Java source code.

Inside the `CancellableTask` class, we used several of the NetBeans APIs to ensure that we were attempting to modify a class. We then created a new method, and added a `@Test` annotation to it and a default body. We added the new method into the class tree and rewrote the source for the class so that NetBeans was aware of our changes.

Finally, we grabbed a reference to `JavaSource` from the currently open document and then executed the task, committing it when completed. If any errors occurred during processing, we simply displayed the stack trace.

For more information on the NetBeans Platform APIs, check out the documentation at `http://bits.netbeans.org/dev/javadoc/`.

Packaging a NetBeans module for deployment

As we've seen in the previous recipe, NetBeans provides us with the ability to extend the functionality of the IDE by creating new modules. NetBeans modules are stored as .nbm files (which are essentially zipped archives), which can then be uploaded directly to the NetBeans plugin portal, or can be distributed via other techniques to other developers.

In this recipe, we'll show what we need to do to a module project to allow us to create a distributable NetBeans module.

Getting ready

To complete this recipe, you'll need the Add JUnit Test project created earlier in this chapter in the *Creating a NetBeans module* recipe. If you have not completed that recipe, the source code is available as part of the code download bundle for this book.

How to do it...

To create a distributable NetBeans module, perform the following steps:

1. The first stage when getting a NetBeans module ready for deployment is to specify the license that the module will be deployed under. We need to store the license within a text file in the project so that anyone who gets a copy of our module can see the license conditions. Right-click on the **Source Packages** node of the Add Unit Test project within the **Projects** explorer and create a new blank file called license.txt. Since this module is available under the Apache 2 license, enter that into the license.txt file.

> The Apache 2 license boiler plate text is available as part of the code download bundle for this chapter. The Apache 2 license can be found online at http://www.apache.org/licenses/LICENSE-2.0. Information about the Apache Software Foundation can be found at http://www.apache.org.

2. Now that we've added a license file to the project, we can configure the project properties ready for building the module. Right-click on the Add Unit Test project within the **Projects** explorer and select **Properties**.

3. On the **Project Properties** dialog, select the **Display** category and enter the following information:

   ❑ **Display Name**: Add Unit Test

- **Display Category**: `Testing Tools`
- **Short Description**: `Quickly add an empty JUnit test into your code`
- **Long Description**: `Add JUnit Tests allows the developer to quickly add a JUnit test into their code via the Insert Code option within the NetBeans code editor window.`
- **Show in Plugin Manager**: Ensure this option is checked

We can see our **Project Properties** dialog in the following screenshot:

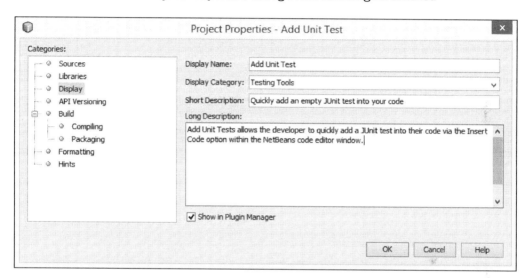

>
> Always ensure that the **Show in Plugin Manager** option is checked during development; otherwise, you'll find it very difficult to uninstall a module once you've installed it!

4. Select the **API Versioning** category and ensure the **Specification Version** field is set to `1.0`.

5. Select the **Build** category and then **Packaging** and enter the following information:

- **License**: Click on **Browse...** and select the `src/license.txt` file
- **Home Page**: `http://www.packtpub.com/netbeans-ide-8-cookbook/book`
- **Author**: David Salter

We can see our **Project Properties** dialog in the following screenshot:

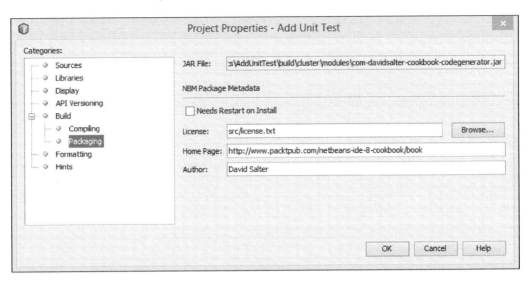

6. Click on **OK** to store the project properties.

7. We've now defined all of the metadata needed to package our plugin, so let's generate the .nbm file.

8. Right-click on the Add Unit Test project within the **Projects** explorer and click on **Create NBM**.

9. NetBeans will now take a few seconds to compile and package the module.

10. Click on the **Files** explorer and expand the Add Unit Test and build nodes. The com-davidsalter-cookbook-codegenerator.nbm module file has been generated within the build folder of the project, as shown in the following screenshot:

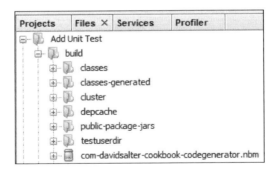

How it works...

When generating a packaged module, NetBeans creates a `.nbm` file. This file is a `.zip` archive like many other Java deployment files (`.jar` and `.war` files for example). The `.nbm` file has the following folders/files within it:

- `Info/info.xml`: This contains metadata about the module such as its license, the project's home page, and author.
- `META-INF/MAINFEST.MF`: This contains information about the tools that created the module file.
- `netbeans.config.Modules`: This contains information about whether the module is enabled and whether it needs a restart upon loading. The path to the module's `.jar` file is supplied within here.
- `netbeans.modules`: This contains compressed versions of the compiled module's `.jar` files.

There's more...

Using the NetBeans plugin mechanism (selecting **Tools** and the **Plugins** option from the main menu), we can add the `.nbm` file into a running instance of NetBeans to test it out. Note that all of the information we entered about the plugin (author name, URL, version, and plugin description) are all shown within the plugin manager, as shown in the following screenshot:

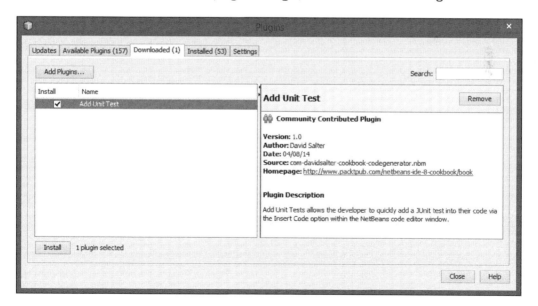

[It's best to test your plugins thoroughly using the techniques shown in the *Creating a NetBeans module* recipe rather than creating a `.nbm` file and loading it into your development IDE. If your plugin crashes, for example, or even worse, temporarily breaks NetBeans, its best if this is done to a standalone instance rather than your development instance.]

So what's next? I've created a plugin, how can I let other users know about it? When you've completed development and testing of your own plugins, you can deploy them to the NetBeans Plugin Portal at `http://plugins.netbeans.org`. The following screenshot displays the welcome screen of the NetBeans Plugin Portal:

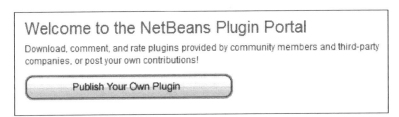

By logging in to the NetBeans Plugin Portal, you can upload your plugin and categorize it so that other developers can easily find it.

Submitting your plugin to the NetBeans Plugin Portal is the first step to increasing awareness of your plugin and allowing other developers to use it. To provide the optimal experience to users, and allow your plugins to be discoverable directly within NetBeans itself, you need to sign your plugins and ensure that they pass the plugin quality criteria.

Signing a plugin is a relatively straightforward task, but must be completed from the command prompt rather than inside NetBeans itself. The procedure is:

1. Open a command prompt or terminal and change directory to the NetBeans project.

2. Execute the following command to create a keystore, answering all the questions asked during execution:

   ```
   keytool -genkey -storepass <password> -alias <your name> -keystore
   nbproject/private/keystore
   ```

3. Edit the `project.properties` file located in the `nbproject` folder to reference the keystore:

   ```
   keystore=nbproject/private/keystore
   nbm_alias=<your name>
   ```

4. Edit the `platform-private.properties` file located at `nbproject/private` to contain:

   `storepass=<password>`

5. Rebuild the module and it will be signed.

Once your plugins have been signed and passed the quality criteria, they then become discoverable directly within NetBeans itself, so you no longer have to distribute `.nbm` files manually.

Full details of the quality criteria required for plugins can be found at `http://wiki.netbeans.org/PluginPortalQualityCriteria`.

Index

Thank you for buying
NetBeans IDE 8 Cookbook

About Packt Publishing

Packt, pronounced 'packed', published its first book "*Mastering phpMyAdmin for Effective MySQL Management*" in April 2004 and subsequently continued to specialize in publishing highly focused books on specific technologies and solutions.

Our books and publications share the experiences of your fellow IT professionals in adapting and customizing today's systems, applications, and frameworks. Our solution based books give you the knowledge and power to customize the software and technologies you're using to get the job done. Packt books are more specific and less general than the IT books you have seen in the past. Our unique business model allows us to bring you more focused information, giving you more of what you need to know, and less of what you don't.

Packt is a modern, yet unique publishing company, which focuses on producing quality, cutting-edge books for communities of developers, administrators, and newbies alike. For more information, please visit our website: www.packtpub.com.

About Packt Open Source

In 2010, Packt launched two new brands, Packt Open Source and Packt Enterprise, in order to continue its focus on specialization. This book is part of the Packt Open Source brand, home to books published on software built around Open Source licenses, and offering information to anybody from advanced developers to budding web designers. The Open Source brand also runs Packt's Open Source Royalty Scheme, by which Packt gives a royalty to each Open Source project about whose software a book is sold.

Writing for Packt

We welcome all inquiries from people who are interested in authoring. Book proposals should be sent to author@packtpub.com. If your book idea is still at an early stage and you would like to discuss it first before writing a formal book proposal, contact us; one of our commissioning editors will get in touch with you.

We're not just looking for published authors; if you have strong technical skills but no writing experience, our experienced editors can help you develop a writing career, or simply get some additional reward for your expertise.

open source
community experience distilled

Getting Started with Lazarus IDE

ISBN: 978-1-78216-340-4   Paperback: 116 pages

Get to grips with the basics of programming, debugging, creating components, and documenting projects with the Lazarus IDE

1. Create new projects.

2. Create components for use in Lazarus.

3. Document Lazarus projects.

Java EE 7 with GlassFish 4 Application Server

ISBN: 978-1-78217-688-6   Paperback: 348 pages

A practical guide to install and configure the GlassFish 4 application server and develop Java EE 7 applications to be deployed to this server

1. Install and configure GlassFish 4.

2. Covers all major Java EE 7 APIs and includes new additions such as JSON Processing.

3. Packed with clear, step-by-step instructions, practical examples, and straightforward explanations.

Please check **www.PacktPub.com** for information on our titles

[PACKT] open source ✿
PUBLISHING
community experience distilled

Instant JRebel

ISBN: 978-1-84969-880-1   Paperback: 46 pages

Accelerate your code development dramatically with this practical guide

1. Learn something new in an Instant! A short, fast, focused guide delivering immediate results.

2. Use your favorite tools without spending much time on compilation and deployment.

3. Enable JRebel on Tomcat and Glassfish.

4. Utilize JRebel to greatly improve your Java SE and Java EE projects.

Instant NetBeans IDE How-to

ISBN: 978-1-78216-344-2   Paperback: 70 pages

Develop different Java applications such as desktop, web, enterprise, and mobile applications using NetBeans IDE

1. Learn something new in an Instant! A short, fast, focused guide delivering immediate results.

2. Explore the drag-and-drop features of NetBeans IDE to write bug-free code without writing anything.

3. Generate different code snippets and files with only a few clicks.

4. Easy to use images and various controls within projects.

Please check **www.PacktPub.com** for information on our titles

41721908R00221

Made in the USA
Lexington, KY
24 May 2015